# Filling the Hole in the Nuclear Future

# AsiaWorld

### Series Editor: Mark Selden

This series charts the frontiers of Asia in global perspective. Central to its concerns are Asian interactions—political, economic, social, cultural, and historical—that are transnational and global, that cross and redefine borders and networks, including those of nation, region, ethnicity, gender, technology, and demography. It looks to multiple methodologies to chart the dynamics of a region that has been the home to major civilizations and is central to global processes of war, peace, and development in the new millennium.

### Titles in the Series

# Filling the Hole in the Nuclear Future

## Art and Popular Culture Respond to the Bomb

EDITED BY ROBERT JACOBS

LEXINGTON BOOKS
A division of
ROWMAN & LITTLEFIELD PUBLISHERS, INC.
*Lanham • Boulder • New York • Toronto • Plymouth, UK*

Published by Lexington Books
A division of Rowman & Littlefield Publishers, Inc.
A wholly owned subsidary of The Rowman & Littlefield Publishing Group, Inc.
4501 Forbes Boulevard, Suite 200, Lanham, Maryland 20706
http://www.lexingtonbooks.com

Estover Road, Plymouth PL6 7PY, United Kingdom

British Library Cataloguing in Publication Information Available

**Library of Congress Cataloging-in-Publication Data**
Filling the hole in the nuclear future : art and popular culture respond to the bomb / edited by Robert Jacobs.
    p. cm. — (AsiaWorld)
  ISBN 978-0-7391-3556-3 (cloth : alk. paper) — ISBN 978-0-7391-3557-0 (pbk. : alk. paper) — ISBN 978-0-7391-3558-7 (electronic)
  1. Arts and society—United States—History—20th century. 2. Arts and society—Japan—History—20th century. 3. Art and nuclear warfare—United States. 4. Art and nuclear warfare—Japan. 5. Popular culture—United States—History—20th century. 6. Popular culture—Japan—History—20th century. 7. Atomic bomb—Social aspects—United States. 8. Atomic bomb—Social aspects—Japan. I. Jacobs, Robert A., 1960–
  NX180.S6F55 2010
  700'.4581—dc22                                             2009050432

Printed in the United States of America

For my wife Carol.

# Contents

# Acknowledgments

This book is the result of a research project funded by the Hiroshima Peace Institute (HPI) and the citizens of Hiroshima, Japan. The book would not have been possible without the hard work and support of the entire HPI administrative staff, but specifically it is very much the result of the tireless professional commitment of Michiko Yoshimoto. From the first day of the research project until the placing of the last period mark at the end of the manuscript, Michiko never stopped working to make this book as perfect as possible.

The book began as a unique research project at HPI, bringing together both scholars and artists in a collaborative effort centered on the iconography of nuclear weapons. Meeting twice, in Chicago and also in Hiroshima, project members shared ideas and critiqued each other's work. HPI President Motofumi Asai addressed the group to stress his sense of the importance of our work, and lent the full support of HPI throughout the research and production periods. Hiroko Takahashi joined us for many of the workshop sessions and offered critical insights at key junctures. Atsuko Shigesawa contributed the translations of the two manga chapters. Kazumi Mizumoto helped to bring the work of essential participants to the group's awareness. Narayanan Ganesan and Sung Chull Kim also offered advice on how to organize, manage, and complete the tasks of such an unwieldy group of contributors.

Mark Selden oversaw the process of guiding the work generated in our research project into the holistic form of a coherent book. Mark's familiarity with the disparate topics; his support for the unusual structure of scholarship, manga, photographs, and poetry in one book; and his editorial guidance are clearly visible throughout the book. Michael Sisskin at Lexington Books has offered both patience and guidance in bringing the book to fruition. I am grateful for his commitment to the book and its unusual format, and for the strong support he and Lexington have shown for this work.

This book contains the work of a group of scholars and artists who found productive and new ways to work with each other. Coming from different disciplines, and even from different worlds, their common devotion to the issues of nuclear weapons and to the work of their fellow collaborators is an inspiration. Crossing barriers of language and training, they all worked for the quality and success of each other's work. Our meetings together were productive, and extremely fun. Special thanks go to Jerome Shapiro, Margot Henriksen, Tom Altherr, and Brian Johnson, who attended many of the workshop sessions and contributed valuable insights, many of which have found their way into the final work.

And finally, my thanks go to my family—Kaya, Ocea, Gwynne, Levi, Yolanda, Carol, and Muriel—whose support provides the ground on which I walk every day.

# Foreword

## HIROSHIMA STORY[*]

*Tom Engelhardt*

Even though we promptly dubbed the site of the 9/11 attacks in New York City "Ground Zero"—once a term reserved for an atomic blast—Americans have never really come to grips either with the atomic bombings of Hiroshima and Nagasaki or the nuclear age they ushered in.

There can be no question that, as the big bang that might end it all, the atomic bomb haunted Cold War America. In those years, while the young watched endless versions of nuclear disaster transmuted into B-horror films, the grown-ups who ran our world went on a vast shopping spree for world-ending weaponry, building nuclear arsenals that grew into the tens of thousands of weapons.

When the Cold War finally ended with the Soviet Union's quite peaceful collapse, however, a nuclear "peace dividend" never quite arrived. The arsenals of the former superpower adversaries remained quietly in place, drawn down but strangely untouched, awaiting a new mission, while just beyond sight, the knowledge of the making of such weapons spread to other countries ready to launch their own threatening mini-cold wars.

In 1995, fifty years after that first bomb went off over the Aioi Bridge in Hiroshima, it still proved impossible in the U.S. to agree upon a nuclear creation tale. Was August 6, 1945, the heroic ending to a global war or the horrific beginning of a new age? The *Enola Gay*, the plane that dropped the Hiroshima bomb, and a shattered school child's lunchbox from Hiroshima could not yet, it turned out, inhabit the same exhibit space at the Smithsonian's National Air and Space Museum in Washington D.C.

---

[*] Courtesy of Tom Englehardt, TomDispatch.com.

Today, while the Bush administration promotes a new generation of nuclear "bunker-busters" as the best means to fight future anti-proliferation wars, such once uniquely world-threatening weapons have had to join a jostling queue of world-ending possibilities in the dreams of our planet's young. Still, for people of a certain age like me, Hiroshima is where it all began. So on this August 6th, I would like to try, once again, to lay out the pieces of a nuclear story that none of us, it seems, can yet quite tell.

In my story, there are three characters and no dialogue. There is my father, who volunteered for the Army Air Corps at age thirty-five, immediately after the Japanese attack on Pearl Harbor. He fought in Burma, was painfully silent on his wartime experiences, and died on Pearl Harbor Day in 1983. Then there's me, growing up in a world in which my father's war was glorified everywhere, in which my play fantasies in any park included mowing down Japanese soldiers—but my dreams were of nuclear destruction. Finally, there is a Japanese boy whose name and fate are unknown to me.

This is a story of multiple silences. The first of those, the silence of my father, was once no barrier to the stories I told myself. If anything, his silence enhanced them, since in the 1950s, male silence seemed a heroic attribute (and perhaps it was, though hardly in the way I imagined at the time). Sitting in the dark with him then at any World War II movie was enough for me.

As it turned out though, the only part of his war I possessed was its final act, and around this too, there grew up a puzzling silence. The very idea of nuclear destruction seemed not to touch him. Like other school children, I went through nuclear attack drills with sirens howling outside, while—I had no doubt—he continued to work unfazed in his office. It was I who watched the irradiated ants and nuclearized monsters of our teen-screen life stomp the Earth. It was I who went to the French film *Hiroshima Mon Amour*, where I was shocked by my first sight of the human casualties of the A-bombing, and to *On the Beach* to catch a glimpse of how the world might actually end. It was I who saw the mushroom cloud rise in my dreams, felt its heat sear my arm before I awoke. Of all this I said not a word to him, nor he to me.

On his erstwhile enemies, however, my father was not silent. He hated the Japanese with a war-bred passion. They had, he told me, "done things" that could not be discussed to "boys" he had known. Subsequent history—the amicable American occupation of Japan or the emergence of that defeated land as an ally—did not seem to touch him.

His hatred of all things Japanese was not a ruling passion of my childhood only because Japan was so absent from our lives. There was nothing Japanese in our house (one did not buy their products); we avoided the only Japanese restaurant in our part of town, and no Japanese people ever came to visit. Even the evil Japanese I saw in war movies, who might sneeringly hiss "I was educated in your University of Southern California" before they met their suicidal fates were, I now know, regularly played by non-Japanese actors.

In the end, I followed my own path to Hiroshima, drawn perhaps to the world my father so vehemently rejected. In 1979, as an editor, I published *Unforgettable Fire*, the drawings of Hiroshima residents who had lived through that day. It was, I suspect, the first time any sizable number of images of the human damage there made it into mainstream American culture. I visited Japan in 1982, thanks to the book's Japanese editor who took me to Hiroshima—an experience I found myself unable to talk about on return. This, too, became part of the silences my father and I shared.

To make a story, thus far, would seem relatively simple. Two generations face each other across the chasm of a war and an act that divided them. It is the story we all know. And yet, there is my third character and third silence—the Japanese boy who drifted into my consciousness after an absence of almost four decades only a few years ago. I no longer remember—I can't even imagine—how he and I were put in contact sometime in the mid-1950s. Like me, my Japanese pen pal must have been eleven or twelve years old. If we exchanged photos, I have no memory of his face, nor does a name come to mind. If I can remember half-jokingly writing my own address at that age ("New York City, New York, USA, Planet Earth, the Solar System, the Galaxy, the Universe"), I can't remember writing his. I already knew by then that a place called Albany was the capital of New York State, but New York City still seemed to me the center of the world. In many ways, I wasn't wrong.

Even if he lived in Tokyo, my Japanese pen pal could have had no such illusions. Like me, he had undoubtedly been born during World War II. Perhaps in his first year of life he had been evacuated from one of Japan's charred cities. For him, that disastrous war would not have been a memory. If he had gone to the movies with his father in the 1950s, he might have seen Godzilla (not the U.S. Air Force) dismantle Tokyo and he might have hardly remembered those economically difficult first years of American occupation. But he could not at that time have imagined himself at the center of the universe.

I have a faint memory of the feel of his letters; a crinkly thinness undoubtedly meant to save infinitesimal amounts of weight (and so, money). We wrote, of course, in English, for much of the planet, if not the solar-system-galaxy-universe, was beginning to operate in that universal language which seemed to radiate from my home city to the world like the rays of the sun. But what I most remember are the exotic-looking stamps that arrived on (or in) his letters. For I was, with my father, an avid stamp collector. On Sunday afternoons, my father and I prepared and mounted our stamps, consulted our *Scott's Catalog*, and pasted them in. In this way, the Japanese section of our album was filled with that boy's offerings; without comment, but also without protest from my father.

We exchanged letters—none of which remain—for a year or two and then who knows what interest of mine (or his) overcame us; perhaps only the resistance boys can have to writing letters. In any case, he, too, entered a realm of silence. Only now, remembering those quiet moments of closeness when my father and I worked on our albums, do I note that he existed briefly and without discussion in our lives. He existed for both of us, perhaps, in the ambiguous space that silence can create. And now I wonder sometimes what kinds of nuclear dreams my father may have had.

For all of us in a sense, the Earth was knocked off its axis on August 6, 1945. In that one moment, my father's war ended and my war—the Cold War—began. But in my terms, it seems so much messier than that. For we, and that boy, continued to live in the same world together for a long time, accepting and embroidering each other's silences.

The bomb still runs like a fissure, but also like an attracting current—a secret unity—through our lives. The rent it tore in history was deep and the generational divide, given the experiences of those growing up on either side of it, profound. But any story would also have to hold the ways, even deeper and harder to fathom, in which we lived through it all together in pain, hatred, love, and most of all silence.

In this sixty-fourth year after Hiroshima, a year charged with no special meaning, perhaps we will think a little about the stories we can't tell, and about the subterranean stream of emotional horror that unites us, that won't go away whether, as in 1995, we try to exhibit the *Enola Gay* as a glorious icon or bury it deep in the Earth with a stake through its metallic heart. For my particular story, the one I've never quite been able to tell, there is a Japanese boy who should not have been, but briefly was, with us; who perhaps lives today with his own memories of very different silences. When I think of him now, when I realize that he, my father, and I still can't inhabit the same story except in silence, a strange kind of emotion rushes up in me, which is hard to explain.

# Introduction

## FILLING THE HOLE IN THE NUCLEAR FUTURE

*Robert Jacobs*

Among the most powerful visual symbols of the atomic age was the "Doomsday Clock" of the *Bulletin of the Atomic Scientists*, which imagined how close we were to nuclear war. The Doomsday Clock told us how many "minutes to midnight" we had: the number would vary depending on the state of world affairs. As the political and military situation shifted, those tensions would be reflected by how close the minute hand came to midnight. In 1947, the first clock showed humanity to be at "seven minutes to midnight," a gap that would fluctuate from two minutes as the race to build an H-bomb intensified during the height of the Cold War in 1953, to seventeen minutes after the Cold War ended in 1991. While the Doomsday Clock was a useful visual aid to communicate the risk of nuclear war, its power came from what is left unsaid: after midnight, there was nothing—nuclear midnight was the *end of time*.

This was one vision of the future implicit in the nuclear standoff of the Cold War—that there might be no future. The fact that it was as easy to believe that there might be no future or that there might soon be a world government, as it was to believe that the future would just be a steady continuation of the present, shows how disruptive nuclear weapons were to human societies. This sudden uncertainty about what lay ahead for civilization was a spiritual and a philosophical crisis as well as a political crisis.

Art and popular culture have played an essential role interpreting nuclear issues to the public and investigating the implications of nuclear weapons to the future of human civilization. While political and social forces often seemed paralyzed in thinking beyond the dilemma posed by this apocalyptic technology, art and popular culture were uniquely suited to grapple with the implications of the bomb and the disruptions in the continuity of traditional narratives about the human future endemic to the atomic age.

What Godzilla carried with him into Tokyo Bay, and what the giant ants in *Them!* brought up out of the sewers of Los Angeles, was a message—a message about the future. With human technological abilities far outpacing human social abilities, if society didn't change quickly, atomic weapons would fuel a war to end civilization. Human society was at a fork in the road: one path led to atomic holocaust; the other led to a future of peace and plenty. This was the nuclear dilemma, navigating past the danger and accomplishing the transformation to a new Eden.

Through this breach in the line of continuity from the present to the future, artists cast their visions. Many were dystopian, but others were fantastical. With the traditional narrative broken down, envisioning the future became an area of wild speculation. The presence of nuclear iconography in a work of art made the impossible suddenly plausible.

However, the value of nuclear art and culture was always considered suspect. Theodor Adorno famously wrote about the impossibility of poetry after Auschwitz. He was not saying that no one should write poetry; he was saying that if a society filled with poetry and culture could spawn the Nazis, what was the point of producing art? A dozen years later Susan Sontag wrote that in some ways science fiction films were complicit with the bomb. It was a hard burden that was placed on artists who tried to respond to or describe the place of nuclear weapons in society. Were they supposed to help save the world from the bomb? Was their work just trivializing it and making people complacent?

Critical discussions of the appropriateness and even the possibility of nuclear art resembled nothing so much as earlier discussions of attempts to represent the presence of the divine. Religious scholars in many faiths had long decried the impossibility of representation of the ineffable. This, of course, didn't stop the masses of artists and artisans who worked at producing just such work throughout recorded history.

Here we can see the level at which nuclear themes had to be approached by artists and producers of popular culture: it was like representing the holy. There were even many critics who spoke of the "nuclear sublime." This awe was rooted in attempts to contain a fear so complete that its imagined power of destruction left only shadows cast against stone from what had been human beings. The complete erasure of beings, and quite possibly of societies, was a power that had previously been reserved for gods. No painting or science fiction movie or poem could contain such horror, or such power. So what was an artist to do?

This book is an examination of a number of answers to that question. It examines various impacts of the bomb on art and popular culture in the two countries for which the use of the atomic bomb was historically real, Japan and the United States. It contains both scholars and artists presenting their work about the bomb, side by side. Several of the artists have also contributed written essays. The book cuts a broad path through its topic and is not meant to be comprehensive. It is not a history of nuclear-themed art. It is illustrative of both the diversity of art being done that integrates nuclear iconography and of the breadth of current nuclear scholarship.

The book, which is one outcome of a research project funded by the Hiroshima Peace Institute, opens with "Hiroshima Story," written by American editor, author and blogger Tom Englehardt on the fifty-ninth anniversary of the bombing of Hiroshima. Englehardt tells a story that will not let itself be completed. He examines aspects of the relationship of three people: himself as a boy, his father (a World War II Pacific veteran), and a childhood Japanese pen-pal. The bomb remains an ineffable presence between the three people, unspoken of, yet obscuring the view of each.

American John Canaday approaches nuclear history and culture from both the artistic and scholarly perspectives. Canaday, an award-winning poet, explores the history of the Manhattan Project and the use of nuclear weapons in Japan through narrative poems written in the personas of the historical figures that populate that history. Canaday draws out the human presence in the unfolding of events that gave birth to the atomic age. From Otto Frisch mulling over the results of the first nuclear fission experiments in Germany in the late 1930s to Edward Teller driving Leo Szilard to talk Einstein into signing the letter to Roosevelt that began the Manhattan Project, to Edith Warner considering the international physicists who became regulars at her remote teahouse near Los Alamos, Canaday gives face and interior life to people we know only through historical impact. Canaday explores these historical moments as lived human experience.

Canaday also muses on the place of metaphor and image in nuclear discourse. Much as has traditionally been said about religious and mystical experiences—that language cannot bridge the gap between the reality and representation—nuclear weapons are invariably spoken of through abstraction and metaphor. Canaday provides a fascinating examination of the centrality of metaphor to nuclear discourse exploring both how this has maintained the supernatural veneer of nuclear weaponry and become an aspect of how humans can act with a sense of normalcy in presence of the sublime.

Japanese historian of science and technology Kenji Ito examines the relationship of Japanese identity to technology in the twentieth century and how it revolves around the atomic experience. Ito compares the place of robots in Japanese popular culture from before and after World War II and argues that a clear shift can be seen between the threatening and foreign robots of the pre-war period and the benevolent and native robots of the post-war period. Before the war, robots in Japanese popular culture are often the tools of foreigners who employ the robots to gain power over Japan. Here we see the belief that technology was not as advanced in Japan as it was in foreign militaries, and therefore was a threat. After the war, robots, typified by Astroboy (Atomu), were depicted as of Japanese origin and were benevolent, often fighting against evil threats to humankind. Ito shows what a complex and delicate set of ideals lay behind this shift. The pole around which this change pivots was the wartime experience, and specifically the experience of the atomic bombings of Hiroshima and Nagasaki.

Minorou Maeda is a Hiroshima-born animator. His chapter, "The Day the Sun was Lost," is taken from his animated film by the same name. Maeda has taken his anime and turned it into manga form for this book. The story is about his father's experience of the bombing of Hiroshima as a young boy. Maeda's document is especially interesting because rather than being art about the experience of the bombing, it is art about the experience of inheriting that history as family history. It is about being second-generation to historical trauma. In the film, the bomb does not go off until almost the very end. Most of the film shows his father playing with his friends on the morning of August 6, before the bomb went off. It is a joyful and mischievous tale of boys at play. The story is not directly about the impact of the bomb; it is about the long-term view of that impact. Maeda has made a film, not about what his father experienced on that day, but about what he lost: his innocent childhood. Maeda-san tries to give him back just a few minutes of that childhood, before those years turned into a story about devastation and survival. In this story we can see the experience of the atomic bombing as inherited history.

The chapter by Naoko Maeda, Minoru's sister, shows this process from another perspective. Naoko Maeda has made a manga about the time in her life when her brother was making his anime. One focus of her manga, the part reproduced here from a much longer and broad ranging work, is on the debates in the family about Minoru's choice to focus the film on his father's playtime rather than on his experience of the bombing. To their father, it seemed trivial to spend so long depicting boys playing, which was not historically significant at all. Naoko's chapter is fascinating in that she has taken the negotiations within a family about the meaning and correct form in which family history is to be remembered and retold. In this case, the family history is a history that has affected all of our families. While we all grapple with the place of these weapons in our world, the Maeda family has had to also grapple with it as personal history. In this process they have both laid a foundation for all of our struggles about what the bombings of Hiroshima and Nagasaki mean, and created several great pieces of art.

Australian media and film scholar Mick Broderick examines the role of the Truman White House in shaping the narrative of the development and use of nuclear weapons during World War II presented in the 1947 MGM film *The Beginning or the End*. This film, the first major Hollywood presentation of the history of the Manhattan Project and the decision to drop the bomb, established an influential early narrative of that history for consumption by the American public. Working with records of the film's production and of meetings between Truman and other administration officials with MGM executives, Broderick details the nuances and negotiations of establishing the narrative of the bombings which the White House preferred be presented to filmgoers. Noting that this history betrays a "conflict of historical and artistic agendas between the filmmakers/screenwriters and the Truman administration," Broderick reveals the intensity with which the president worked to create a portrait of himself and the decision to use nuclear weapons that was both sympathetic and demonstrative of enlightened leadership.

Japanese historian Yuki Tanaka weaves the history of the first Godzilla movie (*Gojira*, 1954) to the history of the test earlier that year of the first deliverable hydrogen bomb by the United States in the Pacific—the Bravo test. This test would result in the exposure of hundreds of Pacific islanders, the crew of the Japanese fishing trawler the *Lucky Dragon*, and countless U.S. service personnel to heavy amounts of fallout radiation. This incident proved too big for the U.S. government to contain, and put the word "fallout" into common usage. While the whole crew of the *Lucky Dragon* would become sick, one person would eventually die from this exposure, creating intense fear and anger in Japan just as *Gojira* was in preproduction.

Tanaka examines the film *Gojira* for clues about its relationship to the Bravo test experience, as well as other nuclear and anti-nuclear expressions in the film. In addition, Tanaka details how such references were stripped out of the American release of the film as *Godzilla! King of the Monsters* in 1956, making a neutered and more politically palatable film for the American market.

The American photographer Carole Gallagher focuses on the toll of the human encounter with nuclear weapon testing. Her contribution details this encounter in two different ways. The photographs, taken from her book and exhibition *American Ground Zero*, detail the impact of nuclear weapon testing on those who endured it. Gallagher photographs people: her work on this project is exclusively portraits. The people Gallagher has chosen to photograph for this work all encountered the bomb at or near the Nevada Test Site in the United States. The Nevada Test Site was the United States' sole continental test site, though they also tested larger thermonuclear (H-bombs) weapons in the Pacific. The people in Gallagher's photos include downwinders (those who lived downwind of the test site and were therefore affected by fallout radiation), atomic soldiers (those who participated in military maneuvers during nuclear tests), and test site workers. The intimacy of their experience of nuclear weaponry is revealed in their faces, and frequently by the artifacts that they display while being photographed. Her work honors the nobility of those whose experience of nuclear weapons has altered their lives in ways that they must cope with alone, without the recognition and support of their government they served or supported.

Carole Gallagher's essay documents her experiences in researching and photographing *American Ground Zero*. She lived in the downwind communities of (mostly southern) Utah for almost ten years while working on her project. While allowing her to produce what would become her magnum opus, the experience took an enormous toll on her personally. Writing about that experience for the first time, we are allowed a view into the devastated personal landscape left behind long after the fallout clouds had passed. In a world in which victims can become victimizers, the depth to which such experiences penetrate and mutate the human spirit are starkly depicted and exact their toll on the artist seeking to work with the materials left behind by nuclear testing.

My own chapter discusses the origins of the image of the whole Earth as seen from space, arguably one of the most ubiquitous visual images of the second half of the twentieth century. The chapter focuses on the content of this visual icon, and argues that much of this content can first be seen expressed in editorial cartoons published in the immediate aftermath of the atomic bombings of Hiroshima and Nagasaki. This initial visualization rendered in ink and paper rather than as a photograph, imagines the *whole* Earth as the target, and therefore victim of a possible nuclear war. The Earth is seen as a single entity, one being, that will live or die depending on its interaction with the bomb. While not specifically referring to the image of the Earth as seen from space, the content that would later be so familiar in the image of the whole Earth are present: the Earth as a single living organism, the absence of political/national borders, the common destiny of all the nations and inhabitants of the planet, the interdependence and the fragility of life on Earth. The cartoons that I consider were all published within a year of the bombings of Hiroshima and Nagasaki, and most within one week.

Japanese American visual artist Judy Hiramoto's installation artwork addresses the issues and imagery of the nuclear age head on. Her work is densely layered with the history of the experience of a world filled with nuclear weapons. The content is filled with both visual and conceptual references to the nuclear experience from the Manhattan Project, to the bombings of Hiroshima and Nagaskai, to the subsequent development and proliferation of nuclear weapons, rendered in historical forms as well as traditional Japanese and American motifs. Hiramoto expresses this content through a variety of media in three dimensions to create an interactive experience. Oppenheimer's statement to Truman after the war that physicists had "blood on their hands" takes life in a sink that runs with red water accompanied by a towel to wipe dry the hands on which Hiramoto has printed the names of Japanese and Korean victims in Hiroshima. Her

*Garden for a Nuclear Age* is planted with a variety of plants that were the first to regenerate in Hiroshima and Nagasaki after the bombings.

Meticulously detailed and constructed, Hiramoto's installations create from nuclear history a visceral experience that challenges the observer to stand unflinchingly aware of the world in which they live. Yet through this act, one participates in the beauty and consciousness need for the world to survive and endure the nuclear experience.

American historian of physics Spencer Weart examines nuclear culture and imagery in the United States during the last two decades. Weart's 1986 book *Nuclear Fear* is the primary text in the field of nuclear cultural history in the United States, and his chapter updates this classic book by examining what has changed since its publication. The end of the Cold War shifted nuclear culture profoundly because of the elimination of the direct conflict between the two "superpowers" that fueled its first half-century. Thus does Weart conclude that the end of the Cold War "changed everything." Weart's analysis does not stop here. Continuing to connect the cultural motifs that resonate around nuclear weapons to older tropes which supply its imagery and story lines, he shows equally how "nothing has changed."

Weart brings a very important analysis to his work by integrating relevant advances in neurobiology and what they reveal about the nature and functioning of the human brain. When discussing issues of perception, fear, and anxiety, all critical for understanding the manifestations of nuclear culture, a deeper understanding of how the brain relates thoughts to emotions, and perceptions to beliefs offer essential clues that are typically lost in most historical analyses. In this sense, Weart's work informs us both on the level of content and on the level of historical methodology.

Nuclear weapons have toyed with long held assumptions about the continuity of the human future to the present and the past. Our collective global destiny seemed dependent on the benevolence of human governments and militaries—the same institutions that had just led humanity through World Wars I and II. Against this dire backdrop, art and popular culture have played a very powerful role: they have looked back to what happened in 1945, they have imagined the nuclear and post-apocalyptic landscapes of the future. While the bomb tore a hole into traditional narratives about the future, art and popular culture began to populate that vacuum with stories and images, material and visions. John Canaday points out that most of us primarily encounter nuclear weapons through story. Spencer Weart has used the framework of a "history of images" to guide his nuclear scholarship. Minorou Maeda and his sister have used anime and manga to tell their tales. Art and culture are at the center of our experience of nuclear weaponry, and our sense of agency in response to the disruptions they have created in our lives.

# CHAPTER 1

# Fetch-Lights and Grocery Lists

## METAPHORS AND NUCLEAR WEAPONS

*John Canaday*

> Upshot, Knothole, Teapot, Plumbob—
> Lesbos, Athos, lost, lost, and Sounion . . .
> These are—these have become—the fixed stars' points, the fetch-
> lights shining through our dreams.
>
> Richard Kenney, "The Invention of the Zero"[1]

In 1998, Christopher Felver released a short film celebrating the sculptor Donald Judd. Footage of Judd talking about his work alternates with commentary by a poet, John Yau, who begins the film with these words:

> [Judd] would be against metaphor because he would understand, instantly I think, that metaphor could not in any way be a vehicle of meaning after the Holocaust and the dropping of the atom bombs; that metaphor had been called into serious question and serious doubt; and that he had to find a way to make art that could exist on its own terms without the support of metaphor, one may say, without the scaffolding of metaphor.[2]

Yau may be thinking of Theodor Adorno's famous dictum, "To write poetry after Auschwitz is barbaric," though he substitutes "metaphor" for "poetry," which transforms Adorno's highly debatable claim (he more or less retracted it in 1966[3]) into pseudo-intellectual folderol. Evidence of the continuing vitality of metaphor since 1945—in art, literature, popular culture, even Yau's own work—belies the claim. Yet Yau's assertion, like Adorno's, points to something real. The cataclysms of World War II haunt the creative imagination. Urgency and inadequacy twine in us, along with a sense that something essential in the human condition has changed. Though metaphor remains a powerful means of expressing many different kinds of meanings, can it in fact help us to understand

9

the bombings of Hiroshima and Nagasaki? In what ways might it help us to envision, and ultimately to create, a livable future in the long shadow of those events?[4]

Why might someone believe that the bombings of Hiroshima and Nagasaki had negated the ability of metaphors to convey meaning? It is the sweeping character of Yau's assertion that robs it of sense. If we put it in less drastic terms—for instance, if we suggest that metaphorical representations can seem inappropriate, inadequate, even distasteful in the face of the suffering caused by the use of nuclear weapons—Yau would not be alone in experiencing a degree of anxiety. Writers who use metaphors to describe the bomb often seem uncomfortable with them. They try to limit their scope and control their reach, striving, apparently, to produce tracts of clear meaning—but at what expense? And what causes this anxiety? I will begin by considering the problem of representing the bombings of Hiroshima and Nagasaki before turning to attributes of the weapons themselves.

# Challenges of Representing Nuclear Weapons

The most immediate challenge involved in representing the bombings of Hiroshima and Nagasaki is obviously the scale of human suffering they caused. How can we convey the immensity of the horror? The fullness of a single victim's experience is beyond our representational reach; multiply that by hundreds of thousands; string it out over years, over decades, in all its agonizing shadings: the task is beyond us. Yet this does not mean we should (or can) abandon it. Works like Masuji Ibuse's *Black Rain* and John Hersey's *Hiroshima* demonstrate the power and importance of such attempts. Even if any single work must fail to capture the scale of these events, each adds to our collective effort to open ourselves, to reach out, to understand.

Most people who attempt to write about these events are also hampered by a lack of direct experience. As the years pass, fewer and fewer people (we hope) will have personal experience of a nuclear attack, and without firsthand knowledge, we must rely on the accounts of those who have such experience. From this position of dependence, what can we add to eyewitness accounts? And why should readers trust the authority of someone who has not directly observed what he or she writes about? These questions are, in a sense, the motivation for this essay, and answering them will be a rather lengthy process. For the moment I will simply suggest that although eyewitness accounts will always be a crucial resource—and we should return to them often, as touchstones for our work—our task is to grapple with these events on behalf of readers who, like us, have no direct experience of nuclear weapons. For it is important to understand not only what these weapons meant to those who built and used and suffered them, but what they mean to all of us, in our own disparate contexts.

Why would we want to undertake this difficult work? Concern for the future of humanity seems a compelling answer. Yet there is anxiety even here, in the midst of this noble undertaking, because in our efforts to grapple with history and make it speak to our future, we are acting in an essentially selfish fashion. There is immense presumption involved in appropriating the experiences, the suffering, the lives and deaths of the inhabitants of Hiroshima and Nagasaki. By what right do we turn them to our own purposes? Though most people (the hibakusha foremost) will insist that we must redeem the horror by learning from it, anyone who has attempted to do this will recognize the danger. We walk a fine line between honoring the dead and misunderstanding, misrepresenting, misappropriating their experiences. We must approach the task cautiously, respectfully. Yet too much caution can hobble our efforts, cause us to second-guess ourselves, prevent us from the necessary daring. The endeavor requires an artful balance of humility and hubris.

In addition to the challenges of representing the bombings of Hiroshima and Nagasaki, there are a number of peculiar features associated with nuclear weapons themselves that would seem to set them apart from other kinds of weapons, potentially rendering them more difficult to represent. As the Fat Man and Little Boy bombs demonstrated, the magnitude of their destructive force dwarfs conventional weapons. With the development of fusion bombs, the yield of nuclear weapons increased even further. The United States has produced bombs with a yield-to-weight ratio approaching six kilotons TNT equivalent per kilogram.[5] This is six million times the energy release of TNT. Likewise, the largest nuclear weapon ever tested, the Soviet Union's Tsar Bomba, produced a yield equal to fifty million tons of TNT—comparable to two and a half thousand Fat Man bombs. Such destructive power defies self-defense and overwhelms imagination, frustrating our descriptive efforts; perhaps this is why some people assume it also cripples our modes of description themselves.

Nuclear weapons not only undermine the hope that we can defend ourselves, they also unsettle confidence in our ability even to detect an approaching threat. Two bombs, each carried by a single aircraft, destroyed Hiroshima and Nagasaki. Today, a single Trident submarine carries twenty-four Trident II (D5) ballistic missiles, each with a range of more than 4,600 miles, and each capable of carrying eight independently targeted warheads, such as the 475 kiloton W88 (with an explosive force greater than twenty-three Fat Man bombs).[6] This means each Trident submarine can carry the equivalent of over ninety-one million tons of TNT (four and a half thousand Fat Man bombs) and is capable of utterly destroying 192 cities. Since Trident missiles travel at approximately four miles per second, they can reach targets four thousand miles away in about twenty minutes.[7] The apparent speed and ease with which nuclear weapons can reach and destroy any location on earth is indeed terrifying.[8]

With the development of nuclear weapons came the realization that we now have power of an entirely new kind: the means to destroy ourselves, to destroy, indeed, the entire world. At the height of the Cold War, the United States and the Soviet Union had approximately seventy thousand warheads between them; since then, the numbers have lessened dramatically. Today there are approximately twenty-six thousand to thirty thousand nuclear warheads in the world.[9] Before we congratulate ourselves on our improved safety, however, we should recall that this represents the equivalent of approximately five billion tons of TNT, or roughly 250,000 Fat Man bombs—more than enough to do ourselves in.[10] If describing the bombings of Hiroshima and Nagasaki tests our representational resources, how are we to cope with the prospect of a quarter million such cataclysms? And beyond that, how are we to imagine and embody in language not only our own end but the end of our species?

A more subtle but no less daunting challenge to our representational methods is the fact that nuclear weapons employ a recently discovered and "mysterious" source of energy. Most people do not understand how these weapons work—or even, despite exposure to these concepts in high school science classes, how atoms are structured. Even with such knowledge, describing subatomic processes is immensely difficult, simply because they are beyond our ability to observe directly. Indeed, not only are they too small for us to see, but they do not, in fact, "look" like anything.[11] Although we are made up of them, atoms are entirely outside our experience of the world, behaving in ways that defy common sense. Scientists struggle with this difficulty as they seek ways of describing entities that are inaccessible to our senses and have no consistent analogs in the human world.[12] This would seem to be a considerable obstacle confronting anyone who wants to write about nuclear weapons.

In addition to the explosive release of energy, the physical processes underlying nuclear weapons have another threatening and even more mysterious manifestation: radioactivity. Our senses cannot detect it, yet it can kill us. Its effects can be immediate or delayed. It can cause hair loss, cataracts, internal bleeding, bruising, fatigue, weakness, nausea, and blistering. It can linger in the body, cropping up years after initial exposure, resulting in cancer, infertility, and organ failure. Radioactive debris can permeate the ground, rendering it dangerous long after the initial detonation of a bomb. Plants, in turn, can absorb the contamination, rendering the grains we eat toxic, poisoning our livestock and tainting their milk. Radioactive dust can rise into the atmosphere, descending as a deadly rain of fallout on distant places. Not only are these phenomena horrifying, but they present their own challenge to our representational facilities.

Ironically, nuclear weapons are a particular manifestation of physical processes that also have beneficial applications. In fact, benign uses of nuclear technology appeared long before the malign,[13] and development of humanitarian applications continues side by side with nuclear weapons research. Nuclear power plants, for instance, offer the potential of vast, long-term sources of energy that—despite important concerns regarding operating safety, expense, and the creation of hazardous waste—merit serious consideration, especially in light of the environmental threats posed by global warming. Radiation treatments, likewise, have revolutionized medical practices, while radiochemistry has extended our understanding of biological processes, opening up new possibilities in the study of DNA and other molecular structures. There are potentially even productive applications of bomb technology, such as the possibility of breaking apart large meteors before they hit the earth. Yet despite the benefits of these applications of nuclear technology, they, like nuclear weapons, though more subtly, are also attended by a good deal of anxiety—as anyone who has undergone radiation treatments, or lived near a nuclear power plant, or had a loved one who worked in radiation research can testify.

# Responses to Representational Challenges

Nuclear weapons clearly involve significant challenges to our representational efforts. I think it is important to recognize, however, that none of these challenges—on its own—is quite as unprecedented as we often allow ourselves to assume. The enormous destruction caused by the bombings of Hiroshima and Nagasaki was prefigured, for instance, in the fire bombings of Dresden, Hamburg, and Tokyo. The potential for surprise involved in the use of nuclear weapons echoes the attack on Pearl Harbor. The ability to destroy the planet—or at least render it uninhabitable by humans—exists in the form of global warming, to which each of us contributes every day. The mysterious character of nuclear processes is hardly more of an impediment to our understanding than larger scale atomic interactions, since most people do not understand how conventional explosives (including handguns) work any more than nuclear ones. The insidious threat of radioactivity is no more difficult to detect and defend ourselves against than the innumerable carcinogens and pathogens, both natural and artificial, that surround us (and pass through us) every day. Though each of these analogous examples tests our representational abilities, none make us opine that metaphors simply don't work the way they used to.

Of course there are differences inherent in each of these comparisons. The bombings of Hiroshima and Nagasaki *were* different from the attacks on Dresden, Hamburg, Tokyo, and Pearl Harbor. Nuclear annihilation *is* distinct from global warming, nuclear reactions from chemical reactions, radiation poisoning from cancer. But none of these differences are sufficient to account for a belief that nuclear weapons cripple metaphorical representation while the analogous instances I have mentioned don't. Only in combination do the phenomena associated with nuclear weapons constitute something "new"—only together do they provide a satisfactory explanation for the almost divine powers we have ascribed to nuclear weapons.

The difficulty involved in representing the range and variety (and, of course, the power) of these attributes helps explain our complex, often contradictory responses to nuclear weapons. They are variously interpreted as promising the end of war and as threatening the end of the world; as diabolical devices and as agents of divine will; as practical tools of war and as immoral weapons of genocide; as mere technological artifacts and as proof of the epistemological supremacy of science. Contradictory attitudes towards nuclear energy permeate post-war culture, appearing in the public pronouncements of scientists, political debates, the manufacture of commodities, and the full range of popular entertainments, from music to movies to pulp fiction. Everywhere we look, we can see ourselves struggling to make sense of the forces—physical and social—embodied in nuclear weapons: the dark humor of Dr. Strangelove and the macho slapstick of *True Lies*; Joseph Rotblat's Pugwash conferences and Edward Teller's response to Three Mile Island; Atomic Fireball candies and Brumm's Fat Man and Little Boy toys; Radioactive Records and the song "5 Minutes" by Bonzo Goes To Washington; Raymond Brigg's *Where the Wind Blows* and Russell Hoban's *Riddley Walker*; the Bulletin of the Atomic Scientists and Los Alamos National Laboratory. Instances of such ambivalence toward nuclear weapons are widespread, and they have proven remarkably resistant to overt attempts at logical resolution as well as to the implicit forces of cultural consensus.

Given the range and incongruity of the characteristics we associate with nuclear weapons, it is not surprising that writers often feel the inadequacy of any particular metaphor, preferring the relative safety of literal narratives. Though narratives also feel inadequate—unable to convey the immensity of the subject, or even fully account for a given individual's experience of it—they can claim a factual grounding in events (if only those of a fallible individual). Metaphors, on the other hand, though used in both fiction and nonfiction contexts, have a fictional, aesthetic feel to them. They impress us as willful creations of the writer's mind. In *Hiroshima Diary*, for instance, Michihiko Hachiya describes a "bundle" of medical supplies as "no bigger than the tears of a sparrow."[14] This simile stands out as a rare instance of authorial license: in the midst of the terrors and suffering Hachiya describes, this shift into self-conscious linguistic play feels odd, almost disturbing. A part of us whispers: *These things are too awful to make art out of.* Yet the straightforward narrative mode that characterizes the book, founded on Hachiya's direct experience of the events he describes, gives him the authority to indulge in this moment of authorial creativity.

But is metaphor the decorative trifle that this attitude suggests? Or can it be a medium for the serious exploration of human experience? Given that our society valorizes the processes of logical analysis and causal narratives—in science, the social "sciences," academic discourse, and even our interactions with one another—can metaphorical representation complement rather than negate these dominant modes? If so, then it is imperative that we "make art" out of precisely those experiences we deem most important yet, least accessible to human reason. Answering these questions requires that we consider carefully the dynamics of metaphorical representation—how it works and what it offers us.

# How Metaphor Works

Metaphors are linkages between symbols—though we generally ignore the intermediary role of the symbols and focus instead on the links between what the symbols represent. Thus in Hachiya's comparison of medical supplies and sparrow tears, we do not think of the metaphor as a linking of symbols (the actual words "bundle" and "tears of a sparrow") but of the objects to which those symbols point. Though this is a simplification of the actual processes involved in metaphorical uses of language, it is a useful one for our purposes—and it is so common as to be unavoidable in any case.

The ostensible purpose of a metaphor is to convey understanding of an unfamiliar object, event, or idea (the tenor) by linking it to something familiar (the vehicle). For instance, "Mary is a crab" tells us something new about Mary by equating her with a familiar animal. These linkages can take the form of comparisons, equations, or replacements: "Mary is acting like a crab"; "Mary is a crab"; "The crab came by today." Metaphors used as overt comparisons tend to be the most highly circumscribed, in several senses: they make the act of linking obvious by means of comparative terms ("like," "as"); they link less forcibly, stopping short of asserting actual identity; and they often narrow the focus of the linkage (in this case by identifying behavior as the basis of similarity). Replacement metaphors, on the other hand, are the most intensive, far-reaching, and "poetic."

As this suggests, an essential feature of these linkages is that they involve multiple comparisons and contrasts in a single verbal gesture. Though the writer usually has a small number of similarities in mind when formulating a metaphor, the actual link involves a practically unlimited number of connections. Mary might look like a crab in any number of ways, from beady eyes to thin, bony arms. She might move in a crablike fashion. She might behave aggressively. She might like pinching people. She might maintain a strong social "shell," rendering her difficult to get to know. She may be a scavenger. She might prefer to live by the shore. Though some of these possibilities will seem more likely than others, the relative likelihood is a function of social conventions and prior uses. Since each of us has encountered and absorbed these precedents differently, any given metaphor is "open to interpretation" along a wide variety of lines, depending on which threads resonate with a given individual's particular memetic makeup.[15]

Metaphors therefore induce a curious state in a reader, requiring the recognition, evaluation, selection, and rejection of connecting threads. This is work each of us does all day, every day, without "thinking" about it—at least, not consciously. Often the process is fairly straightforward: social conventions and repetition in effect vet popular metaphors ahead of time. When someone says, "I left the car running," for instance, she does not pause to select the metaphor, nor does anyone listening expend energy considering in which ways a car might be "running" or what the comparison is intended to convey about the state of the car. Metaphors of this sort have become static, their multiple semiotic threads snipped and woven into a single strand of meaning. Many metaphors, however, remain dynamic even after repeated use—and all "original" metaphors require active interpretation. In what ways is Mary like a crab? Processing this metaphor—retrieving and unpacking the meaning it is meant to convey—requires an active mental engagement involving a complex set of steps. Luckily, our brains have been wired to perform these tasks quickly and efficiently, as is evident in the fact that we spend relatively little time thinking consciously about the myriad metaphors we encounter every day.

Not surprisingly, despite our rather astonishing metaphorical skills, we generally sacrifice some precision in favor of speed. Told that Mary is a crab, we don't actually consider all the possible bases of comparison. Instead, we quickly eliminate large categories, narrow in on others, and apply the gist of the similarity, as we interpreted it, to our ever-flowing "stream of thought."[16] As we might expect in such a seat-of-the-pants process, mistakes are often made and may later be discovered: "Oh, you meant the way she walks! I thought you meant she was irritable." Yet mistaking a speaker's intent is only one way in which metaphors can surprise us. Even after a metaphor has been processed and its meaning "extracted," innumerable rejected or overlooked possibilities remain, and seemingly static threads can regain their dynamism in surprising or significant ways. Even the framer of a metaphor can discover unforeseen and unexpectedly apropos threads, and in some important senses, the precise contours of a metaphor's meanings are never firmly fixed.

Furthermore, metaphors are not unidirectional linkages. Although the ostensible purpose of a metaphor is to increase our understanding of the tenor, the comparison ultimately goes both ways. It is a given that the vehicle must be familiar in order to convey information; yet the tenor cannot be entirely un-known, either. To say "———— is a crab" is not a metaphor. It gives us no basis for discrimination. We must map *all* the qualities of a crab onto the unknown noun. For all we know, it *is* a crab. This suggests, of course, that the differences between the vehicle and tenor of a metaphor are as important as the similarities. It also points out that metaphors are only viable when it is possible to map the properties of the tenor back onto the vehicle, if only as a means of determining which of the vehicle's properties may be appropriately mapped onto the tenor. Practically, it will often be the case that we will have a much more detailed knowledge of the tenor than of the vehicle: the tenor is, after all, the primary object of interest. In the case of our working example, for instance, we are likely to know a lot more about Mary than about *Brachyura*.

Literary uses of metaphors explore these properties and turn them to the service of expressing the meanings of human experience in nonlinear ways. Liter-ary metaphors, for instance, tend to resist our efforts to narrow their scope and, instead, keep a wide variety of meanings in play at once. They also emphasize semiotic mapping in both directions, from tenor to vehicle as well as from ve-hicle to tenor. In short, they create webs of meaning—as opposed to the linear sequences generated by the causal structures of narratives. When, for example, Eleanor Wilner writes in "High Noon at Los Alamos"[17] that "our thoughts, however elegant, were fire," she uses the metaphor to map a number of proper-ties associated with fire onto human thought: energy, light, beauty, speed, the consumption of whatever fuels it, its destructive capacity. But the metaphor also maps the other way, creating what is, in this case, perhaps an even more powerful and disturbing link. Our thoughts not only share some of the qualities of fire, Wilner implies, they also stoke it, spread it, and manufacture it. Our thoughts *become* fire—from the burning of Troy to the bombings of Hiroshima and Nagasaki.

It should be clear that metaphor is far more than "simply" a shorthand way of expressing a complex set of related ideas. It is obviously possible to list the qualities woven into a metaphorical web, as I have done. It would even be pos-sible to attempt to untangle the threads, examining each at length and arguing for its relative weight and its relation to those around it. But while it is likely that many people would agree on the issues involved, at least in broad terms, it would remain an argument. Though I think my characterization of Wilner's metaphor is correct, it would be possible for a reasonable reader to disagree, either substantially or in terms of the details, and there is, in any event, a great deal more to be said about the matter. As anyone who has attempted an exegesis of a poem knows, there are many ways to interpret a metaphorical web. Fur-thermore, its meanings are not static. They shift and shimmer as one examines them. A literal gloss cannot capture this interplay, for a metaphor is, in the end, a process of thought—a dynamic balance in our minds—rather than a fixed set of meanings.

# Metaphorical vs Narrative Modes of Thought

Scientists tend to be suspicious of metaphors precisely because of this plasticity of meaning—an attitude worth mentioning because it has spread widely throughout our culture, among scientists and nonscientists alike. Science in general privileges stable meanings, the elimination of variables, and fixed mathematical relationships among those that remain. The ambiguity of metaphors, and the shifting matrix of variables they juggle, makes them an inefficient medium for the production of symbolic structures suited to the manipulation of natural processes. Science builds its semiotic structures, instead, on the predictability of causal narratives (in a mixture of mathematical and "natural" languages) that unfold the same way each time.

Such repetition is not boring; in fact, scientists often apply aesthetic terms to the manifestation of phenomena predicted by the narrative structure of a pet theory, calling such underlying orderliness "beautiful." Nor is narrative repetition confined to science: the Greeks staged the same tragedies over and over; religion endlessly rehearses its peculiar narratives; Jung's archetypal narratives replay themselves from one generation to the next; and every one of us finds it comforting to refresh the "software" of consciousness by rereading a beloved book or watching a favorite movie yet again. Narrative is the foundation of causal thought, and, partly as a result of the powers granted us by the scientific method, our culture has gradually placed an increasing emphasis on narrative while decreasing its reliance on metaphor.

Metaphor has not disappeared, however; nor will it. For one thing, science is also founded, though more subtly, less comfortably, on metaphor. The webs of metaphor are the first nets scientists cast into uncharted waters, because metaphors provide a powerful way of grouping and organizing disparate phenomena. When Benjamin Franklin, for instance, proposed that electricity could be thought of as a single fluid, the metaphor provided an essential conceptual framework, establishing a theoretical foundation and guiding subsequent research. But in what ways did the metaphor apply? After the first metaphorical cast, scientists compete with one another to pick out relevant threads, snip those that seem extraneous, and convert the dynamic linkages into static causal narratives. The vast majority of scientific papers are of this kind, and so the methods of science appear antithetical to metaphor, effacing its crucial role in grappling with complex, unfamiliar phenomena. Yet for all our efforts to limit, contain, and define the scope of metaphoric linkages, we cannot shake our dependence on them.

The persistence of both metaphoric and narrative modes of representation, as well as the differences between them, stems from their roots in the two primary modes of human thought. The human brain is a parallel processor—that is, it allows the "deployment of several neuron groups or several pathways to convey similar information."[18] Our neural structures allow us to process information by means of "simultaneous"[19] manipulation of redundant data sets, or different parts of a data set, or different data sets altogether. At any given instant, for example, our brains are responding to information received by our retinas, cochlea, taste buds, olfactory nerves, and tactile nerves, as well as processing abstract data regarding a book we are reading or what we want to eat for lunch, and at the same time controlling the muscles that move and focus our eyes, keep us balanced, and guide our hands, all while keeping our hearts beating, regulating our body temperature, and managing dozens of other automatic nervous functions.

Meanwhile, our conscious minds are aware of (and able to process) only a small fraction of this information. As Daniel Dennett has pointed out, "Conscious human minds are more-or-less serial virtual machines implemented—inefficiently—on the parallel hardware that evolution has provided for us."[20] Our conscious minds, therefore, experience the world sequentially, as a series of events, thoughts, and reactions, and the primary mode of this experience is narrative. We turn our daily experiences into stories around the dinner table; we employ alternate hypothetical narratives to reason through difficult decisions; we evaluate (and revise) our psychological state by examining, with the aid of a therapist, the narratives that grant us a sense of self; the very language we use is organized around sequential narrative units called sentences; even the theorems and postulates of mathematics are constructed as "If . . . then" narratives, which we combine to form elaborate causal chains echoing the process of thought that led from the simplest axiom to the most anti-intuitive conclusion.

Metaphor, on the other hand, engages the dominant parallel structures of the brain. We have already seen that metaphors form complex comparative webs, including both similarities and differences, linking vehicle and tenor. We have also seen that the links involve semiotic mapping in both directions. And we have noted that absorbing a metaphor requires rapid comparison, evaluation, and selection of relevant threads. All of these features are most efficiently and effectively handled by parallel processing. Furthermore, even if one believes it is possible to translate the simultaneous back-and-forth mapping of a metaphor into a series of narrative declarations, the power of a metaphor depends on the simultaneity of the experience. We *feel* the force of a metaphor, such as Wilner's "our thoughts, however elegant, were fire," because it allows us to hold a particular set of meanings in mind together—for the most part without additional explicit verbalization (though we may subsequently seek to express pieces of the experience in the narratives of rational thought). Metaphors are therefore tailor-made for (by) the brain's parallel processing, because such processing allows us to experience the multiple threads linking vehicle and tenor as a temporally unified mental experience.

It is worth bearing in mind that the serial functions of the brain are not synonymous with "consciousness" per se. They form, more specifically, our rational consciousness. Other animals are also conscious, but theirs is a consciousness that does not depend on narratives (or metaphors, for that matter—though it may be closer to a metaphorical way of thinking). Most animals, lacking complex language, experience each moment as a plethora of stimuli, which they sift in simultaneous relation, rather than breaking them down into components and considering each separately, sequentially. We retain this form of consciousness as well, though it is often difficult to access, being "shouted down" by the verbal facility of our serial consciousness. Meditation is one way of attempting to access the parallel portion. Metaphor is another—though because it is a function of language, it also engages the serial portion of our brain. The linking function of metaphor therefore acts not only on symbols, but on our different modes of mental processing as well. Metaphors, in effect, allow the two modes of our brains to talk to one another.

These characteristics of metaphor, along with those I outlined earlier, make them particularly suited to expressing complex relationships among phenomena, especially those involving contradictory or incompatible elements that resist representation by means of causal narratives. Nuclear weapons, as we have seen, fit this description: they combine attributes of such power and diversity that narrative representations invariably become convoluted, confusing, and contradictory. Far from being undone by the bombings of Hiroshima and Nagasaki, metaphor remains an essential tool for dealing with the conceptual challenges presented by nuclear weapons, because metaphors increase the kinds and range of ways we can think about these weapons by engaging the brain's parallel functioning directly.

# Metaphor, Narrative, and Nuclear Weapons

It is not surprising that metaphorical representations of nuclear weapons have proliferated in popular culture: those of us with no direct knowledge of these weapons will naturally turn to metaphor as we try to express imaginatively what we have not experienced actually. What is perhaps more surprising is that even scientists with an intimate knowledge of these weapons, despite a prejudice in favor of causal narrative, turn again and again to metaphor as they search for ways to understand and express their experiences. Alice in Wonderland, the resurrection of Christ, Columbus's arrival in the New World, the Hindu god Siva, "a red-hot elephant standing balanced on its trunk"[21]—each of these vehicles is both an expression of disorientation and an effort to reorient the self in response to a radically unfamiliar experience. Although they strive to focus on narrative renderings of their experiences, the writings of scientists who have participated in the construction of nuclear weapons offer an embarrassment of metaphorical riches that reflects the utility of the mode as a means of navigating the unfamiliar conceptual terrain.

Amidst these riches, there is one form that occurs more frequently than any other, in various guises: the bomb is like God. It is an immediately compelling link, referencing the power of nuclear weapons, their apparent omnipresence, the actual omnipresence of the nuclear processes that engender them, the role of fusion in creating all of the heavier elements that make up the world, and the fact that fission and fusion reactions underlie the properties that lead us to call the sun "the giver of life." These are important associations, and they tell us a great deal about our relationship to nuclear weapons, as well as about the nature of God; but ultimately the metaphor is most compelling not in what it says, but in what it does not say.

Perhaps the most significant link between the bomb and God is the mystery that surrounds each. So far, God has eluded rational observation (although there have been many mystical sightings); nuclear weapons, being products of our own handiwork, existing as physical entities in stockpiles around the world, ought to be less resistant. We can watch film footage of nuclear explosions, look at photographs of warheads, and read the accounts of the hibakusha. Yet few of us, we pray, will ever see a nuclear weapon "incarnate"—either in use or repose. They exist for most of us only as textual entities, like God. And while fewer people may doubt the reality of nuclear weapons than question the existence of God, almost all of us who believe do so for reasons that bear an unsettling similarity to religious faith: because we grew up in households that believe, because we trust the evidence of books and films, because other people share their belief with us. Even the causal mode of scientific description that "justifies" our belief grew out of the narrative tradition of biblical exegesis.

I'm not suggesting, as I hope the sensible reader already assumes, that nuclear weapons don't exist. Nor am I suggesting that the evidence for their existence is not far more trustworthy than a religious text. But the fact remains that nuclear weapons are inaccessible to most of us. Even the military personnel and technicians who tend to these weapons have only limited access. Indeed, nuclear weapons exist within elaborate physical and institutional structures of compartmentalization and procedure designed specifically to maintain their inaccessibility.

This leaves us in the curious situation of spending, worldwide, trillions of dollars to build, transport, store, and service objects we intend never to use.

Surely they must have, in Marx's phrase, some "use value." If so, that value would seem to be the value of a symbol—in addition to what we commonly call "symbolic value." These weapons stand for the unimaginable damage and suffering they can inflict; for the power and prestige of the society capable of building them; for the determination to "defend" a nation (or exact revenge on its enemies) at any cost; for the Faustian bargain of scientific knowledge; for the abuse of power. Precisely what they mean is, of course, an ongoing debate; but there is no doubt that they mean, and with unusual force. Indeed, it is their unrestrained capacity to mean that makes us value them so highly and fear them so intensely. While unused, they function as markers for what they might do. When used, they flood our lives with irresistible meanings—meanings so potent they destroy everything, including meaning. And so we fear them as we fear madmen, never quite confident that we understand them or what they will do. And so madmen are drawn to them as a means of imposing their mad meanings on the world.

The ability of nuclear weapons to perform these symbolic functions depends on a curious feature of the way in which they respond to metaphor. As I mentioned previously, metaphors usually involve knowledge of both the tenor and vehicle; when one has no knowledge of the tenor, the effect of a metaphor is a complete mapping of the vehicle onto the inscrutable tenor. Though we have some knowledge of nuclear weapons and their effects, it is limited and secondhand, like our knowledge of God. Because of this, nuclear weapons tend (incompletely, in inverse proportion to our knowledge of them) to swallow the metaphorical vehicles applied to them, as a black hole swallows light. This renders them both difficult to know in themselves and immensely effective as symbols. They become, in effect, reservoirs of the meanings we apply to them: symbolic entities stocked with an abundance of metaphorical vehicles, ready to echo our meanings back to us, in the most profound or trivial ways: mutually assured destruction, Atomic Red Hots, the Second Coming in Wrath, the Atomic Cleaners of Beaumont, Texas.

Here is the real danger inherent in metaphorical treatments of nuclear weapons. It is not that our metaphors will demean or trivialize these weapons or the experiences of those who suffered because of them. Though this is possible and should be guarded against, the more significant danger is the inverse: not the metaphors we apply to the bomb, but the ways in which we use the bomb itself as a metaphor. Like God, the bomb is a symbolic entity we have stoked with meanings that can be used to justify any argument: the United States is God's chosen nation; the United States is the great Satan; our government officials are merchants of death; our government officials are saviors, backed by their godlike bombs. Each of these dogmatic narratives can be supported by the symbolic flexibility that characterizes the inaccessible vehicle of nuclear weapons.

The problem, therefore, is not metaphor in isolation, but particular inter-actions of metaphor and narrative. There are good reasons to apply each mode cautiously, and the twentieth century produced plenty of examples of writers and artists who mistrusted one or the other.[22] But they did so in a wide range of contexts, and for reasons that were not peculiar to the representational challenges presented by nuclear weapons. Chief among these reasons were the insights that narrative is dangerous because it fixes meanings; metaphor because it grants them dynamic range. Yet we continue to rely on both for the essential functions they perform—functions we can't, in fact, live without. What we need to do, and urgently in the case of nuclear weapons, is find a way to use each in a mea-sured, appropriate fashion.

The representational practices of science and religion offer convenient poles to guide our efforts. It is important, for instance, to recognize the danger of loose and imprecise applications of scientific representational modes in nonscientific contexts. While scientists do very well constructing narratives out of meta-phorical insights, they are able to do so only by virtue of rigorous experimental verification of those narratives. In general, basing narratives on metaphors is imprecise, sloppy, even destructive, because it fixes certain arbitrary features of the dynamic linkages established by metaphors. On the other hand, we should also avoid metaphors lacking a solid narrative foundation. In the case of nuclear weapons, the only way to keep the bomb from being an indiscriminate and in-satiable symbolic reservoir is to ground our metaphor-making in narratives from authoritative sources, including the hibakusha and other eyewitnesses.

Religions, likewise, weave metaphor and narrative into representational webs; and their efforts to know unknowable gods offer a cautionary example for those of us who hope to apply these modes to the remote but imminent power of nuclear weapons. The importance of authorizing narratives is everywhere evident in religion: the Torah, the New Testament, the Quran, the Vedas—each offers narratives purporting to define its faith. The relative veracity of these narratives is, of course, subject to violent debate. Yet these narratives would not result in intolerance, holy fervor, and an effort to impose belief and behavior on others if they were understood to be essentially metaphoric, based on God as a symbol of a dynamic truth rather than God as a fixed, prescriptive set of narratives. Dogmatic adherents believe the narratives of their faith literally, and they are correspondingly inflexible in their attitudes and behavior. Metaphorical relations to God (favored by mystics) are less dangerous because they remain fluid and emotional rather than fixed and "logical." When a religious devotee believes faith is "reasonable" (which narrative encourages), faith turns dangerous.

Science and religion are often considered utterly incompatible disciplines, yet the metaphorical power of nuclear weapons links them inextricably, and some of the most interesting and instructive literary treatments of these weapons recognize and explore the conjunction. *A Canticle for Leibowitz*, for example, begins with the discovery of a bomb shelter by Brother Francis, a novice monk, during his Lenten fast in the desert. Inside the shelter, he finds tools, a grocery list, a racing form, and a circuit diagram, among other artifacts dating from before a nuclear apocalypse six hundred years earlier. These artifacts belonged to Isaac Edward Leibowitz, an engineer who survived the "Deluge" and converted to Catholicism, founding a monastic order dedicated to preserving pre-war knowledge from the destructive rage of the "Simpletons." Although the monks can read and write Latin, and even some English, these objects are mysteries to them. When Pope Leo asks Brother Francis if he understands the meaning of the circuit diagram, for instance, he replies: "'No, Holy Father, my ignorance is complete.' The Pope leaned toward him to whisper: 'So is ours.'"[23] The novel, therefore, depicts a world in which the symbolic meanings of nuclear weapons, unleashed in a horrific incarnation, have overwhelmed all other meanings (including, ironically, the knowledge of how the weapons were made, or even what they really were). The monks can read Leibowitz's words, but their original meanings have been erased. Everyday objects mingle indistinguishably with the specialized tools of science, all of them reduced to blank slates that the monks overwrite with their own narratives.

This metaphorization occurs in two steps. First, the people who set off the nuclear conflagration did so because they imposed certain meanings on their weapons, and those meanings, whether we consider them right or wrong from our vantage point, trumped all others. Second, the monks, encountering objects from which the nuclear bombardment had stripped all meaning, and needing to extend and strengthen their faith, metamorphosed those objects into metaphorical vehicles capable of mapping religious narratives back onto the vast experiential blank of the nuclear apocalypse. So the monks preserve Leibowitz's grocery list as a relic, using it along with all the other artifacts to make a case for their founder's canonization.

Russell Hoban's *Riddley Walker*, written twenty-one years after *Canticle*, offers a very different vision of a post-apocalyptic world, yet one in which the power of metaphor and metaphors of power play an equally important role. Like the southeastern United States in which Brother Francis lives, Riddley's England has been utterly transformed by nuclear war. Most pre-war knowledge has been lost, and the fragments that remain are a hodgepodge, indiscriminately uniting scientific and religious narratives and metaphors. At the center of these fragments is a twentieth-century informational leaflet describing a fifteenth-century fresco of St. Eustace's life. The original meanings of the leaflet have been obliterated by nuclear fire, like those of the grocery list or the circuit diagram in *Canticle*, and so the descendents of the survivors (over the course of some three thousand years) read it metaphorically, applying their own experiences, hopes, and fears to the bomb's erasures.

Out of these fragments they construct a set of narratives with which they attempt to shore up the fragments of their society in turn. These narratives are the special property and care of an educated elite; as Riddley tells us, "You wunt have seen the woal thing wrote out without you ben a Eusa show man or connexion man or in the Mincery. No 1 else is allowit to have it wrote down the same which that dont make no odds becaws no 1 else knows how to read."[24] The show men travel from community to community, retelling their stories by means of an elaborate Punch and Judy show, which are then interpreted by the local connexion man. The cycle of retelling and reinterpretation binds the various communities in a web of shared meanings, creating a larger political entity in much the same way individual religious communities are bound into a single religious institution by the semiotic glue of sanctioned metaphors and narratives.

The "Eusa story" in *Riddley Walker* is neither quite scientific nor fully religious, but it combines clear elements of both. It includes, for instance, the pre-apocalyptic discipline of chemistry, now known as "chemistery"—part scientific discipline, part religious mystery—that tells, among other things, of "the Littl Shynin Man the Addom." Here and elsewhere, Hoban brilliantly reconstructs the historical links between religious myth and scientific theory, in this case by merging pieces of the narrative of Adam and Eve with bits of atomic theory to create a kind of doubled metaphor. By "doubled" I mean that it functions as a metaphor both within the world of the novel—a narrative figure that serves as a vehicle for the mysterious forces of the "1 Big 1"—and for the reader—a trope linking the religious and scientific narratives of Adam and atom. In each case, the metaphor is rich with meaning and practical implications. For Riddley's people, it represents both a means of social cohesion and a step on the long road of (re)constructing (religious, scientific) narratives that constitute understanding of the natural world. For us, it reveals some of the ways metaphors and narratives function—as modes of finding and making meaning in the world; as means of imagining how our world might be laid waste by the ways we have construed it; as tools for reimagining a world in which the threat of nuclear weapons is not simply a matter of megatons but of how we think and write and speak.

A crucial component in the doubling of Hoban's metaphor is that we know things that Riddley and his compatriots do not. The original meanings of St. Eustace, Adam, and atom are still accessible to us, while Riddley's knowledge is limited to the reconfigured narratives and metaphors of the novel. We therefore see two sets of meanings "side by side" (though separated by ninety pages): the originals and those revised by nuclear war. From the leaflet:

> 1. At the bottom of the painting St. Eustace is seen on his knees before his quarry, a stag, between whose antlers appears, on a cross of radiant light, the figure of the crucified Saviour.[25]

And from the Eusa story:

> 8. In the dark wud Eusa seen a trak uv lyt he follert it. He cum tu the
> Hart uv the Wud it wuz the Stag uv the Wud it wuz the 12 Poynt
> Stag stud tu fays him & stampin its feat. On the stags hed stud the
> Littl Shynin Man the Addom in be twean thay horns with arms owt
> strecht & each han holdin tu a horn.[26]

In a fascinating passage, unfortunately too long to reproduce here, a character named Goodparley offers an interpretation of this doubled text that reveals both how far he and Riddley are from grasping its pre-apocalyptic meanings and yet how slowly and surely they are constructing new, viable metaphoric and narrative structures that will lead from an unlikely foundation in the life of St. Eustace to the rediscovery of gunpowder. Our ability to see both the old and the new structures of meaning allows us to recognize not only what we stand to lose, but the narrative and metaphoric processes by which it came to be created in the first place.

# Conclusion

All of this suggests a number of answers to the question I asked earlier: What can our metaphoric representations add to the narratives of those with firsthand knowledge of nuclear weapons? Without Hoban's novel (and other metaphoric explorations of all sorts), we would be more likely to accept the metaphors of eyewitnesses as exclusively authoritative, to treat narratives based on these metaphors as fixed, to find ourselves stuck in outmoded ways of thinking. Einstein famously said, "The unleashed power of the atom has changed everything save our modes of thinking, and we thus drift toward unparalleled catastrophe."[27] By "modes" he did not mean either metaphor or narrative in itself, but rather the particular ways we used them immediately following World War II. Einstein saw that we were allowing ourselves to become dependent on old, obvious metaphors and the overly rigid narratives they inspired. But *Riddley Walker*, and works like it, grant us a second perspective—imaginary, yes, but based on a wide-ranging knowledge of the facts as we know them. In doing so, the novel functions as a single, enormous metaphor itself, linking the narratives and metaphors of our experience with those of Hoban's imagined world. Such metaphoric acts of imagination can help us to see our own "modes of thinking" more clearly, as well as where they might lead, and ultimately contribute to a potential transformation, or at least revision, of how we think and act in response to nuclear weapons.

# Notes

1. "The Invention of the Zero," in Richard Kenney, *The Invention of the Zero* (New York: Alfred Knopf, 1995).

2. "Two Sculptors: Donald Judd's Marfa Texas; Tony Cragg: In Celebration of Sculpture." Directed by Christopher Felver. Palm Pictures. 2006.

3. Adorno wrote, "Perennial suffering has as much right to express itself as the martyr has to scream; this is why it may have been wrong to say that poetry could not be written after Auschwitz." *Negative Dialectics*, trans. Dennis Redmond, www.efn .org/~dredmond/ndtrans.html, 2002.

4. These are, of course, enormous questions. In the hope of finding a way toward practical insight, I will limit the scope of the issues I consider, focusing on the functions of metaphor relative to nuclear weapons and leaving issues of representing and responding to the Holocaust to others. I will also look at metaphor in its verbal manifestations rather than its use in the plastic arts.

5. Nuclear Weapon Archive, "The B-41 (Mk-41) Bomb: High yield strategic thermonuclear bomb," nuclearweaponarchive.org/Usa/Weapons/B41.html (updated 10/21/97).

6. United States Navy, "Fact File: Fleet Ballistic Missile Submarines," www.navy .mil/navydata/fact_display.asp?cid=4100&tid=200&ct=4; Lockheed Martin, "Navy Team Celebrates 10th Anniversary of Trident II D5 Missile System," www.lockheedmartin .com/wms/findPage.do?dsp=fec&ci=12491&rsbci=0&fti=0&ti=0&sc=400; Nuclear Weapon Archive, "The W88 Warhead: Intermediate yield strategic SLBM MIRV warhead," nuclearweaponarchive.org/Usa/Weapons/W88.html.

7. United States Navy, "Fact File: Trident Fleet Ballistic Missile," www.navy.mil/ navydata/fact_display.asp?cid=2200&tid=1400&ct=2.

8. It is worth remembering that 120,000 people worked for two years to build the first three atomic bombs and that an ongoing massive collaboration between government, military, academic, and industrial institutions is required to design, produce, and maintain these weapons.

9. Bulletin of the Atomic Scientists, "5 Minutes to Midnight: Nuclear," www .thebulletin.org/minutes-to-midnight/nuclear.html.

10. Nuclear Age Peace Foundation, "Nuclear Stockpiles," www.nuclearfiles.org/ menu/key-issues/nuclear-weapons/basics/nuclear-stockpiles.htm.

11. Sight is a process involving the transfer of information from an object to an eye by means of huge numbers photons. Atoms are over a thousand times smaller than the smallest wavelength of visible light, so an interaction between a photon and a subatomic particle can convey only partial information—and none that our brains can register. The photon's impulse changes the behavior of the particle it is "reporting on" anyway.

12. In fact, despite the scientific emphasis on literal over metaphorical language, it is precisely this lack of analogs that proves most troubling to scientists, since the process of constructing literal descriptions of the world involves initial forays into highly metaphorical conceptions. I will return to this point later.

13. Radiation therapy was first used to treat cancer in 1899. American Cancer Society, "The History of Cancer" (accessed 2/15/07), www.cancer.org/docroot/CRI/content/CRI_2_6x_the_history_of_cancer_72.asp?sitearea=CRI. (revised 3/25/02).

14. Michihiko Hachiya, *Hiroshima Diary* (Chapel Hill: University of North Carolina Press, 1955), 43.

15. I'm coining "memetic" based on Richard Dawkins notion of "memes" as patterns of information (ideas, metaphors, behaviors) that reproduce throughout a culture. We are the medium of their reproduction, as of our genes'. And as our genes are, collectively, a blueprint of our bodies, memes structure our noninherited behaviors and identities. See Richard Dawkins, *The Selfish Gene*, third ed. (Oxford: Oxford University Press, 2006).

16. This metaphor is, itself, an excellent example of the complex, ongoing processing involved in the creation and consumption of symbolic linkages, having been the subject of considerable exploration and debate since it was formulated so memorably by William James in his *Principles of Psychology*.

17. Eleanor Wilner, *Sarah's Choice* (Chicago: University of Chicago Press, 1989).

18. Eric R. Kandell, James H. Schwartz, and Thomas M. Jessell, *Principles of Neural Science*, fourth ed. (New York: McGraw Hill, 2000), 34.

19. The term is vexed, both relativistically and when applied to neural processing, in the latter of which there is approximately a fifty-millisecond range during which two events are effectively "simultaneous." See Daniel C. Dennett and Marcel Kinsbourne, "Time and the Observer: The Where and When of Consciousness in the Brain," in *The Nature of Consciousness*, Ned Block, Owen Flanagan, and Güven Güzeldere, eds. (Cambridge, Mass.: MIT University Press, 1997), 143.

20. Daniel Dennett, *Consciousness Explained* (Boston: Little, Brown and Company, 1991), 218.

21. Robert Serber, correspondence with the author, March 8, 1993; Victor Weisskopf, *The Joy of Insight: Passions of a Physicist* (New York: Basic Books, 1991), 152; Arthur Compton, in *The Cosmos of Arthur Holly Compton*, Marjorie Johnston, ed. (New York: Alfred A. Knopf, 1967), 248; Robert Oppenheimer, quoted in Richard Rhodes, *The Making of the Atomic Bomb* (New York: Simon and Schuster, 1986), 676; Otto Frisch, *What Little I Remember* (Cambridge: Cambridge University Press, 1980), 164.

22. James Joyce, T. S. Eliot, and Samuel Beckett come to mind as examples of writers who questioned conventional narratives; Ernest Hemingway, Theodor Adorno, and Donald Judd mistrusted metaphor.

23. Walter M. Miller Jr., *A Canticle for Leibowitz* (Philadelphia: J. B. Lippincott, 1973), 112.

24. Russell Hoban, *Riddley Walker* (New York: Summit Books, 1980), 29.

25. *Riddley Walker*, 123.

26. *Riddley Walker*, 31.

27. Albert Einstein, *The New York Times* (May 25, 1946), 13, col. 5.

# CHAPTER 2

# Poems from *Critical Assembly*

*John Canaday*

The poems in this chapter are taken from John Canaday's work titled *Critical Assembly*. These poems focus on the specific events that are part of the history of the advent of nuclear weapons, and are written in the voices of historical participants in those events. Biographical notes of those invoked in the poems follow at the end of the chapter.

## Leo Szilard Imagines a Nuclear Chain Reaction (London, 1933)

In 1913, H. G. Wells produced *The World*
*Set Free*, a novel that describes a global war
fought with atomic bombs. Moonshine, Ernest Rutherford
would say, with all the Cavendish to echo him.
An expert is a man who knows what can't be done.
Wells is a dilettante, no doubt—his books chock full
of wild imaginings—and yet he does his homework,
foreseeing consequences of another man's
discoveries more clearly than the man himself.
We met once at a dinner party. He was fierce
in his pursuit of truth. He cared more for ideas
than men—and so he dedicates *The World Set Free*
to Frederick Soddy's book on radium and not
its author. Individuals will come and go,
but what we think and write lives on to bless or haunt
the future. Lately, Wells's work haunts me more. I thought
at first, like Rutherford, I knew reality

from make-believe. But Wells foresaw the birth of man-
made radioactivity in '33—
he named the very year! And when this fiction proved
a fact, the rest seemed . . . plausible. And so I sipped
Wells's moonshine. Lounging in my hotel bath past noon,
I bribed my body with hot water, let my mind
float free—what better place to think than in a tub?—
until the maid descended. Then I dressed and strolled
through London, wondering. One day I wandered down
Southampton Row. A red light broke my chain of thought.
I balanced on the curb, and when the light turned green
I felt the swift, sweet surge of inspiration hit
and knew the missing piece must be an element
that would absorb a single neutron when it split
and then emit two more. I knew this element,
assembled in sufficient mass, might well sustain
a chain reaction. Only slowly did the joy
of insight give way to a more foreboding thought.
I couldn't publish this. Instead, I patented
the concept and assigned it to the Admiralty
and prayed that no one in the Reich read H. G. Wells.
But if all knowledge comes through individuals,
it comes to answer questions asked by history.
I knew that one day soon I'd have to make a choice,
or sit back in my bath and have it made for me.

# Otto Frisch's Fission (Kungälv, 1938)

Rare earth sparks the clouds
　　　　between two wars.
Fermi, Hahn and Strassman,
　　　　Joliot-Curie—
all chemists, physicists,
　　　　track protons now.
But Hitler's blinders point
　　　　to Austria:
the occupation interrupts
　　　　Aunt Lise's
parting of nature's mists.
　　　　When she departs
for Sweden, isotopes
　　　　of radium
(she thinks) sit on her desk,
　　　　unanalyzed.

Lonely, she summons me
⠀⠀⠀⠀north to Kungälv
for our Christmas ritual.
⠀⠀⠀⠀Her colleague's letter
intercepts festivities.
⠀⠀⠀⠀The body's tagged,
identified by Hahn.
⠀⠀⠀⠀It's barium.
I strap on skis; she demurs,
⠀⠀⠀⠀makes good her claim
to move as fast without.
⠀⠀⠀⠀The woods that wall
the Göta älv become
⠀⠀⠀⠀our conference room;
a fallen spruce's trunk
⠀⠀⠀⠀our sticky seat,
my pockets stocked with scraps
⠀⠀⠀⠀of hotel paper.
We know uranium
⠀⠀⠀⠀can't crack in two
against the grain of Gamow's
⠀⠀⠀⠀alpha theory.
Yet it does. We turn
⠀⠀⠀⠀to Schrödinger
for insight: particles
⠀⠀⠀⠀are waves. Then Bohr:
a nucleus is liquid,
⠀⠀⠀⠀like a drop. Our thought:
that heavy nuclei
⠀⠀⠀⠀must undulate
like water molecules,
⠀⠀⠀⠀collectively.
In larger elements
⠀⠀⠀⠀charge balances
the surface tension. Struck
⠀⠀⠀⠀even lightly,
in neutron capture,
⠀⠀⠀⠀the pseudo drop
will wobble, waist, and split.
⠀⠀⠀⠀Sometimes physics
lacks words for what we think.
⠀⠀⠀⠀Its abstract paths—
quantum tunnel effects,
⠀⠀⠀⠀packing fractions,

and disintegration—
    lead to thickets
where neutrons multiply
    like rabbits, wildly.
The winter woods are gone.
    The mind's meadows
bloom as I calculate
    the energy
released: two hundred million
    electron volts.
Now atoms break and breed
    like living cells.
I name their splitting "fission"
    and publish it
where even Nazi stooges
    can read the news.

# Robert Serber Roughs It (Pecos Wilderness, 1938)

Robert and his brother spent their summers
in the Pecos Mountains north of Santa Fe.
They had a ranch they called Perro Caliente—
Katie Page's Spanish double take
on Robert's first words when he saw the place.
In '35 he summoned us to make
the pilgrimage, and though our city blood
felt like the sap of potted plants, I'd learned
to pity men who disappointed Oppie.
So we headed down Route 66,
with Charlotte riding shotgun, primed to find
high mountain meadows, a canopy of stars.
We crossed into New Mexico, and bang!
the highway turned to dirt. We wondered if
we'd underestimated how much zeal
we'd need. We wondered for two hundred miles.
But once we'd passed the cabin and the small
corral half-hidden in the aspen, twice,
before we grasped it must be Oppie's "ranch,"
we thought we knew the worst. What did we know?
The place was "picturesque." Two rooms. In one
a battered couch, a Navajo throw rug
beside the huge stone hearth, and that was it.

The kitchen housed a wood stove and a pot
of chili left to ripen all week long.
No sink. No plumbing, period. No place
to sit. They all slept on the bare board floor.
It daunted us at first, until we learned
our worry was unfounded, since a few
"old friends" had happened by that afternoon
(the way Scott must have happened by the Pole)
and commandeered our spots on Oppie's floor.
Instead, our kind host loaned us horses. "Ride
straight north, toward Jicoria Pass," he said.
"Blue and Cumbres know the way." We tried
to smile. "In three days you'll reach Taos, where
they always have a room for friends of mine."
Well, I'd seen photographs of horses, once,
so who was I to look these in the mouth?
We mounted gingerly and said goodbye
to Oppie. Almost as an afterthought,
he handed us a fifth of scotch, a box
of crackers, and two bags of oats. "The oats
are for the horses," he admonished us.
We gave the beasts their heads and off we went
into the Pecos wilderness, two rubes
trusting in God as they had never done before.
By afternoon our fears had eased, replaced
by pain: the stirrups bruised our city feet,
the saddles rubbed our thighs and buttocks raw.
We camped that night beneath the canopy
of stars, but hardly noticed them as sore
legs stiffened, backs cramped, tender blisters swelled.
The first two days remain a nightmare blur.
Then on the third day Charlotte lost her grip
and fell. I ran to help, but she got up,
said she was fine, and seemed to be, except
for what appeared to be a bloody straw
stuck in her cheek. I tried to pluck it out
and found it was a fountain of her blood.
A pine needle had pierced her cheek and hit
an artery. I tore strips from my shirt
and bound her jaw. The bleeding wouldn't stop.
What could we do? We mounted our horses
and urged them on toward Taos. Two hours
later, a cluster of adobe houses
appeared on the horizon. Charlotte broke
into a gallop. When she reached the town

she reined her horse in by a wide-eyed group
of local men and fell off at their feet.
They called a doctor, and he sewed her up.
So ended our adventure: a small taste
of life in Oppie's world, which might, you'd think,
have left me soured on my boss. But no:
we'd reached past every possibility
we had imagined for ourselves, inspired
by Oppie's expectations and his blunt
refusal to allow that we might fail.
He drove us past all inhibition. So
when Oppie called six thousand scientists
together in the Jemez range, among
the cottonwoods above the Rio Grande,
to do his secret weapons work, we came,
trusting what he would make of it, and us.

# Edward Teller Chauffeurs
# Leo Szilard (Long Island, 1939)

Now Einstein knows me as Szilard's
chauffeur. I warm the stoop
while great men talk of physics, bombs.
Fame is a used Ford coupe.

A mere post doc, I heard Einstein
expound God's mysteries
at Kaiser Wilhelm Institute
in 1929.

Later, at der Berliner Zoo,
the sweet spring sun fell mute.
Wigwam inquired, made me confess
I was a brainless brute.

"Apes. Men. Stupidity's a trait
all fauna share." Kind words.
Though sad, I sometimes wish them true.
Then no one would be great.

A guest at Bohr's colloquium,
I sat beside him, awed,
and watched his face fall as I spoke
of Newton's physics' flaws.

He closed his eyes. Sat silently.
Then murmured, "Better say
we do not sit here drinking tea
but only dream your words."

Why strive for Truth? Humility
whispers a choice: take less
and add, mechanically, to top
what passes for success.

I tried that route. Great Heisenberg
assigned my doctoral work—
compute the $H_2$ ion's states—
as though I were a clerk.

The Thales in the common room
groaned unmusically,
despite the oil I wooed it with,
and physics lost its bloom.

But most when Heisenberg pranced through
complaining he had solved
the last great question. "Nothing left
that needs genius." I stewed.

And then resolved to prove him wrong.
In increments. Stumbling,
perhaps. But finding it. The next
big thing. The biggest thing.

# Albert Einstein Sails
# (Peconic Bay, Long Island, 1939)

Life is finite
                                and improbable.
The wooden tiller smooth as living skin
trembles under my fingers' calcite grip.

What was the chance of my appearing here
and now? And yet my sail has only filled
as nature wills, and as its laws decree

my prow points out across Peconic Bay.
The water, white-capped, wrestles with the wind.
I wrestle both, though each of us obeys

and manifests the selfsame laws.
The instruments are mortal, what we measure
infinite. Mankind's proper posture

must be awe: our bodies' currents carry us,
like Newton (grant we travel half so far),
toward revelation of the limits God

has set on nature. Are we fit to know
such secrets? We cannot resist the sweet
temptation of the possible: we eat

the apple, build machineries of war,
reshape the world in our short-sighted image;
yet no physicist could have a soul so poor

he would not do as much to see God's face.
Nostra culpa! The more we know, the less
we feel. Man cools more quickly than the earth.

# Eugene Wigner Thinks of His Family in Hungary (Princeton, 1939)

Hatred's homicidal.
Hitler knows. He makes
what most men mean by hate
a tepid sentiment,
though at the time,
no one seemed inclined
to notice, and I wondered,
When will my Hungarians
awaken? I waited
for the Jews to rouse
themselves. But only
slowly were they moved
to anger; even then
most merely said,
"depose the madman."
Moderation's suicide.
A whimper while the butcher
spreads fresh paper.
Even in translation
in the *Times*, he aims

his hate at me, my family
trapped in Budapest.
Our decades-old conversion
meaningless. In Nazi law,
I could become a *hausfrau*
more easily than Lutheran.
Why should I hesitate
to bend my skills to kill?
My colleagues here
at Princeton wince.
I challenge them
to say which wrong
they disapprove of more:
the braying Nazi donkeys,
or this Jew who has
the questionable taste
to corner them.

# Albert Einstein Imagines Atomic Bombs (Peconic, Long Island, 1939)

The Czechoslovak state is occupied,
the Nazis stockpile its uranium,
and Leo claims they plan to make a bomb.

He's had some crazier ideas. And if
I listened when he pitched induction flow
refrigerators, why not now? Perhaps

God has designed the world as I have thought,
and firing neutrons at the nuclei
of heavy atoms is like shooting birds

at night. But if I'm wrong, my data old?
It's not improbable that novel sources
of enormous energy exist. And if

we follow, then . . . . O grant us no such then!
If Leo's right, then all bombardments all
together since the first men used firearms

would be child's play to what we will unleash,
and we will build ourselves a future age
to make our coal-black present shine like gold.

# Louis Slotin Remembers the Spanish Civil War (En Route to Los Alamos, 1943)

On the train from Oak Ridge down to Lamy
we talked about our new assignment
at Los Alamos, the doubled frontier
of A-bombs and wild west escapades.
We savored the thought of living side by side
with pioneers like Bethe and Niels Bohr
though, after hours in the same cramped seats,
our aching backsides made us squirm
and dampened our enthusiasm some.
But still we feigned a manly disregard.
So when Bill kvetched about the food, or lack of it,
I mocked his daintiness and asked
what he expected in a war. I figured
I would give him food for thought. I said
I'd been a regimental engineer in Spain
resisting Franco's fascists. This trip was nothing
next to riding in a cattle train turned hell-
hole troop transport from Quinto to Ambite.
The ancient Falstaff-bellied boiler choked us,
coughing coal smoke and a froth of oil.
We had no food at all until we stopped
abruptly by a truck parked in thick scrub
near no road I could see. We climbed out, baked
and aching. Dust had painted us to match
the khaki-colored earth. A troop of cooks
stood by the tracks—a brigade of golems
with grub buckets tilted on their shoulders.
Up and down the train they lugged
the metal pails of rice and beans.
Cup measures dangled from their belts
like sidearms. In our half-starved state,
the flies that swarmed around their heads
glistened like halos in the setting sun.
Funny how time and distance make
privation sound romantic. Bill shut his trap,
his hunger blunted by a few choice words.

# Robert Serber on How to Build a Bomb (Los Alamos, 1943)

When Oppie's first recruits arrived in March,
few knew what we were working on. Rumors
stitched bits and pieces of the facts to pure
conjecture: radium-laced poison gas,
electric rockets, windshield wiper blades
for submarines. So Oppie had me write
some talks to bring our colleagues up to speed.
We used the lab's unfinished library.
While carpenters stomped in and out, and cursed
and hammered, hanging drywall, doors, and shelves,
I raised my voice above their senseless noise:

"The object of our work is to produce
a bomb—"
                    But Oppie stopped me cold. He said
I'd better pitch that word. I tried again:

"A gadget of the kind we hope to make
is likely to result in several kinds
of damage, which I'll outline briefly here.
With fifteen kilograms of 25
we can expect that this device will yield
a range of pathological effects
within a thousand meter radius.
The radioactivity will be
a million curies ten days afterwards,
tending to render the locality
unfit for habitation for some time.
The gadget also will initiate
acoustic waves, and their velocity
will superpose on the velocity
with which the vaporized material
will be convected from the blast in jets,
and so the wave will overtake itself
and build a well-defined destructive front.
Thus, if destructive action is regarded
as a function of the pressure amplitude,
it follows that the likely radius
of noteworthy mechanical destruction
will be about a mile. As you can see,
these are not insignificant results.

But they involve considerable cost.
Since the materials this work requires
are precious, they constrain us to maintain
as high efficiency as possible.
Our aim is, simply put, the maximum
release of energy per nucleus."

Who would have thought mere words—so technical
and flat the workmen never blinked—could sketch
the pattern of a star to singe the earth?
But first, of course, we had to step aside
and let the work crew build our library.

# Richard Feynman Joins the Manhattan Project (Los Alamos, 1944)

Once people thought that angels
beat their wings to push the earth
in its ordained track around the sun,
as easily as we might move a blackboard
covered with Serber's latest figures.
That view has now been somewhat modified.

The blank, unassuming face of a blackboard
makes it easier to calculate the sun's
mass, and gravity's figures
speak louder than the handful of earth
in a man. Numbers don't change
their minds, like people or angels.

As a boy, I thought I'd been left on earth
by aliens. I could figure
the rotational velocity of a changeup,
but my aim was a radian off. While the sun
arced through the blue vault like an angel,
I scrawled resonance equations on a blackboard.

On my first drive up to Los Alamos, the sun
on cottonwoods and sandstone transformed
me. I'd been thinking of Arline
in the TB ward in Albuquerque. The doctors figured
she had a year. My heart was a blackboard
covered in odds. The naked earth

rose before me then like the figure
of an angel.
I could spend my life slaving at a blackboard
and never quantify the way light shifted
in her eyes. I lay down on a bare patch of earth
to think. My chest was heavy with sun.

I chose the smaller job: alter
the course of a war. Armed with a blackboard,
I would earn my place on earth.
Behind me, an angel
beat her wings. I circled the sun
with a lasso of figures.

# Edith Warner Runs Her Tea Room (Otowi Bridge, 1944)

Venus hangs low above the mountains. After a long night's sleep
I feel less like a toy in constant need of being wound.
My headache's gone. My cracked lens bothers eyework, but I read
a little Lattimore. Tilano combs and braids his hair
after his Sunday riverbath. The chicken water pans
need cleaning. I will pickle winter pears, tomatoes, squash,
and then lay out tobaccy Dukey, lemons, and sardines
against the herders' ritual return, driving their sheep
down from the pastures of the Valle Grande.

                                        Much I thought safe
is lost already. War drives innovation, justifies
a hasty, thoughtless excess. Dump trucks rut the riverbank:
the Army steals its gravel for construction on the Hill
and forces farmers from their beanfields on the high plateau.
Power can be so many things. The rivers, sky, trees, fields,
and even mountains take into themselves what we give off—
and give it out again. Niels Bohr would understand. Last night
his eyes drew fire from the pine knots burning on my hearth—
a golden brilliance that the Israelites thought heaven had—
a light that is the legacy of long forgotten trees,
the essence of the elements they gathered and release,
a living circle closed. "What lingers in your heart to say?"
I longed to ask, thinking he had a magic word for me.
But now I know there is no magic word—or need for one.
Only endurance, trust. He cannot tell me what they do.

As if he needed to, when Bethes, Fermis, Allisons,
and Tellers dine each night in my tea room; I recognize
the conversation of atomic specialists; I know
the sound of German and Italian natives, what it means
when such men staff a secret Allied military base.

They think I disapprove. They're right. But not of them.
Last summer Army drillers set up an infernal rig
to test what footing my yard's earth would offer for a bridge.
Fear moved in as a boarder, as it hadn't in past years
when peach trees failed to bloom or hoppers ate the pueblo crops.
But in the end they oiled the Española road instead.
The gods send fat and lean times. Always rain will follow drought.
But men are slow to learn. They trust their ingenuity;
they think their needs are paramount. And so our pueblo boys
ship out for England, Africa, and Guam. Hilario
was burned when his destroyer took a shell; Slim saw two friends
draw sniper fire; and 5 Cents lost a leg. Pity the soul
who doesn't know enough to disapprove.
                                        This afternoon
we'll spend our rationed gas to gather wood on the plateau,
where sky and aspens vie in beauty. Soon hoarfrost will crisp
the smallest weedstalks, quieting the cries of canyon wrens.
Tonight I'll write a note to Brownie in the Philippines
on Peter's diabolical contraption. What the hunt
system will do to thought's another thing. I promised him.
Tomorrow Kitty comes for vegetables. Pronto will hunt
white turkey feathers with Tilano while our women's talk
brightens my kitchen. Later, Compton, Tuck, and Segre grace
my table. Levity and wisdom, laughter, somber words.
And I will serve them lamb ragout with cloves, posolé, sweet
tomato relish in an earthen bowl, and chocolate cake.
My "contribution to the war," they call it. "To the peace,"
I'd say, but don't. I'm grateful for the honor they intend.
I've listened to their talk and learned that what I thought beyond
man's compass can be so strong in some it radiates from them.


# Robert Serber and the Impact of the Gadget (Los Alamos, 1944)

Most days it was easy to forget
that we were building bombs. In fact, we weren't.
My group in T-Division spent its time

comparing tamper scattering results
from Manley's Cockcroft-Walton measurements
with half-baked estimates we'd jury-rigged
out of gut feelings, guesswork, and little more.
Our conversations ranged through new, exciting
territory: spark gap switches, spalling,
mean free paths, backscattering, and neutron
populations. Who had time to talk
of bombs? Technically, the job was sweet
enough, as Oppie said, to put your heart
and soul in—and we did. We took to sleeping
in the lab. Charlotte said she knew the loss
a widow feels. Even brushing your teeth
became a luxury. So when Bob Wilson
put aside his work one winter night
to host a meeting he sententiously
referred to as "The Impact of the Gadget
on Civilization," not many people
took the bait. I wasn't pinched by any
moral qualms, but out of friendship left
a stack of calculations on my desk,
wrapped up in my mackinaw, and went.
Besides, Priscilla told me Oppie planned
to go, and that, as everybody knew,
would make it an occasion. I can't say
in any detail what was said. Incidentals
dominate my memory: the cold snap
early in the week that set the sea of mud
churned by autumn rains and army boots
as if in stone, the waning gibbous moon,
and Pegasus high overhead. Inside, the air
was fogged with warm breath as we talked
in the shadow of the idle cyclotron.
As I recall, we talked awhile about
the imminent defeat of Germany.
Someone alluded to Dumbarton Oaks
and said the new United Nations should
be founded on full knowledge of our work.
But who could tell our story? We were bound
to silence by our army oaths, the slaves
of military secrecy. Then Oppie said,
so softly, so intensely, no one thought
to disagree: "A demonstration. Let
the bomb speak for us." It seemed obvious.
And left us even less time to discuss

the moral ins and outs of weapons work.
We followed Oppie from the lab like moths
drawn by the flame of his sweet eloquence.
Behind us, Wilson slowly powered up
the cyclotron. Its giant magnets hummed
their siren's song. Please God,
we weren't monsters. But we loved our work.

# Richard Feynman Sniffs Out a Code
# (Los Alamos, 1944)

Man's main concern is man—so artists
in the Renaissance believed. Scientists
think otherwise. Like bloodhounds
we sniff out invisible codes:
what goes on under the hard
surface of nature. *Mycobacterium tuberculosis*,

for instance. That bacillus broke the code
of Arline's body so badly she spit blood
on the collar of her nightgown. She tried hard
to hide the stains. She fooled the doctors.
For months they thought she had Hodgkins.
They liked to say that diagnosis is an art.

Once I read a book on bloodhounds
while the doctors fussed over Arline's tubercles.
It made those mutts seem like artists
with their noses, but I wondered how hard
it could be. I spent weeks sniffing out their codes,
crawling around on all fours, like a scientist.

Sometimes, I admit, I tried too hard
to pass the time. Arline was the real artist.
Each week she mailed me a new code.
She wouldn't let me pity her TB
by pretending to be stumped. "You're not a scientist
if you can't be dispassionate." I was a good dog.

I let her lose. We watched the TB's
progress. It became a kind of code
of honor for me as a sissy scientist
to match her artistry

in dying, to not let on how it dogged
my dreams. She hated when I took it hard.

So I devoted myself to the science
at hand. I rode my assistants so hard
they nicknamed me TB
(That Bastard) Feynman. But mostly I hounded
myself, as though I cared only to perfect the art
of killing; as if I understood death's code.

# Major John Dudley Requests a Transfer (Los Alamos, 1944)

By then I'd had it up to here
with stuck-up, smart-ass scientists.
For months I'd asked to join the war
and been mañanaed by the Corps
with lines a moron wouldn't buy:
"Your work here just might win the war."
So when Lebow turned my request
for transfer down again and said
instead I'd have to babysit
these prima donnas while they played
at building bombs, I really blew
my stack. "Six months," he promised me.
Alright, I thought, I'll give it that.
But three months nearly did me in.
They were children—smart as hell,
of course, with all their theories and
the laws of atoms and all that,
but when it came to common sense,
the Lord had clearly passed them by.
Somehow they couldn't understand
that requisitioning supplies
took time. They wanted everything
the day before they asked for it.
They didn't seem to understand
what safes were for. I used to find
thick stacks of classified reports
left lying on their desks, their safes
wide open a few feet away?
And then they'd clam up when I asked
for stats to help me build a shed

to house their precious cyclotron.
Later, I'd find them in the bar
at the La Fonda, arguing
top secret information with
a dozen locals listening.
I've had some physics in my day:
it doesn't take an Edison
to figure out that something's up
when words like "fission," "nucleus,"
and "bomb" are thrown around for free.
I tried to tell them even I
was not supposed to know these things.
I couldn't get them to shut up.
Some days my biggest job was just
to keep their secrets from myself.

# James Nolan in the Maternity Ward (Los Alamos, 1944)

What were we making: babies or . . . ? That joke
wore thin, though no one ever finished it.
We read the punch line in each other's eyes,
wanting to laugh but only managing
weak smiles, if that. Tight-lipped, our hearts sank. We
walked around towing blank thought bubbles like
wind-fretted barrage balloons. Our numbed minds
were blacked-out burgs. We hunkered down, silent,
watching G-men in snap-brim straw hats
quicken the thick shadows in every door-
way. So when Weisskopf stormed the hospital
with a letter to his sister some half-
witted censor'd chopped to hell and back and
wondered, really meaning it, "How can you
work in a place like this?," all I did was
wink (or wince?), and whisper, "Mum's the word."

# Ruth Marshak Mourns (Los Alamos, 1944)

Tech was a pit that swallowed up
my husband, day and night, and left

his better half, an untrained soldier, fighting
heartache. Finally I gave up
waiting dinner. Often he came home
at three or four a.m. Or not at all.
He said since all we had were Army cots,
he might as well sleep in the lab.
I think the Army knew what it was doing
when it only gave us single beds.
What made it worse was that this sacrifice
was not a sacrifice for him. He loved
his work. It overcame all scruples,
all familial feeling. Few of us knew
the thing our husbands sought,
its magnitude, or why it had aroused
such passion. "There's a war on, love," Bob said
each time I asked, until I learned
to shut my mouth, and wait, and spend my energy
on the mechanics of my daily life.
The alternation of the seasons: mud
to dust and back to mud. Teaching
third grade prima donna kids.
Learning to cook at 7,000 feet
with vegetables and fruits long past
their prime. A total absence
of fresh eggs. I chose my battles. This
was one that I could win. I howled for months
until the Army veterinarian agreed
to candle every egg before it hit
the Commissary shelves. I'd had enough
of finding grim reminders
of what they wanted to become, and failed.

# Edith Warner Visits Her Neighbors (Ildefonso Pueblo, 1944)

Over the years I learned their rituals. Tilano joined
the dancers for each new year's festival. On the fourth day
before the dawn the dancers disappeared into the hills.
Slowly women gathered in the plaza. I pressed close
against the wall of an adobe house. They stood in silence,
waiting for the sun to rise above the broad, dark shoulders
of the mountains. That first light seemed to free them, and they formed
a chorus, chanting to the living sun. Its power spilled

into the plaza, filling them. And then the men appeared,
their bodies painted black and white, with mottled turtle shells
tied at their knees and red yarn on their legs, embroidered kirtles
and the skins of foxes, great collars of fir, and feathers bound
into black hair. They moved in unison as animals,
as deer and mountain sheep and buffalo. Their moccasins
beat on the ground with lifted steps that took strength from the earth.
My body seemed to whirl and turn with them, until I thought,
were I an Indian, I'd be a man and dance with men.
But as I watched, I saw their dance revolved around the women,
who softly, slowly, with feet scarcely lifted from the ground,
held men and children, lightly, in the dance. And as they passed,
the women touched the dancing forms and mingled powers
of the earth and sun.
                    But then a distant sound of blasting
echoed from the canyons near Los Alamos. The tombe throbbed
and the chorus raised its voice. I watched a long plumed serpent
of grey smoke rise from the hills and spread above the pueblo.

# Louis Slotin Tickles the Dragon's Tail (Los Alamos, 1944)

My work required grace. It daunted some.
Feynman himself dubbed my experiments
"Tickling the Dragon's Tail." The theorists knew
in theory how these active elements
behave—or misbehave—as they explode.
But someone had to test their bright ideas:
how quickly slower neutrons multiply,
which tampers we should use, even the mass
a bomb required—it all involved guesswork.
At first when every microgram of twenty-
five had fifty people clamoring
for precedence, I used uranium
polystyrene pseudospheres. Later
I worked with nickel-plated hemispheres
of Hanford's delta-phase plutonium
set in a half-shell of beryllium.
The trick was lowering an upper shell
until it nearly touched its mate below.
Too much space and no chain reaction—but
too little and I'd rather hold a bomb.
Some delicate adjustments were involved,

I will admit. No wonder I declined
the gross mechanical contrivances
my colleagues recommended—winches, clamps,
thumb screws, and whatnot—favoring the most
steadfast equipment known to man: my hands.
Grasping the upper shell in my right hand,
I'd rest its rim against the lower shell,
and hold it, hinged like an open oyster,
the pearl between its lips, plutonium.
Slowly I'd let the metal mollusk close.
The Geiger counter stuttered, cleared its throat,
and started chattering. To calm it down,
I'd keep an old slot-headed driver wedged
between the shells. A single metal blade
divided life and death—one slip would send
the whole assembly supercritical—
a sudden spray of neutrons in the gut
and then the long, slow, agonizing wait
as one by one my organs turned to mush.
Yet in those moments, I felt life and death
so fully, so intensely, I was past
all fear. I held a rough beast in my hands
and heard its infant chatter, half amazed
how mild it was and, till it recognized
its own essential terror, beautiful.

# Kitty Oppenheimer in the Maternity Ward (Los Alamos, 1944)

When Robert planted Peter in my gut
at first I felt a flag unfurling. "Claimed,"
my heart said. "Yes," my mouth. A month alone
in Reno earned our marriage, my divorce.
But when fulfillment? What euphoria?
I waddled like a penguin, body gone
all belly, certain I could never love
the slow explosion of these clotted cells,
convinced I would have more luck mustering
maternal feelings for a stone I'd swallowed.
But earth's own mineral accretions smacked,
at least, of duty I could stomach—some.
Then Pronto stalled: still as a granite chunk
he granted my desire, stubborn, sunk

deep as a faultline in my body's dust.
The doctors heard my pleading in the end,
cleft muscle, parted layered fat, and dug
down, lifting free at last the little boy
who waited, smeared and dripping, at my core.
And when I woke, drugged, sluggish, savoring
the sudden emptiness, I swore no man,
no god, not even Robert would seduce
the She in me again.
                Now this. Tyke proves
I am the slave of what is possible.
No one can silence nature. She inscribes
her secrets in our flesh: new tissue blooms
with meanings we can't read, but sense. Genes spell
dependence that our lives sound out—small signs
of larger purposes—prolific and
devouring.
             What we make consumes us. Tyke,
conceived in disbelief, resists confinement,
scratches the greasy membranes binding us,
fights, furious and futile, kicks and twists,
ties knots in my intestines, spends her waste
into my veins. I long to help her, calm
choked motions, still her strangled gestures.
But both of us are trapped like rats inside
the blood-filled bag my body has become.
Each night, I listen to our heartbeats fight
like bitter lovers, waiting for her rage
to build until she finds the strength to tear
her way out, split me open, spill us both
into a harsh and unfamiliar light.

# Rose Bethe on VE Day (Los Alamos, 1945)

We beat the Nazis on a Tuesday
and the lab boys threw a party that same night
as only they knew how.
The theorists were good company, of course,
but lived too much inside their heads
to organize a party on the scale the day deserved.
And yet I didn't want a drink that night.
Not that I wasn't glad
the Nazis had been crushed—

their souls belong in hell—
and not that I was sad
to see my birthplace brought to ruin,
though I was.
My mood was hardly personal.
I felt—how can I say it?—
not outside myself exactly,
but outside us all.
The Nazis forced us here, Gentiles and Jews,
Americans and Russians, Germans, Dutch.
They made us all commit ourselves
to evil. Grant this once there is a God,
so God may grant we chose the lesser evil.
After the party, we went back to work.

# Joseph Rotblat Quits the Manhattan Project (Los Alamos, 1945)

Spay nature. Speed
the spray of neutrons—
prompt, delayed.
Halt fission. Feed
it salt of boron—
scattered, stalled.

Vain wish. Chiggers,
sharks reign. Men. Life sows
selves, greed, pain.
Looms lust. Prefers
ripe wombs to calm—blows,
grapple, bloom.

Silence science.
Defy fact. Ignore
ears, hands, eyes.
Scrap evidence.
Unmap Einstein, Bohr.
Knowledge traps.

Worse: when Brits thought
Hitler's tanks were fake,
missed Panzers.
Furor, flaws, faults,

seizures, gaffes, mistakes—
science cures.

Leave the lab. Seek
naïve work and save
the heart. Grieve.
Bless lost years. Speak
low, less. Count light waves'
darker crests.

Humble Doctors
succumbed. Proud, they placed
faith in sums.
Fascists. Better
self-shush than bomb blast,
hush of ash.

# Louis Slotin Assembles the Trinity Core (Alamogordo, 1945)

The core assembly was as riveting
as watching someone bake a birthday cake
at first. I did the whole thing sitting down.
And yet the smallest details somehow still
are luminous. The table top was masked
with long, brown sheets of butcher's paper strewn
with the gadget's gold and nickel-plated guts.
It felt as though I moved in thickened light,
each gesture so precise it almost hurt,
shifting the metal parts as others watched.
My focus narrowed to a small sphere
of beryllium. I cupped it like an egg
between two hemispheres of hollowed-out
plutonium, womb-shaped, as warm as flesh
from random fissions. Then the tamper's curved
plum-colored calyx closed to form a bud.
I felt a world take shape between my hands.
The Geiger counter clicked. My palms grew slick.
My fingers tingled, slowly growing numb,
gripping the heavy chunks, more dense than gold.
I shifted my grip abruptly. Everybody
jumped. My back ached. Were my fingers freezing
or on fire? I tried to blink away the sparks

from my exhausted retinas. I leaned
close to the sphere, only to see it shrink
to a speck far out of reach. Or had it swelled
to planet size? Great jagged mountains stabbed
my hands—yet smaller than a single pin
between my fingertips. And I began
to fall. I closed my eyes. My stomach lurched.
The taste of rotten lemons stained my tongue.
The core gone critical. Air glowing blue
as radiation ionized my eyes.
Now I would die.
                        Then Serber spoke. "Louis,
are you all right?" He touched my arm. My eyes
were wet. I opened them. In my clenched hands
was the completed core. It seemed that I
was not among the ones about to die.

# Norris Bradbury Oversees the Trinity Test (Alamogordo, 1945)

I choose my luck. We start
        at midnight, Friday the 13th.
Lt. Shaffer signed off
        on the V-site charge assembly.
Dual replacement castings
        for the dummy trap door plug
are boxed, all booster holes
        Scotch sealed, the unit wrapped
in Butvar water-proof.
        Shaffer's lashed the gadget
to its padded truck bed—minus
        core, X-unit, and HE.
Two G-2 escort cars
        wait, idling, fore and aft.
Luck's physics. Nothing more.
        Except a million hours
sweating details, second-
        guessing snags and foul-ups,
anticipating every
        accident and glitch.
The final hot run starts:
        we'll haul the tarp off, hoist

the gadget from its cradle,
　　　rig a canvas tent
to ward off dust and rain,
　　　remove the polar cap,
insert the active core.
　　　G-engineers will chain tongs
to the tentpeak, latch the trunnion,
　　　lift and turn the sphere.
The HE people keep
　　　on hand a shim stock shoe horn
and hypodermic grease gun
　　　to aid the HE fit.
Jercinovic will bring
　　　a small dishpan and footstool.
Lift to the tower top.
　　　The detonator group
cables the X-unit's
　　　switches and informers.
Where they get the springs
　　　and fittings is their business.
Once the gadget's live,
　　　we'll spend all Sunday rubbing
rabbit's feet and finding
　　　four-leaf clovers. Perhaps
I'll bring the Chaplain down.
　　　Then, come Monday: Bang!


# Frank Oppenheimer Prepares for Trinity (Alamogordo, 1945)

In the lulls between cloudbursts
I set off smoke bombs on the cliffs
to watch the winds. I geared up
for disaster, planning routes
across the desert to escape
the fallout. All night long,
frogs squalled nearby,
copulating in the sudden mud.

# Victor Weisskopf at Trinity (Alamogordo, 1945)

I looked at zero through dark glass.
The night was cloudy. Nothing showed.

I'd climbed a little ridge 100 yards
from camp to find a view, and solitude.

The base camp water tower's shadow aped
a blunt, hunched steeple with each lightning stroke.

A group of SEDs appeared, noisy,
fervent. They fidgeted like kids in church.

Eager to estimate the fireball's
diameter, they measured, argued, mapped.

They struck sticks upright in the ground, each half
foot staking out 1000 feet at zero.

Perhaps I wondered where they found the sticks
when—suddenly—a sun's acetylene.

Despite my welder's glass, the indirect
light blinded me long seconds, stupid, stunned.

But when the brightness died a bit, I saw
a yellow-orange fireball ascend.

An aureole of bluish radiation
bruised the air, haloed the bomb with ions.

Against all reason, it reminded me
of Grünewald's altarpiece at Colmar:

Jesus folded in a bright ascending sphere
of yellow, head framed by a turquoise glow.

Here in the desert of New Mexico
that abstract image clothed itself in flesh.

The resurrection of our Lord in wrath.
1000 billion curies scalding earth.

That awful vision haunts me still,
a forced faith burned into my retina.

# Kitty Oppenheimer Visits Louis Slotin After an Accident in the Lab (Los Alamos, 1945)

I hadn't seen Hiroshima myself
or Nagasaki, though I'd heard Bob Serber's
stories. They seemed like fairy tales or myths—
fables to frighten children, or at best
efforts to cast the inexplicable
in human terms. But then I tended Slotin
his last nine days and saw. Saw him vomit
till his stomach bled. Saw him try to grip
the white enamel bowl in the crotch of his thumbs,
his hands so swollen that his fingers wouldn't bend.
Saw him retch clear strands of spit, green flecks
of bile, too tired to wipe them from his lips.
He hiccuped for ten hours straight. At first
he almost laughed; later we strapped him down
to stop him clawing at his diaphragm.
Blisters grew like toadstools on his hands,
between his fingers, up his arms. The skin
peeled off his chest. His hair came out in clumps.
His liver failed. His kidneys. Bowels blocked.
Blood filled the bedpans. We gave him codeine.
Morphine. Nothing helped. Pain paced his body.
His fingers and his toes turned blue. His face
bloated, blistered, thick as a mask. A rind.
He seemed unconscious—so we had to think.
He might have been a thousand different men.
A hundred thousand. Only, when he died,
no cities burned. Friends grieved. His parents took
a lead-lined coffin back to Winnipeg.

# Eugene Wigner Remembers His First Wife (Oak Ridge, 1946)

We are all guests
here in this world.
As for the next?

Better, perhaps,
that we not wear
our earthly welcome out.
I learned to love
America in Madison.
Exiled from Budapest
because I wished
to be a physicist,
and from Berlin
by Hitler, then
from Princeton by the men
who coveted my job,
I settled in the midst
of wheat fields in
Wisconsin, fields
like those of Belcza-Puszta
where I learned to talk
when I was three
by walking with
my uncle, laughing at
his homespun jokes.
In Madison, I learned
another language
from Amelia. She
surprised me—not
her beauty but
her love. What curious
animals we are
to need romantic love.
But then I've never been
the quickest to intuit
nature's laws.
But when one stares me
in the face? That was
the first of many things
I learned from her.
A few months saw us
married. Then her heart,
which was, I thought,
the stronger, suddenly
went wrong. No one
could tell us why
or how. Nine months
I lived in her
sweet light. I learned

to read by it
my own heart's flickerings.
Then darkness fell,
and I went back to work.

# Edith Warner After the War
# (Otowi Bridge, 1945)

As season follows season, I sense a change,
though subtle, in the earth. Like the thin veil of green
that mantles the desert after rain, a change
has come upon the land. Or else, I hope, the difference is in me.
Now when I smell the Russian olive's bloom each May,
when the woods along the river fill with its rosy scent,
another odor teases my palate, faint, vague, but inescapable—
like the hint of bitterness in milk that will soon sour.
Now when I hear the wind in the salt cedar's feathery leaves,
another sound frets gently in my ear, almost inaudible,
like the whispered passing of a rattlesnake across dry sand.
And now when I see children in the pueblo spreading sheets
beneath the piñon trees to gather nuts, high on the edge of sight
a brief metallic glint catches my eye, then vanishes,
and I stop, and the veil falls, and I listen for the bee drone
fading in and out on the drifting wind. And if
I have not heard it yet, I know, I can't forget, I might.

# Robert Oppenheimer After the War
# (Crossing the Rio Grande, 1945)

We lost the moon among mountains,
urging our horses forward, watching ribbons
of steam rise from their flanks as they climbed in the midnight cold.
We had left the trail. Crisis' steel shoes sang
on the sandstone outcrops. High slopes
barred the sky.

The moon was waiting down by the river
where the boatman slept in an old alder shack
between two palms. We pulled ourselves
across the wrinkled water. Slick, moon-silvered planks echoed
when our horses stamped. The wet ropes

chafed our hands.

On the far bank, soaptrees bloomed, pale, odorless.
We called farewell to the sleeping boatman. The salty breath
of desert tamarisks replied
as the moon set behind Los Alamos.
Their dry leaves flickered like candles
and went out.

# Biographical Notes

Rose Bethe was the daughter of German physicist Paul Ewald and wife of Nobel physicist Hans Bethe, who led the Theoretical Division at Los Alamos. At Robert Oppenheimer's request, Bethe preceded her husband to Los Alamos, where she headed the Housing Office.

Norris Bradbury, a physicist and lieutenant commander in the Navy, oversaw assembly of the high explosive charges that would detonate the plutonium bomb in the Trinity test. When Robert Oppenheimer resigned after the war, Bradbury took over as the scientific director of Los Alamos.

John Dudley was the Army Corps of Engineers major charged with finding a location for the secret laboratory where the first atomic bombs would be designed and built. His choice, Jemez Springs, was rejected by Oppenheimer and Groves in favor of Los Alamos. He was later transferred, at his request, to an engineer regiment in the Pacific theater.

Albert Einstein signed a letter in August 1939 alerting Franklin Roosevelt to the possibility that nuclear fission might be used to make "extremely powerful bombs of a new type" and that Nazi Germany was probably already working on them. At the time, Einstein was living on Long Island, where he spent the summers sailing and working on his "hobbyhorse," the unified field theory. *Tinef,* Yiddish for "junk," was the fifteen-foot sailboat in which he navigated the waters of Peconic Bay.

Richard Feynman was the youngest group leader at Los Alamos. His wife Arline lived in a tuberculosis sanatorium in Albuquerque during most of Feynman's time on the "Hill." She died in 1945, shortly before the Trinity test.

Otto Frisch, along with his aunt, Lise Meitner, interpreted, in December 1938, the experimental results produced by Otto Hahn and Fritz Strassman in their work on radium and, in the process, "discovered" (and named) nuclear fission. He later joined the British bomb project and was part of the contingent that moved to Los Alamos to support the Manhattan Project.

Ruth Marshak accompanied her husband, physicist Robert Marshak, to Los Alamos. Like many of the scientists' spouses, she was not privy to the purpose of the work being done there.

James Nolan was the army obstetrician at Los Alamos.

Frank Oppenheimer, brother of Robert, was an experimental physicist who came to Los Alamos late in the war to assist with preparations for the Trinity test.

Kitty Oppenheimer, wife of the scientific director of Los Alamos, worked there as a biologist. Robert was her fourth husband. She gave birth to their second child, a daughter named Katherine (nicknamed Tyke, later Toni) in December 1944.

Robert Oppenheimer was the scientific director of Los Alamos. He and his brother Frank bought a cabin, which they called Perro Caliente, across the Rio Grande Valley from Los Alamos, in the Pecos Mountains. Before the war he had written to a friend, "My two great loves are physics and desert country. It's a pity they can't be combined."

Joseph Rotblat, a Polish physicist, was a member of the British mission to Los Alamos. After the defeat of Germany, he was the only senior scientist to leave the project. He was awarded the Nobel Peace Prize in 1995.

Robert Serber studied under Robert Oppenheimer at Berkeley before joining the Manhattan Project as a theoretical physicist. In March 1943, he delivered a series of lectures, later mimeographed and nicknamed the "Los Alamos Primer," to incoming scientists to "bring them up to speed" on the bomb project. Immediately after the war, he visited Japan as part of a scientific team gathering data on the effects of nuclear weapons.

Louis Slotin, a Canadian physicist, had little luck finding an academic job after receiving his PhD. He worked for a couple of years as a lab assistant before transferring to Los Alamos, where he ran critical mass experiments nicknamed "Tickling the Dragon's Tail." He was killed by radiation in a lab accident shortly after the war ended.

Leo Szilard, a Hungarian physicist, recognized the possibility of a nuclear chain reaction in 1933. He drafted, and convinced Einstein to sign, the letter to Franklin Roosevelt warning him that it might be possible to make "extremely powerful bombs of a new type."

Edward Teller is best known as "the father of the hydrogen bomb." In 1939 he drove Leo Szilard to Long Island where Einstein signed the letter to Roosevelt. Teller later worked as a physicist at Los Alamos, where he devoted more of his time to fusion theory than to the more practical business of designing a workable fission bomb. "Wigwam" is the nickname of his fellow Hungarian friend, Eugene Wigner.

Edith Warner moved from Philadelphia to New Mexico before the war, seeking a place to recover from tuberculosis. She established a tea house by the Rio Grande River, near Los Alamos, where she lived with an older Native American man named Tilano. During the war, she served scientists from the mesa exclusively, providing a secure location in which they could relax and escape for a few hours from the pressures of their work.

Victor Weisskopf, an Austrian physicist, served as a group leader in the theoretical division at Los Alamos.

Eugene Wigner, another Hungarian physicist, worked for the Manhattan Project in its Princeton, Oak Ridge, and Chicago divisions. After the war, he accepted the position of director of research and development at the Oak Ridge laboratory. He won a Nobel Prize in Physics in 1963.

**Grateful acknowledgment is made to the editors of the following publications, in which some of these poems first appeared, sometimes in slightly different form: *At Length, The Autumn House Anthology of Poetry, The Cincinnati Review, The Hudson Review, The New Republic, Poetry Daily, Prairie Schooner, Raritan, Salamander, The Southern Review, The Southwest Review, Slate,* and *The Virginia Quarterly Review.*

# CHAPTER 3

# Robots, A-Bombs, and War

## CULTURAL MEANINGS OF SCIENCE AND TECHNOLOGY IN JAPAN AROUND WORLD WAR II

*Kenji Ito*[1]

# Astroboy's Birthday[2]

Astroboy was born on April 7, 2003. The date is, of course, a fiction, created by the comic's author Tezuka Osamu. The effects of this fictitious date on the real world were, however, substantial. Around this date, various ceremonies were held, a new animation series of Astroboy was released, and a website created by one of the largest newspaper companies in Japan displayed a countdown of how many days were left before Astroboy's birthday. People compared Tezuka's robots with contemporary robots, wondering how little modern robotics had achieved. Tezuka was in no way an expert in robotics, yet people talked about his imagined robots as a measure of the progress of robotics.[3]

Imagination is sometimes inseparable from reality and exerts real effects on the real world, especially when "futuristic" technologies, such as robotics, are concerned. Imagination about science and technology constitutes one of the bases of cultural meanings of science and technology in a given society. This chapter examines what science and technology meant in Japan, or what place science and technology occupied in the culture and society of modern Japan around World War II. The answer to this question provides an important basis for understanding research, development, dissemination, and the use of science and technology in modern Japanese society. I seek a partial answer to this question through studying images of robots in popular culture in 1930s and 1950s Japan.

Images of robots in the 1930s and in the 1950s reflect what science and technology meant to the Japanese public in these eras. These images, I argue, indicate that there was a dramatic change in the public perception of science and technology after World War II. In the 1930s, robots, and therefore science and technology, belonged to the enemy and hence were a threat to the Japanese. In the 1950s, science and technology were viewed as the basis of democratic values and Japan's future prosperity. Science and technology gained an extremely positive image and constituted one of the perceived goals of the Japanese. This change resulted from the war, and perceptions of the A-bomb played an important role. The positive perception of science and technology embodied in the image of robots persisted, if not always dominated, in Japan since World War II.

Robots are an excellent example in which technology and culture overlap. Robots are technological products, and at the same time can have close ties to humanity. Robots by definition have some resemblance to humans, and have a certain place within human society. In this way, robots represent a means by which humans relate themselves to machines. Therefore, the way robots are conceived, designed, or constructed at a given time reflected the way people of that time perceived machines (and therefore technology, as well as science to some extent) and the relationship between machines and human beings.

Here, I treat images of robots as an anthropomorphism of science and technology. By looking at the perception of science and technology through images of robots, we can see embodiments of science and technology. Moreover, as it happens, there are rich materials related to robots in Japanese popular culture.

Images of robots appear in various places, but most prominently they appear in various genres of popular culture, and in particular science fiction. Analyzing representations of science and technology in popular culture is useful to understand popular perceptions of science and technology. If a work of science fiction is extremely popular, it is likely that its depiction of technology is in accordance with popular perceptions of technology. The relation between them is not simply a reflection. To be commercially successful, writers of science fiction must be aware of what ordinary readers know and feel about science and technology.[4] Otherwise, readers might not accept their work.[5] In addition, it is likely that a widely circulated work affects and shapes perceptions of technology that its audience has. This is particularly true in the case of juvenile literature, whose readers are impressionable young people. Not only do fictions affect values attached to technology, they also shape people's perception about what technology is like, how it functions in society, and what relation it has to humankind. Whereas public perception of science and technology might be ephemeral and easily affected by external events, products of popular culture have a stabilizing effect by making them part of collective memory.

As it turned out, popular perceptions of science and technology and images of robots have a lot to do with the atom bomb. The reason is that the most powerful image of robots in Japan is Astroboy, whose original Japanese name is Tetsuwan Atomu (Mighty Atom). In the formation of the images of robots and in the images of science and technology in Japan, the war and the atomic bombs played a crucial role.

Too often, scholars and others talk about science and technology in Japan in very essentialist terms. By essentialism, I mean an idea that some people, in this case Japanese, have certain essential qualities that make them different from others. Japanese scientists themselves are responsible for this to some extent because some of them are very fond of fashioning themselves as exotic oriental thinkers, who have a different way of thinking about science than western scientists. A typical example is Yukawa Hideki, but he is not alone. My approach here aims to de-essentialize cultural meanings of science and technology in Japan.[6] First I will discuss a representative image of robots in science fiction in each era. Then, I discuss how these images match the historical situations of these eras. I describe relevant events of the time to provide an interpretive context from which meanings of robot images can be understood.

This approach might arouse suspicion, especially from those who are familiar with comics critique in Japan. Seeing comics as reflecting society was once a dominant methodology of intellectual discussion of comics in Japan, presented by the group around *Shisō no kagaku*, such as Tsurumi Shunsuke and Fujikawa Chisui.[7] Since the mid-1990s, however, Japanese comic critics have been paying much closer attention to "expressions" in comics, in order to understand what makes a comic a comic. Natsume Fusanosuke, for example, a prominent comic critic, expresses his discontent with the cultural critics in the 1970s that wrote about comics. According to Natsume, those critics discuss comics in terms of how comics reflect society, for example, Astroboy as symbolizing popular worship of the omnipotence of science and technology. Since then, an apparent dichotomy of "expression" approach (*hyōgen ron*) and "social reflection" approach (*shakai han'ei ron*) has been one of the central foci of manga studies in Japan.[8]

This debate over the two approaches is not necessarily a conflict between mutually exclusive positions. Rather, *hyōgen ron* and *shakai han'ei ron* are complementary, and both approaches can be combined. Ito Go, for example, attempts to synthesize both approaches by treating a comic as a system of expression that includes diverse forms of expressions, narratives, and environment, and allows multiple readings.[9] At stake, however, is whether we take manga seriously as a specific genre of expression, distinct from other genres of culture. Therefore, *hyōgen ron*'s criticism of *han'ei ron* focuses on the attitudes of cultural critics who discuss comics as if they are the same as novels or movies, rather than their methodological validity. Since the goal of this chapter is not to discuss the expressions of comics per se but some aspects of social reality reflected in comics, the social reflection approach is in fact more relevant to the aim of this chapter.

This, however, does not mean that the social reflection approach is devoid of its own internal problems. There are at least a few methodological limitations and problems. The first concerns how to differentiate public perceptions of science from the individual peculiarities of the authors. If authors are extremely talented and original, it is possible their works transcend time and place and therefore do not necessarily reflect the thinking of most people. My strategy to cope with this problem is to focus on popular culture and juvenile literature that were relatively widely accepted by a large population at the time, rather than highbrow artistic masterpieces whose value had to wait to be recognized by later connoisseurs. In addition, examining the authors' possible biases might help filter out their peculiarities and calibrate the results to some extent.

The second problem is more serious. Asking a question about the public perception of science and technology in terms of how ordinary people see it entails a danger of positing a monolithic category of "ordinary people." People are never homogenous and have different views. For example, there might be a huge difference between men and women's perceptions of science and technology. I have to admit that I do not get to that level of differentiation in this chapter.

With all these limitations, however, the popular culture approach is useful because there aren't many other ways to investigate popular perceptions of science and technology in the past. We cannot just go back to the 1930s and take a poll.

# Robots Before the War: Unno Jūzo and Mr. F.

The idea of robots was introduced in Japan already in early 1920s. Karel Capek's *R.U.R.*, which was published in 1920 and staged as a play in New York in the next year, was then translated and staged in Japan in 1923. In 1929, Fritz Lang's *Metropolis* was screened. Soon, Japanese writers and painters began disseminating images of robots in Japan. In the 1930s, the idea of the robot was fairly trendy.[10]

Accompanied by this was a modernist cultural movement then gaining momentum, and a form of popular culture for the youth emerging in this modernist cultural milieu of 1930s Japan. The literary magazine *Shinseinen* (New Youth) represented this cultural trend. Originally *Shinseinen* started as a moral and educational magazine for rural youth. In the 1930s, the magazine became the principal forum of urban modernist youth culture.[11] In this modernist culture, natural science was one of the main concerns, and the genre of the detective story was then closely tied to science.

One of the most prominent writers of detective stories around *Shinseinen* was Yumeno Kyūsaku (1989–1936). He is best known for *Hakuhatsu kozō* and *Dogura magura*, and many of his works were published on *Shinseinei*. In his discussion of detective stories entitled "New Missions of Detective Stories," Yumeno writes that the detective story is "a newer, deeper, and more painful genre of literature that has evolved from all the kinds of literature fashionable a couple of hundred years ago. It is an unlikely form of art that was born to depart from all the traditional spirits and forms of conventional arts, penetrate into human psychology even more deeply and boldly, and analyze it, poison it, and then atomize it, and electronize it."[12] According to Yumeno, such attitudes of detective story writers are parallel to that of the scientist's attitudes to nature, yet he contends that the same attitude works as an "antidote" to problems of scientific mentality. Yumeno claims that conventional arts are like a celebration of the beauty of costumes, whereas detective stories open up human bodies, scoop up intestines, and analyze bodily fluid including blood and excretions. Such "taste" of detective stories coincides with "instinct" of scientists, because science also attempts to analyze all the beauty and the mysteries of nature. According to Yumeno, the mission of the detective story is to apply this analytical tendency on the social systems that produce science itself, infiltrate into materialistic and utilitarian ethics of science, to expose its ugly and bizarre aesthetics, and, by doing so, to give a shock to the remaining conscience and innocence.[13]

Whereas Yumeno's position toward science might be ambivalent, his locution indicates a clear attempt to bear "scientific" ambience in his approach to detective stories. Certainly, Yumeno's view of detective stories was not shared by every author of his time. Yet, considering his importance in *Shinseinen*, it was at lease one of the conspicuous views in the contemporary youth culture about science and its affinity to the genre of the detective story, as well as the youth culture of the time.

Scientific ambience is indeed abundant in some of his novels, in particular, his magnum opus *Dogura magura*, published in 1935. This work might be considered as a kind of psychological thriller, although it is difficult to put this unusual novel into any category. The novel has elements of science fiction or science fantasy, with a fictional scientific theory as the basis of the story. Taking place at a mental hospital of the faculty of medicine at Kyushu Imperial University, the story revolves around the protagonist and narrator, the heroine, and two psychiatrists. The story hinges on the notion of psychoheredity, a theory that mental states can be inherited over generations, which is not unlike the fictional use of the notion of genetic memory found in some contemporary science fiction.[14]

More directly related to science than the detective story was the genre of science fiction. Coming from the same progenitor, Edgar Allan Poe, detective stories were much more popular in the interwar modernist literature, as Edogawa Rampo (named after Edgar Allan Poe) was primarily a detective writer rather than a science fiction writer. It is probably safe to say that science fiction as a distinct genre was clearly established in Japan only after World War II. Yet, writers already began to incorporate elements of what we now call science fiction in the prewar period and called their work "science novels"(*kagaku shōsetsu*) or "science fantasy novels" (*kūsō kagaku shōsetsu*). The earliest prominent writer in this genre was Oshikawa Shunrō (1876–1914), who was known for novels about an underwater battleship.[15] Oshikawa, however, died young, and among the writers in this period, the leading figure in Japan's emerging science fiction world was Unno Jūza. Born in 1905 as Sano Shōichi, he studied electrical engineering at Waseda University (one of the most prestigious private universities in Japan) and got a job at the National Electrotechnical Laboratory in 1923. The Electrotechnical Laboratory (later the National Institute of Advanced Industrial Science and Technology) was, and is, one of the most important national technological and industrial laboratories. There, Sano conducted research on wireless technology, in particular vacuum tubes. He, however, received discriminatory treatment because of his not being a graduate of Tokyo Imperial University, and began to spend more energy on his activities as a writer. He started his career as a science writer with his real name Sano Shōichi. Then he began writing detective stories for magazines like *Shinseinen*, and later science fiction. He became one of the most popular writers of that time, whose novels found enthusiastic readers in the younger generation. For example, a magazine called *Shonen kurabu* (Boys' Club), one of the magazines for which he was one of the principal writers, boasted a circulation of eight hundred thousand copies.[16] Unno was also a frequent contributor to *Shinseinen*, and a part of the modernist movement in arts and literature in the 1930s.

Unno wrote many novels about robots, including "Jinzōningen jiken" (The Robot Case), "Jinzōningen shissō jiken" (The Disappeared Robot Case), "Jinzōningen efu-shi" (The Robot Mr. F), "Jinzōningen no himitsu" (Secret of the Robot), "Jinzōningen sensha no kimitsu" (Secret of the Robot Tank), "Jinzōningen yashiki"(Mansion of the Robot), "Jūhachi-ji no ongakuyoku" (Music Treatment at Hour Eighteen), "Chikyū yōsai" (Fortress Earth), "Kurogane tengu" (Iron Tengu), and so on.[17]

In Unno's novels, robots are imagined as having foreign and specifically Western origin. In particular, there is no imagined connection to *karakuri ningyō*, Japan's traditional automata in the late Edo period. *Kurogane tengu*, published in 1935, is one of few period novels by Unno, in which the story takes place in the Edo era, but even in this novel there is no mention of *karakuri ningyō*. *Kurogane Tengu* (Iron Tengu) is the robot in this story. The tengu is a Japanese (originally Chinese) mythical creature, portrayed as having wings and a long nose. Iron Tengu detects the brain waves of its creator, a man called Hannojō, and behaves as he wishes. Hannojō used the Iron Tengu to kill another man called Gonshirō, who stole Hannojō's girlfriend. The "Western" character of *Kurogane Tengu* manifests also in its appearance. The robot wears *nanbantesu*, Japan's medieval appellation of Western-style iron armor. Unno does not use the word *karakuri*, a traditional Japanese word in the Edo era to designate machinery. Instead, he employs the terms *kikai* and *kikai ningen*, which connote Western-style modern machines.[18]

It is not rare that a science fiction novel has elements of a detective story. The most prominent example would be Isaac Asimov's robot novels. This aspect is also evident in Unno's science fiction: *Kurogane tengu* has the plot of a detective story. Apparently, Unno was making a transition from detective stories to science fiction. This is clearer in "Jinzōningen jigen" (The Robot Case) in 1935. Dr. Takeda is an authority of robotics, and his nephew Jōtarō works as an assistant to him. Jōtarō, who loves Takeda's beautiful wife Kurara (Clara), attempts the perfect murder by using a robot. Knowing that Takeda's robot is programmed to react to certain words, Jōtarō creates a radio drama using those words, and the robot kills Takeda, giving Jōtarō an alibi. The private investigator Homura Sōroku sees through the plot and solves the case. Seen as a detective story, this work is a failure, using the unlikely trick of a robot, which serves as a deus ex machina, yet it is suggestive of the perceived relation between robots and humans in Unno's fictions. In this plot, the robot is used as a tool and substitute. The robot does not have an independent mind, but is a tool controlled by a specific individual and can be used for criminal purposes. Curiously in Unno's fictions, it is not only robots but also humans that are controlled. In his "Fushiginaru kūkan dansō," published in 1935, the culprit accomplishes the murder of his wife using a mentally retarded friend Tomoeda Hachirō. Tomoeda cannot distinguish between dream and reality, so the husband hires an actor who resembles Tomoeda and makes the actor play the role of shooting a woman. Repeatedly seeing himself shooting a woman in what he believes a dream, Tomoeda comes to believe that it is his role to shoot a woman in his dream. Then, the husband creates a similar situation in reality, and Tomoeda, believing that he is dreaming, kills the wife.

The motif of controlling humans and robots takes an even more striking form in his famous *Jūhachiji no ongakuyoku* (Music Treatment at Hour Eighteen) published in 1937. This can be considered as one of the earliest dystopian novels.[19] President Miruki rules his country as an absolute dictator using the "music treatment" developed by Dr. Kohaku. All the citizens of the country are obligated to receive a daily dose of the music treatment at 6 pm. The music treatment consists of listening to a broadcast of special pieces of music that affects the nervous system of the listeners and invokes superhuman abilities for a short period of time. Moreover, the government can control the behaviors of the people through this music treatment. For example, the piece of music called the "national anthem #39" makes anyone, even a criminal, a "type 39 standard human" who obeys the "thirty-nine rules," which includes not smoking, not drinking alcohol, sleeping only four hours, and being loyal to the country. Miruki governs the country successfully with this music treatment, but his mistress and Minister Asari entice Miruki to kill Dr. Kohaku. Miruki starts administering the music treatment every hour to increase the productivity of his country, a measure that Dr. Kohaku disapproves. Then, alien rockets from Mars attack the country of Miruki. The successive application of the music therapy has completely exhausted the physical and mental strength of the citizens of Miruki, who are unable to respond to the attack effectively. As the last resort to turn the tide of the losing war, Miruki attempts to deploy robots that Dr. Kohaku is believed to have created and hidden deep inside his institute. However, all the people of Miruki die as they try to reach the last gate of the institute. After Miruki and Asari die, the gate opens and Dr. Kohaku and his army of robots appear. The Dr. Kohaku killed by President Miruki was actually a robot. Then, Kohaku and his robots drive back the Martian invading forces, and Kohaku rebuilds the country as a country populated by robots.[20]

The robots in this novel are not mechanical robots, but synthetic organisms composed of artificial tissues and organs with the appearance of humans. They have the body of a young woman and the face of an angel. The prototype is called Anetto, who is found alone in Kohaku's institute after his execution. Because of her beauty, Miruki flirts with her, and his mistress Asari, out of jealously, kills Anetto, feeding her body to birds.

The robots in this novel have only passive roles. The prototype is depicted as feminine, an object of male desire, and a victim of bodily violence. Even the robots that appear and rebuild the country after the extinction of mankind are nothing more than followers of Dr. Kohaku, not independent characters possessing autonomous individuality.

Dr. Kohaku presents an ambivalent image of a scientist. When he comes out of the gate, he is the sole human survivor. With his genius, he could resurrect the dead citizens, but he instead chooses to build a utopia of robots. Here, Unno betrays his deep pessimism about science and technology.[21] The power of science is not used to help humankind here.

For the purpose of this paper, a more important work of Unno is a science fiction entitled "Mr. F the Robot" (Jinzō ningen efu shi).[22] This was published from January to December in 1939 on *Rajio kodomo no tekisuto* (Radio Children's Text), a magazine for young radio amateurs. Its target readership was obviously children with scientific and technological interests, and the main robot character is a boy, therefore this novel makes a good comparison to Astroboy, which I discuss later.[23]

Shōta and Mariko, children of a Japanese trading merchant, are staying in Vladivostok. Russian scientist, Dr. Ivanov, invites them to his house and asks them to teach Japanese to his robot Mr. F. Dr. Ivanov creates the robot Mr. F in the likeness of Shōta. On their return voyage to Japan, Mr. F takes the place of Shōta. Mr. F and a mysterious old man called Ōki abduct Mariko. In Japan, Mr. F carries out subversive activities, destroying, for example, the newest model of a Russian tank seized by the Japanese army. Shōta seeks help from the private investigator Homura Sōroku, and they search together for Mariko. Penetrating the disguise, Homura realizes Ōki is actually Dr. Ivanov, and finds his hide-out, but Ivanov captures both Homura and Shōta. Homura somehow finds the control device of the robot in the hideout and tampers with it. Mr. F goes out of control, destroying everything in his way. In the end, an army of Japanese soldiers surrounded Mr. F, forcing Mr. F to explode himself. Homura manages to rescue Mariko and almost captures Dr. Ivanov, but Dr. Ivanov escapes, fleeing in the sea toward a mysterious submarine with the speed of a torpedo. Homura concludes that the Dr. Ivanov that he has been seeing is also a robot controlled by the real Dr. Ivanov on board the submarine.[24]

In this story, the robot Mr. F is a threat to the country and a tool of the enemy. Far from a benevolent servant, this robot inflicts heavy damages. Not only does the robot resemble humans, the robot can bear the same appearance of a specific individual and steal his or her identity. The theme of a robot taking the place and appearance of a human was already present in Fritz Lang's *Metropolis*. It should therefore have been already familiar in 1930s Japan. It represents the fear that robots might take over human civilization. In fact, as in *Metropolis*, the robot Mr. F takes the place of Shōta and puts him in danger, causing him to be falsely charged for the crimes that Mr. F committed.

This robot has superhuman abilities and poses a grave danger, by being controlled by the enemy or not being controlled at all. Mr. F is not just a hu-manoid robot but is a superhuman robot. He can speak several languages, fly, and read a person's mind. Mr. F has superhuman physical strengths, and can emit high temperatures that melt steel, with which power Mr. F destroys the captured Russian tank. In all respects, the robot is not an imperfect reproduc-tion of a human being, but supersedes men, and poses a grave threat to those who antagonize. Moreover, the robot belongs to the enemy. The very existence of this robot is a symbol of Japan's inferiority in science and technology. Dr. Ivanov never misses a chance to boast Russia's superior science and denounces the scientific capabilities of the Japanese. When Dr. Ivanov captures Homura, he says to the latter, "Does Japan have advanced machines like robots? If you say yes, no one in the world would believe that."[25] When Homura expresses surprise at knowing that Mr. F can read human minds, Dr. Ivanov says, "Huh, you are surprised at such a small thing? That shows how Japan is lagging behind in science."[26] According to Dr. Ivanov, the human brain has electrical functions, therefore it emits electromagnetic waves just like a radio; Mr. F. detects that electromagnetic radio. At the end of the story, when Homura realizes that Dr. Ivanov is actually a robot, he exclaims, "What a terrifying power of science! We Japanese must work harder!"[27]

Whereas Dr. Ivanov and Mr. F symbolize the science of the Soviet Union, Homura Sōroku represents Japan's science. As we have already seen in another story, "The Robot Case," Homura appears as the main private investigator in Unno's stories, like Sherlock Holmes in Arthur Conan Doyle's novels, or Akechi Kogorō in Edogawa Rampo's. Homura's uniqueness is that he is presented as a scientist, with a bachelor's degree in science, possibly an alter ego of Unno himself. He thus represents benevolent aspects of science: whereas the science of the enemy is embodied in hardware, Japan's science belongs in the mind of a human being.

At the same time, Mr. F, as long as it is under control, obeys the orders of its creator or controller. Mr. F does not have an independent will. When the controlling device is out of order, Mr. F runs berserk, destroying everything in sight. Despite its human appearance, Mr. F is not capable of having social ties with humans. It is a robot incapable of offering or receiving friendship or respect. Mr. F can only evoke fear.

Thus, science fictions in the 1930s depicted the robot as a tool that belonged to Japan's enemies, and therefore as a menace. Such a depiction of technology was resonant to external events of that time. From May to September in 1939, overlapping the period of the publication of Mr. F, there was a battle between the Russian army and Japan's Kwantung Army near a village called Nomonhan, located near today's border between China and Mongol. It was a large-scale clash between Soviet Russia's mechanized army under the command of Georgi K. Zhukov and Japan's ill-equipped infantry. Japanese newspapers reported that Japan's Kwantung Army vanquished Russians, by competing against the Russians' "mechanical force" with Japanese "spiritual power."[28] Despite the newspaper report, it was a serious defeat on the Japanese side, and the Japanese army did their best to hide it. But the newspaper was right about Russia's superior mechanical power, which was probably too evident to conceal.[29] Being an engineer himself, Unno's nationalism led him to call for the advancement of science and technology in Japan, as a necessary condition for Japan's economic and military power.

Taking science and technology as a tool well suited the cultural context of pre-surrender Japan. On the one hand, there was Japan's modern myth, a national ideology containing a fair amount of irrationality. On the other, there was the military and economic necessity of greatly increasing national strength with the help of science and technology. These could be compatible when science and technology only served as a tool to achieve nationalist goals. As German-speaking conservative revolutionaries depicted in Jeffrey Herf's *Reactionary Modernism*, science and technology had to be celebrated without committing to the Enlightenment ideals and rationalism.[30] In the late 1930s, Japan experienced the dominance of myth and irrationalism. At the same time, Japanese technocrats mobilized science and technology and attempted to enforce planned economic control in order to carry out Japan's colonial rule and military invasion.[31]

In short, the character of Mr. F was a perfect anthropomorphism of the Japanese view of science and technology on the eve of World War II. Just as Mr. F is under the control of Dr. Ivanov, to the Japanese in the 1930s, technology was a tool of the enemy. Since it was a tool, it was judged according to its utility, rather than its cultural or moral values. Since it belonged to the enemy, it was more a threat than a promise for a better future.

As Japan went deeper into the war, Unno's novels became more militaristic. When the war ended, Unno seriously considered committing suicide along with his family.[32] After the war, he continued writing science fiction and science articles, including famous "Chōningen X-gō," but robots in Unno's fiction during this period do not differ significantly from the pre-surrender period.[33]

# Cultural Meanings of *Atomu*: The A-Bomb and Science in Occupied Japan

World War II ended with Japan's defeat, and the Allied Powers occupied Japan, putting the country under the rule of General Headquarters/Supreme Commander for the Allied Powers (GHQ/SCAP). The occupation came with censorship, imposed from September 1945 to October 1949. The censorship is a mixed blessing to a scholar of popular culture of this period. Because of the censorship, there is an exceptionally good collection of published materials called Gordon E. Prange Collection held at the University of Maryland. The Prange Collection is unusually strong in juvenile literature and comics, the genres that tend to be lost in other collections. At the same time, the censorship complicates interpretation of publications during the occupation. There was the so-called Press Code, in accordance to which information about A-bomb was considered sensitive and suppressed. It is therefore not clear to what extent expressions in popular culture in this period were censored. It is at least clear that public knowledge about the A-bomb was relatively limited at that time, and that there was a very positive image of science and technology at this period.

The Prange Collection has more than eight thousand titles in its collection of juvenile literature, including more than two thousand comics. Many of them are related to science and technology.[34] A separate paper would be necessary to fully analyze these publications. In this section, I briefly survey perceptions of science and technology revealed in the juvenile literature in the Prange Collection. I plan to write more detailed analyses elsewhere.

Publications in the Prange Collection indicate that science and technology were major themes in publications for children, and that they were almost always depicted very positively.[35] In the Prange Collection, there are many biographies of scientists and engineers, many popular science books, and many science fiction comics, related to robots, rockets, airplanes, or other technological artifacts. For example, there are five biographies of Marie Curie. Sawaguchi Ken's biography is entitled *Kyurī fujin: Jinrui no onjin* (Madam Curie, the Benefactor of Mankind).[36] In this biography, positive aspects of radioactivity are stressed. In a biography of Galileo Galilei, he is depicted as "the father of the Earth" in the title.[37] I didn't quite follow the logic, but it is apparent, in both cases, that scientists are celebrated as benefactors to the entire world, or the whole earth.

As for popular science books, many of them are educational and portray practical scientific knowledge related to everyday things. There was a movement to make life more scientific: one book is even titled "Our Scientific Life."[38] There is very little about the A-bomb in popular science books of this period. There is one rare example that is solely about the A-bomb. It is a very neutral description of the scientific principles of an A-bomb.[39]

Relatively few comics have an A-bomb or atomic related topics. There is a comic book about an "atomic ball," a ball with a special atomic power that is used to destroy monsters. So, here "atomic" simply meant scientific technical device with a very strong power.[40]

Before Astroboy, there were several anthropomorphic expressions of the atom in Japan. One such "proto-Astroboy" is Tanaka Shin-ichi's "Chōjin Atomu" (Superman Atom). In this comic, Atomu is a mysterious hero, who can fly and has very strong power.[41]

The next example of a proto-Astroboy is not really like Astroboy. He is also called "Atomu" but he is a normal human boy. This book, *Adventure of Atom*, is a novel written by Suzuki Hiroshi (1921–1951). Suzuki is a physicist and student of Yukawa Hideki. In addition to this novel, he wrote another popular science book on uncertainty relations.[42] Suzuki was also active as a detective story writer with the pen name of Kita Hiroshi.[43] *The Adventure of Atom* is basically a popular science book that conveys knowledge about atomic physics to young people through fiction. The story takes place, the author says, twenty or thirty years in the future. The protagonist is a boy nicknamed Atomu, who is a second-year student of Sēya Middle School in a town called Kusuko. His classmates are Anpēru (Ampère) and Nirusu (Niels). A group of criminals, led by an industrialist and scientist Kiringu-shi (Mr. Killing), steals secret scientific documents from the Institute for Physical and Biological Research, and produces atomic bombs. Using the A-bombs, Kiringu blackmails individuals in the city and attempts to extort a large amount of money. Atomu and his scientist uncle Kosumi work together to apprehend the criminals. Kosumi manages to find the factory that manufactures the atomic bombs and destroys it by detonating the A-bombs.[44]

In the context where science and technology were depicted almost always positively, juvenile literature during this period did not vilify the atomic bomb.

Rather than depicting atrocities that the A-bomb caused, those popular science books, such as *The Adventure of Atom*, presents the A-bomb as a powerful yet ordinary weapon that can be exploded rather casually. In particular, unlike in the mid-1950s, as in the case of the Bikini Atoll explosion and ensuing irradiation of the *Lucky Dragon* fishing boat, mention of radioactivity in relation to the atom or the atomic bomb is not evident. Whereas in the pre-surrender literature, science and technology were closely tied to military technology, juvenile literature during this period refrained from mentioning anything that might be taken as militarism. The atomic bomb or rather the atom was associated with, not necessarily weapons, but some form of extraordinary power.

More generally, the atom (*atomu*) was very often associated with the atomic bomb or atomic energy and had specific cultural meanings in this period. The word *atomu* could simply mean the atomic bomb, as in *atomu no kyōfu* (terror of the atom).[45] It could also mean atomic energy as in *atomu no iryōku*, which is imagined to achieve various technological marvels.[46] As in English, *atomu jidai* (atomic age) is used to designate the post–World War II era.[47] It was fairly often used to indicate nuclear devastation, as in *atomu Hiroshima* or *atomu Nagasaki*.[48]

With the connotation of energy and power, and probably explosion, the word *atomu* was used in sports news, especially the reporting of baseball, as in *Daiei no atomu dasen* (atomic batting of the Daiei team), which probably means a very powerful lineup of batters.[49] In one instance, the word *atomu* seems to have been used to indicate a home run.[50] Similarly, in more everyday context, the word *atomu* was used to indicate strength. According to one article, *atomu man* (atomic man) meant metaphorically a man with an exceptionally strong *shinzō* (heart), which means that this man had nerves of steel.[51]

The word *atomu*'s other connotation was of advanced technology. It was exploited in the names of products and companies. There were products like *atomu chūkan shūha henseiki* (atomic transformer),[52] *atomu bōru pen* (atomic ballpoint pen),[53] and *atomu shinkūkan* (atomic vacuum tube),[54] or company names like *Atomu Rikagaku* (Atomic Physico-chemical),[55] or *Atomu Seiyaku* (Atomic Pharmacy) with *Atomu* in katakana,[56] and another *Atomu Seiyaku* with *Atomu* in hiragana, which sold a product called "pikadon."[57] In addition, science writers used *Atomu* as the name of a scientist. Yokoi Fukujirō, a highly important comic author whom I will discuss in relation to Tezuka in the next section, published an educational comic called *Atomu sensei to Bon-kun* (Teacher Atom and Mr. Bon).[58] There was also a popular science piece in the form of fiction, entitled *Saiensu dorama: aru asa no Atomu hakase* (Science Drama: Dr. Atom on a Morning), in which the protagonist is Dr. Atom, a seventy-year-old scientist, who lives in Neutron City in Uranium Country.[59]

The word *atomu* was also used for magazine titles. Probably the most prominent one was *Atomu* published by Nihon Kagaku Gijutsu Renmei (Union of

Japanese Scientists and Engineers—JUSE). JUSE is an important organization that played a crucial role in the development of Japanese style quality control and it still remains active. The magazine *Atomu* was meant to be commercial, with the goal to supplement JUSE's income. The magazine, however, turned out to be not as profitable as expected; hence, JUSE stopped its publication after its third issue.[60] The magazine shows no explicit explanation for its name *Atomu*; it was probably considered appropriate for a magazine of scientists and engineers. In particular, the first issue has a transcript of roundtable talks entitled *Genshiryoku jidai o kataru* (Conversation on the Age of Atomic Energy) featuring prominent physicists and other intellectuals including Nishina Yoshio, Sagane Ryōkichi, Yuasa Toshiko, and Taketani Mituo.[61]

Another magazine entitled *Atomu* is the organ journal of *Zenteishin Hiroshima Yūbinkyoku shibu* (the Hiroshima Post Office branch of the Japan Postal Workers' Union). Established in 1946, Zeitei (the Japan Postal Workers' Union) was one of the most powerful labor unions in the postwar era, along with *Kokurō* (National Railway Workers' Union) and *Nikkyōso* (Japan Teachers Union). The inaugural issue of this magazine explains the christening of the magazine:

> We at the Hiroshima Post Office are responsible to commemorate for eternity the lesson that the blow of atom gave to the humanity. Our labor union, proudly aware of the responsibility of leading for peace and democratization, declares to name our organ journal *Atomu*, in acknowledging its great significance and emphasizing the gravity of our responsibility.[62]

Whereas the word *Atomu* invoked historical significance among the unionists in Hiroshima, recognizing the historical importance of the A-bomb, people in other parts of Japan were more impressed by scientific connotations of *Atomu*. It became for example the name of a student newspaper published by the chemistry club at the Nobeoka Tsunetomi High School in the southern part of the island of Kyushu. Because the atom is indivisible, the chemistry students took it as implying a strong bond and solidarity among them.[63] Thus, in the immediately post-war era, the word *atomu* had a complex of meanings within a very unique cultural landscape. *Atomu* meant the A-bomb and atomic energy, and at the same time advanced science and technology. Understood as such, *atomu* did not necessarily invoke negative reactions. Rather, it often invoked admiration, to the extent some people find *atomu* congenial enough to name their magazine with this word, or even make it their own pseudonym. This semantic complexity of *atomu* acquired another dimension in the end of the U.S. occupation with the publication and popularization of Astroboy.

# Astroboy and Tezuka Osamu

If Unno virtually founded the genre of science fictions in Japan in the 1930s,[64] Tezuka Osamu (1928–1989) brought the Japanese comics into prominence after World War II. Tezuka was born in 1928, and while being trained as a doctor at a medical school attached to the University of Osaka, he became the most important comic artist in twentieth-century Japan. Tezuka transformed Japanese comics into a genre of entertainment that has a complex movie-like storyline and its own graphical and textual expressions. He was also the earliest pioneer of Japanese animation.[65]

For young readers in the period immediately after the war, who were hungry for reading materials, Tezuka's comics were a godsend. As adults would scramble for *kastori zasshi* (pulp magazines, named after *kasutori shōchū*—cheap moonshine), children longed for their own readings.[66] In this era, there was a genre of publication called *akahon* (red book). It was a cheap comic book published by small publishers with low quality reddish paper. Tezuka became a professional comic author when he started his first series, *Maa-chan no nikkichō* (Diary of Maa-chan) on *Mainichi Shōgakusei Shimbun* (Mainich Newspaper for Primary School Students) in 1946, but his longer comics were first published in the form of *akahon*.[67] In 1950, he met Katō Ken'ichi, the editor-in-chief and publisher of *Manga Shōnen* (Comic Boy), who was a former editor-in-chief of *Shōnen Kurabu* (Boys' Club) but had been purged after the war because of his pro-war activities. Tezuka then decided to publish his *Janguru Taitei* (Kimba the White Lion) in Katō's *Manga Shōnen*, instead of publishing it as a red book. After that, Tezuka continued publishing long comics serially in comic magazines, a media that mushroomed after the war.[68]

In his biographical comics about his memories of Tezuka, Yaguchi Takao, himself a successful comic author known for *Tsurikichi Sampei* (Sampei the Fisherman), describes the context in which Tezuka's comics were read. Yaguchi was born in 1939 in a small village in a mountainous region. During his childhood in the immediate postwar era, Yaguchi was very fond of comics but his family was too poor to purchase as much as he wanted to read. The boy took a part-time job shouldering bundles of cedar bark down from mountains: this bark was in high demand to roof houses in the construction rush of the postwar period. With the money he earned from this hard labor, he would ride down the mountain to a nearby town by bicycle and purchase monthly comics magazines. Yaguchi was exposed to Tezuka through Tezuka's *Ryūsenkei jiken* (The Case of Streamline Shape). Tezuka's comic fascinated him with its ambience of modernity and taste of science. Streamlined vehicles struck Yaguchi, who lived in a village where cars were rare, as very futuristic. Tezuka's aerodynamic explanation about air resistance and turbulence around the streamline shape also made a strong impression on him. To Yaguchi, Tezuka was very closely associated with science.[69] Tezuka's being a "scientist" might have been part of the reception of Tezuka among his readers.[70]

Astroboy, or *Tetsuwan Atomu* (Mighty Atom) in Japanese, is the title of a comic and its main character created by Tezuka Osamu in 1951. The comic, originally entitled *Atomu Taishi* (Ambassador Atom) appeared in a monthly magazine called *Syōnen* (Boy) published by Kōbunsha. The magazine was an entertainment periodical for children that carried various articles, novels, and comics. Around the same time, for example, Edogawa Rampo published a series of episodes of his detective stories featuring Akechi Kogorō, including "Tōmei ningen" (Invisible Man) and "Kaiki Yonjūmensō" (Man of Forty Faces).

Among articles in this magazine, some are about science and scientists. In the first three issues of this magazine, published from November 1947 to January 1948, the scientist Yuasa Akira wrote a series of articles entitled "Kagakusha eno michi" (Path to a Scientist). In this article, Yuasa discusses what science is and what scientific research is, by referring to the history of science.[71] This magazine is also remarkable in its promotion of the romanization of Japanese. The inaugural issue carries a table of romanization of Japanese and an article by Toki Yoshimaro entitled "Minasan wa naze rōmaji o narauka" (Why You Learn Romanization of Japanese), which claims that the Japanese system of writing is waste of time and mental power because of its orthographical multiplicity.[72] Moreover, the second issue published in December 1947 carries a comic strip in *rōmaji* by Yokoi Fukuzirō, entitled "Otenki bōya" (Weather Boy), which explains weather symbols.[73]

A reader opinion poll published in the issue of *Syōnen* in April 1951 (the issue where the first episode of the *Atomu Taishi* was published) tells much about the audience of this magazine and their relation to science. It is a collation of the reader letters stating whom they respected. Here are the top nine and the number of votes that they collected:[74]

| | | |
|---|---|---|
| 1. | Noguchi Hideyo | 3882 |
| 2. | Abraham Lincoln | 2691 |
| 3. | Thomas Edison | 1507 |
| 4. | Yukawa Hideki | 996 |
| 5. | Ninomiya Kinjirō | 724 |
| 6. | George Washington | 603 |
| 7. | Marie Curie | 412 |
| 8. | Edward Jenner | 297 |
| 9. | Fukuzawa Yukichi | 226 |
| | Others | 1410 |

With the sole exception of Ninomiya Kinjirō, all of them are scientists, engineers, or physicians, or those political figures or thinkers whom the readers seemed to consider as democratic. As, for example, one letter states, "I respect Fukuzawa Yukichi as the father of Japan's democracy."[75] Fukuzawa became an object of respect because some of his words were interpreted as democratic, such as the famous beginning of *Gakumon no susume* (An Encouragement of Learning), which begins with the famous line, "It is said that the heaven does not make one above another, or one below another."[76] Another reader writes, "Kinjirō is great, but I respect Abraham Lincoln better, because I think Lincoln is more democratic."[77] Thus, the value systems of the readers of *Syōnen* were based more on democracy and science than Japan's traditional moral values, such as diligence and frugality as represented by Ninomiya.

It is difficult to say how much Tezuka owed to previous images of robots, in particular the robots of Unno. As we see later, it is obvious that the first episode of Astroboy was inspired by the story of Pinocchio, originally in Carlo Collodi's *The Adventure of Pinocchio*, but Tezuka was exposed to this story through the Takarazuka revue. Tezuka spent his childhood in Takarazuka, and lived in the neighborhood where many Takarazuka actresses resided. He frequented the Takarazuka revue and its backstage since his early childhood.[78] According to his sister Minako, Tezuka Osamu was so fascinated by the performance of *Pinochio* (Pinocchio) at this revue that he memorized all the songs and lines.[79]

In general, Tezuka was unwilling to pay credit to other writers and had a tendency to attribute more originality and creativity to himself than was actually the case. For example, in one place, Tezuka writes that he read many of the novels written by Unno Jūza, especially Unno's "Taiheiyō majō" (Magical Castle in the Pacific), in another place, when similarities between "Taiheiyō Majō" and one of Astroboy's episodes entitled "Umihebitō no maki" (The Sea Snake Island) were pointed out, Tezuka vehemently denied reading Unno's "Taiheiyō majō," and stated that he did not read much of Unno's work.[80] As several researchers have already pointed out, Tezuka read many of Unno's novels and owed them many of his inspirations.[81] Moreover, Tezuka's first work, *Maa-chan no nikkichō* was published in *Shōkokumin shimbun* (Newspaper for Children of the Empire), which was later renamed as *Mainichi shōgakusei shimbun*. In his autobiography, *Boku wa mangaka* (I Am a Comic Writer), Tezuka describes it as "a prestigious newspaper for children that carried Unno Jūza's masterpiece, *Kasei heidan* (Martian Corps)."[82] In addition, in some places, Tezuka confesses that he read this novel (*Kasei heidan*) and liked it enthusiastically.[83] He also confesses that in an image in his *Kitarubeki sekai* (The World of Future),[84] he inadvertently imitated from an illustration in Unno's *Chikyū yōsai* (Fortress Earth),[85] which was itself a cribbing from an American sci-fi magazine.[86] These indicate that Tezuka was thoroughly familiar with Unno's science fiction novels.

As for comics, Tezuka admits, and his sister Minako attests that Yokoi Fukuzirō's *Fushigina kuni no Pucchā* (Pucchā in a Mysterious Land) published in September 1946 to March 1948 in *Shōnen Kurabu* (Boys' Club) had a great impact on him.[87] Although completely overshadowed by Tezuka and entirely forgotten today, Yokoi precedes Tezuka as a prominent author of scientific comics, and might have taken a very important place in Japanese popular culture had he lived longer (Yokoi died in 1948 during the publication of *Fushigina kuni no pucchā*[88]). He represents affinity between popular culture and science during this period even more strikingly than Tezuka.[89] In addition to what I have already mentioned above, Yokoi published a series of comic strips entitled *Kūsō seikatsu* (Fancy Life) in addition to occasional cartoons, in a magazine called *Seikatsu kagaku* (Everyday Science) published by *Seikatsu Kakgakuka Kyōkai* (Association for Scientification of Everyday Life). The magazine was originally published by the Mainichi Shimbun starting in 1941, but after the war, the association took over its publication, although the organization itself was under the strong influence of the Mainichi Shimbun. The board members of this association included, in addition to members from the Mainichi Shimbun, prominent figures like Tomizuka Kiyoshi and Matsumae Shigeyoshi. Although established before the surrender, the organization became a part of the post-war movement to make everyday life more scientific.[90]

*Fushigina kuni no pucchā* is Yokoi's finest work as well as his last. With a long story line, it constitutes counterevidence to a common belief that Tezuka started the genre of "story manga," comics with a movie-like long story. The style is an eclecticism of an illustrated novel and a comic; texts and illustrations occupy equal space, and illustrations are in the style of comics, with balloons to indicate character's speech. Tezuka's Astroboy bears many similarities to this comic. The story takes place one hundred years in the future, in which humanity has achieved a technologically advanced society powered by atomic energy. In Yokoi's vision of future, atomic energy is not only a source of energy, but also a symbol of technological advancement and convenience. A line states: "Since automobiles are all powered by atomic energy, no complicated operation is necessary. Rotating a dial is enough to run a car with an appropriate speed from start to finish."[91] The protagonist is a human boy called Pucchā. His father is a robot scientist who creates a humanoid robot Perī (Peree) for Aunt Rorō, who lost her child in a train accident. Perī's appearance is perfectly human, yet, by the mistake of using atomic energy, his power source is one hundred thousand horsepower.[92] Using his superhuman power, Perī saves a girl from a car accident, which makes him famous and popular. Tempted by Perī's superpower, a group of villains steals him. With the help of another scientist, Pucchā rescues Perī. Then, the scientist, Pucchā, and Perī travel to Mars, where another civilization is flourishing. Meanwhile, an empire of subterranean people attacks earthlings, detonating a huge explosion with red radiation, causing a worldwide disaster on Earth. The explosion, later called "the Day of Red," prompts Pucchā and Perī to return to the Earth. Using various technological gadgets such as mantles of invisibility, they fight against the subterraneans. The emperor of the subterraneans sends humanity an ultimatum, threatening the earthlings with another "Day of Red." Using a liquid newly invented on Mars called "Essence of Love," which is capable of invoking conscience even in criminals, Pucchā and Perī manage to turn the emperor of the subterranean empire into a good person and successfully bring peace between humankind and the subterraneans.

In this comic, the android Perī is a friend and partner of the protagonist and has the appearance of a human boy. Just like Astroboy, he has superhuman power, and fights to save humankind or to make peace with aliens. Pucchā's father tells Pucchā that he has put only "good senses" into Perī; therefore, Perī would not do any misdeeds.[93] Just like Astroboy, he is created to substitute for a human boy killed by an accident. Even more than Astroboy, there are many references to science and technology in this comic. When the subterranean empire attacks the earthlings, Perī is told: "Now is the time when the child of science, you the robot Perī should bring your abilities into full play."[94] Not only Perī but also Pucchā is referred to as a "child of science." Pucchā is said to be intrepid and willing to face any difficulty "because he is a child of science."[95] Science is depicted as something that one should trust. Wearing a pair of electric wave boots, with which one is supposed to able to walk in the air, Pucchā hesitates to step out of a window of a tall building into the air high above the ground. When asked by the inventor of the gadget, "Pucchā, don't you believe in science?" Pucchā resolutely steps into the air.[96]

Tezuka's sources of inspiration were not limited to Japanese authors. He was keenly interested in science fiction overseas, especially in movies. Tezuka was a self-professed movie addict, and in addition to his favorite Disney animations, science fiction movies from the United States and other countries made strong impressions on him. His favorite movies included, for example, "The Invisible Man" directed by James Whale.[97] According to Tezuka, he did not watch Fritz Lang's *Metropolis*, but saw a picture of the birth of Maria in a film magazine, *Kinema Jumpō* (Movie Ten-day News), which gave him the inspiration for his comic *Metoroporisu* (Metropolis).[98] He also read the Japanese version of *Amazing Stories*, which was published by Seibundō Shinkōsha from April to July 1950.[99] The Japanese version of *Amazing Stories*, however, probably did not give much inspiration to Tezuka as far as Astroboy is concerned. There are no stories by Isaac Asimov, and the only story where robots play a significant role is "The Flame Queen" by Gaston Derreaux, but the robots in this story are artificially bred organisms rather than humanoid machines.[100]

In his memoirs, Tezuka provides his account of how he came up with the idea for Astroboy, highly contextualized in the post-war Japan under occupation. After the war, when the occupying force landed in Japan, boys of Tezuka's generation were in daily contact with American soldiers. One day, a GI asked him something in English, which Tezuka did not understand and answered by repeating "What?" The angered American soldier gave the boy a punch. Tezuka, shocked and furious, produced various manga on the difficulties of cross-cultural communication and on conflicts between different cultures (between earthlings and aliens, humans and robots, humans and animals, and so on). According to him, this is what Astroboy is about.[101] He was then shocked by the assassination of Mohandas Karamchand Gandhi on January 30, 1948, and deeply concerned by racial conflicts, which he later recalls as the source of the stories of Astroboy.[102]

When asked by the editor of comic magazine *Syōnen*, to start a serial comic in the summer of 1950, Tezuka, thinking about a nuclear bomb test on Christmas Island, came up with the idea of the peaceful use of atomic power.[103] He started thinking of a story about a fictional country called *Atomu Tairiku* (Atomic Continent), where atomic power is used for peaceful purposes, and made it the title of the comic. The editor of the magazine, however, responded that a story about a continent would be too large for this serial. Instead, he recommended that the story could be about one individual. Tezuka, in desperation under pressure from the deadline, changed just the title to *Atomu Taishi* (Ambassador Atom), and then cobbled up the story late. Sometime during this process, Ambassador Atom emerged as a robot character.[104]

The first version of Astroboy entitled *Atomu Taishi* (Ambassador Atom) started in April 1951 and continued until March of the next year. Then, a new series entitled *Tetsuwan Atomu* (Mighty Atom) started in April and continued until the magazine *Syōnen* ceased publication in 1968. Sequels and sporadic spin-off episodes appeared in various places. On TV, Astroboy appeared as a puppet play in 1957, in a live action version from 1959 to 1960, then, in 1963, the monochromatic animation series of Astroboy started as the first serial TV animation show in Japan. The second and in color remake of the Astroboy series started in 1980, and then, in 2003, the third version of the series started. These series are not "seasons," as in North American TV dramas, but two remakes based on the original (or the original comic), with roughly the same stories. Since Astroboy has been created and recreated for such a long period and so many times, it is virtually impossible to talk about Astroboy as a whole. Here, I mainly discuss *Atomu Taishi* the first version of Astroboy, and then use some of the episodes of the early comic version of Astroboy to supplement my argument.

In this story, the protagonists are originally not Astroboy but two boys, whose names are Ken'ichi and Tamao. They are aliens who came from a perished planet to the Earth and find their exact counterparts on Earth. Their world was a distant planet, but just like a parallel universe, these aliens are not only very similar to humans but each alien individual has a human counterpart, and each alien country has a counterpart on Earth as well. For the alien Ken'ichi and Tamao, there are human Ken'ichi and Tamao, who look exactly the same. Similarly, for the alien Japan and the United States, there are Japan and the United States on Earth. After a long journey through space, they arrive on Earth and negotiate their immigration. Earthlings decide to accept the aliens. Fears of a food shortage caused by the immigration lead Dr. Tenma to invent a drug called "Contractor X" that shrinks human cells and, using the secret police of the Ministry of Science, *Akashatsutai* (Redshirts), they start shrinking aliens into tiny pieces of dust in order to resolve the food shortage. With their lives in danger, aliens evacuate to Antarctica and retaliate with their far superior science and technology, reducing the human cities to rubble. Faced with extinction, the earthlings send Astroboy as an ambassador to the aliens. The aliens are ready to launch hydrogen bombs, but Astroboy persuades them to live in peace with humans.[105]

In this story, Astroboy is created at Japan's "Ministry of Science" in the twenty-first century.[106] Dr. Tenma Umatarō lost his son Tobio by a car accident. In his grief, he creates a robot in the likeness of his son bringing together all the advanced technologies available at the Ministry of Science. Dr. Tenma, however, begins to hate the robot, seeing that he does not grow up. Dr. Tenma sells Tobio the robot to a circus, and he starts performing at the circus under the name of *Atomu*.[107]

According to Tezuka, "Ambassador Atom" was unpopular. The story was too complex for readers. Tezuka made Astroboy more central to the story but that did not boost the popularity of the comic. Following advice from the editor of the magazine, Tezuka made Astroboy the central figure in the comic and gave him a more humanlike character in the new series that started in 1952. Then, Astroboy's popularity skyrocketed.

Astroboy has three characteristics. First, Astroboy is a robot created using the most advanced technologies of the time; hence he has superhuman abilities. He has the strength of one hundred thousand horsepower, can fly, and can fire missiles. He can hear sound that humans cannot, and his eyes flash like searchlights. In addition to his physical and combat strengths, he can complete any calculation in one second, and can speak fifty languages. Moreover, he can tell a good person from a bad one just by looking.

Even with all these superhuman abilities nonetheless, Astroboy is a humanoid robot, with the appearance of a lovely boy, and his behavior and life style have superfluously human elements. Astroboy in "Ambassador Atom" retains much more robot-like characteristic and manages to conclude negotiations with the aliens by removing and handing over his own head to them. In *Tetsuwan*

*Atomu*, Astroboy starts to have robotic parents (created by Dr. Ochanomizu) and then a sister Uran (Astro Girl in the English version) and brother Cobalt (Jetto in the English version). He has a family and goes to school just like human kids. Although Astroboy is a model student, and physically and intellectually superior, he still has to learn from a human teacher such as Ban Shunsaku and has various worries similar to those of humans. Unlike Mr. F, Astroboy is like a human; he can be a friend, and can have mutual emotional ties with humans.

Close association between Tezuka's comics, especially Astroboy, and postwar democratic ideology has often been pointed out to the extent that Tezuka expressed his disgust.[108] Yet, in spite of Tezuka's protest, Astroboy is to a great extent a fable of democracy with many specific references to the history of American democracy. One of the early episodes, entitled *Furankenshutain no maki* (Frankenstein), published from 1952 to 1953, is about men's bias and discrimination against robots. Discrimination against black people in the United States and Lincoln's Emancipation Proclamation are mentioned. Villains are dressed with classic Ku Klux Klan outfits.[109] Another episode, *Yūrei seizōki no maki* (Ghost Manufacturing Machine), alludes to Nazi Germany and racial persecution of the Jews. In a country called *Gorugonia Renpō* (Golgonia), an anti-robot dictator called Hitōrin (Hitlin), whose name and appearance obviously resemble Adolf Hitler, persecutes robots. A group of robots mount a resistance movement.[110] Yet another episode, "Burakku Rukkusu no maki" (Black Looks), published in the same year depicts discrimination and the persecution of robots in South Africa and Antarctica.[111] In "Maddo mashīn no maki" (Mad Machine) in 1958, a robot becomes a congressman.[112] In "Deddokurosu denka no maki" (His Highness Deadcross), published in 1960, a robot called Rag overcomes biases and discrimination and becomes elected president of his country.[113] Similar motifs repeatedly appear in various episodes of the Astroboy stories. Astroboy in early stories is a defender of human rights, an opponent of racial prejudice and discrimination, and a proponent of democratic principles, strongly influenced by American history and democratic ideals.

Another obvious strong undertone in Astroboy is its emphasis on science and technology. The comic Astroboy is labeled as *kagaku manga* (scientific comics) on the cover, and the protagonist Astroboy is presented as a crystallization of the future Japan's (advanced) science and technology and a "child of science." There, science is depicted as power; yet it is not mere violence, but the power of justice to punish the evil and recover peace. Astroboy is the power of the atom that in the real world, the power of the United States represented in the immediate postwar era. Astroboy's name *Atomu* signifies not simply the smallest unit of identical chemical property but atomic power, as evidenced in the names of his siblings (Uran and Cobalt). In the world of Astroboy, as with the robots of Isaac Asimov, advanced robots like Astroboy are designed to be incapable of wrongdoing. Only humans and less advanced robots are capable of doing evil—unless an advanced robot is equipped with a special circuit. This idea appears repeatedly in Astroboy. For example, in "Frankenstein," a group of robots commit crimes and attempt to take over Tokyo, but in the end, it turns out that they are not robots but humans who pretend to be robots. It also turns out that Frankenstein, the robot that commits outrages, has a mechanical malfunction caused by the negligence of one of its engineers. The message is clear: the robot (i.e., technology) is inherently good. It becomes evil only when its human user is evil. Even in such a case, the damage is undone by the benevolent power of robots (technology). Thus, the image of Astroboy combines democratic values with positive depictions of science and technology.

Yet, this does not indicate Tezuka's own naïve optimism about science and technology. On the contrary, Tezuka's pessimism, or at least ambivalence, about science and technology is evident in some of the works during this period. *Metoroporisu* (Metropolis) published in 1949 is a prototype of Astroboy, in which the main character is an artificial humanoid youth with changeable gender. According to Tezuka, he conceived this story after seeing a picture of Fritz Lang's film in a cinema magazine, and wrote the comic during the war. At the very end of the comic, one of the character states his concern that humankind might destroy itself because of its overdeveloped science.[114]

So, Astroboy was actually an inversion of Tezuka's own pessimism. This is an important point, because this indicates that Astroboy itself was not simply a reflection of postwar pro-science and technology culture in Japan. Yet the enthusiastic reception of it certainly was. No matter what Tezuka's intentions were, or no matter what a careful reading of Astroboy might reveal, Astroboy was received as a celebration of science and technology.

Astroboy suited the cultural milieu of the immediate postwar era in Japan well. The beginning of *Atomu Taishi* starts with the apocalyptic vision of the death of an entire planet along with the downfall of the alien civilization there.[115] It is an early expression of a recurrent and favored leitmotif in Japanese popular culture—the vision of the end of the world,[116] and it is probably partially based on Tezuka's own personal experience of air raids in Osaka, where he witnessed total destruction of the city.[117] Yet the apocalyptic vision in this comic is not tied to the atomic bomb or science and technology in general.

In *Atomu Taishi*, Dr. Tenma decides to take the extreme measure of eliminating (miniaturizing) aliens because of a food shortage.[118] It is dubious whether a food shortage would still be a serious problem in a future society where humankind has managed to master nuclear energy, but certainly food shortages were a serious and very real everyday problem in immediate postwar Japan. Also in the *Atomu Taishi* episode, after Dr. Tenma's preemptive strikes, humans start a war against aliens. The result is the retaliation of the technologically advanced aliens, resulting in heavy damage by air raids. Here, reckless attempts of a small fraction of villains cause a hopeless war against a more powerful opponent. This is the same as the perception of Japan's war against the United States, according to which Japan, lead by reckless and corrupt military leaders, attempted a hopeless and unjust war against the righteous Allied countries and received due retaliation by air raids and atomic bombs. Moreover, after the air raids and destruction of cities, one of the earthlings tells Astroboy, "You can discern good and evil. Attack those who have caused this destruction!" Astroboy, instead of attacking the aliens, starts destroying the building of the Ministry of Science, and the earthlings say, "I learn from Astroboy who is really responsible."[119] This appears to reflect one of the prevalent views of the time that Americans were not responsible for the civilian victims of the strategic bombardments and nuclear attacks, but Japanese military leaders were.

In addition to memories of the war, various values and norms of the postwar era appear in Astroboy. For example, the United States is often depicted as an example to follow. In *Atomu Taishi*, when the alien Japanese and the earthling Japanese negotiate over aliens' immigration, Japanese representatives, including Dr. Ochanomizu, are initially reluctant to accept the aliens because of various concerns, including, of course, a food shortage, but the earthling United States quickly decides to accept their counterpart aliens. At this news, Dr. Ochanomizu says, "Americans have shown a good example," and changes his opinion, agreeing to allow the immigration of the alien Japanese into the Earth Japan.[120]

In immediate post-war Japan, science and technology had enormous cultural importance. As John Dower shows, politicians, mass media, and the military attributed Japan's defeat to the lack of science and technology in the pre-surrender period.[121] Blaming the perceived pre-surrender lack of science was convenient to exonerate wartime leaders of their responsibilities, and also convenient for scientists to acquire postwar state support for their scientific activities. Culturally, science was relatively easy to conflate with rationalism and democratic ideals. Thus, the wartime mobilization of science and preferential treatment of scientists were obscured.[122]

Through the "democratization" of scientific research, the historian of science Nakayama Shigeru writes that a "happy marriage between science and democracy" took place. Led by deeply sympathetic and understanding officers like Harry Kelly,[123] the occupying allied forces appeared as liberators to Japanese scientists.[124]

The analysis of Astroboy above suggests pushing the arguments of Nakayama and Dower even further. Not only among scientists, but also in the broader Japanese culture in the postwar era, the "happy marriage between science and democracy" took place. For Japanese in the 1950s, science and technology symbolized democracy, and other ideas such as peace, progress, and justice that were believed to accompany democracy. Science and technology, as symbolized by Astroboy, became a friend of the Japanese, rather than the enemy's tool.

The icon that bridges democracy and science was the power of the Atom, or atomic power. As the Japanese name of Astroboy, *Atomu* (or Atom), suggests, Astroboy is closely associated with nuclear power. This is even more evident in the Japanese name of his sister, *Uran*, which means "uranium" in Japanese, and his brother *Kobaruto* or "Cobalt," the name of an element known for its radioactive isotopes. As we have seen in the previous section, Astroboy was not the only reference to nuclear power in popular culture of the time: in *Atomic Ball*, the ball has a very strong power; in *Chōjin Atomu*, Atom has a superhuman power to vanquish the wrongdoers, but he is not a robot.

Considering Hiroshima and Nagasaki, and the still very strong anti-nuclear sentiment of the contemporary Japanese, such an interpretation might be surprising. It seems, however, that the predominantly anti-nuclear atmosphere in Japan emerged only in the mid-1950s, in particular after the *Lucky Dragon* incident. In the immediate post-war period, even in a survey of residents in Hiroshima and Nagasaki, 26 percent of respondents expressed admiration for the bomb, impressed by the scientific power behind it.[125] Many Japanese in the early 1950s were not yet fully familiar with the atrocities and devastations in Hiroshima and Nagasaki. In addition to the American censorship and self-imposed restraints by Japanese publishers and newspapers, graphical accounts of the atomic bomb's damages did not appear until the late 1940s. The Japanese version of John Hersey's Hiroshima appeared only in April 1949.[126] The Japanese government was not yet ready to propagandize and politically exploit Japan's nuclear victimhood, and the process of remembering Hiroshima and Nagasaki required additional time.[127]

It is a matter of debate to what extent information about atrocities in Hiroshima and Nagasaki freely circulated in Japan during the occupation. Monica Braw shows there was a systematic attempt by the SCAP to control the media. In order to expedite implementation of reform and democratization, information that might celebrate the pre-surrender regime or undermine the U.S. authority became subject to suppression. In this context, descriptions of the damage of the A-bombs could suffer forced revision and deletion. In particular, the medical records of hibakusha were taken away to the United States and concealed.[128]

The issue had become inflammatory when Etō Jun wrote an epoch-making book entitled *Tozasreta gengo kūkan* in 1989. The conservative writer Etō discovers and discusses what he called the "War Guilt Information Program" during the occupation, and argues that this program was designed to destroy traditional Japanese value systems, implant war guilt into the Japanese mind, and brainwash Japanese to believe in a masochistic history.[129] Kai Yuzuru, a Japanese censor who worked for the Civil Censorship Detachment of the GHQ, seems in agreement with Etō's contention.[130]

While acknowledging the importance of Etō's work, Yamamoto Taketoshi, one of the leading experts on publishing during the occupation period, responds to his arguments. In his erudite *Senryūki media bunseki* in 1996, he criticizes Etō for not taking the pre-surrender censorship system into consideration, through which the Japanese mass media had become accustomed to censorship before Douglas MacArthur landed on the Japanese shore. Whereas Etō emphasizes the role of the occupation authority in the formation of postwar discourse in Japan and contends that the War Guilt Information Program destroyed traditional Japanese values, Yamamoto points out that Etō ignores the resistance of Japanese leftist intellectuals against the U.S. censorship.[131]

The fact that the Japanese media was used to censorship during the pre-surrender period might be useful for us to evaluate the situation. Criticizing Braw's book, Sasamoto Yukio claims that, in spite of popular beliefs that the U.S. "Press Code" suppressed the circulation of information about A-bombs, in reality, Japanese newspapers wrote a great deal about the damage, disaster, and cruelty caused by the nuclear bombings in Hiroshima and Nagasaki. It is true that vivid descriptions of the horrible situations in Hiroshima and Nagasaki, in particular in literary works, were censored, but, by studying the materials in the Prange Collection, Sasamoto shows that it was not often the case that any reporting of the atomic bomb was wholly or partially deleted because of censorship.[132] Another researcher, Horiba Kiyoko, corroborates Sasamoto's claim. By studying censorship documents in the Prange Collection, Horiba finds that the U.S. censorship was much milder on A-bombs compared to right and left wing political activism, materials related to communism, and criticism of the occupation authority, as far as evidence of deletion and other censorship remarks can reveal.[133]

Eiko Tani studies how censorship affected the publication of juvenile literature. As for publications related to science and technology, three titles did not pass pre-publication censorship, and six did not pass post-publication censorship. Only one of them, Tsuboi Sakae's anthology of children's tales entitled *Jūgoya no tsuki,* suffered heavy revisions of the part related to atomic bomb damages.[134] Another item, *Shōnen shakaika nenkan* (Boys' Almanac for Social Studies), was ordered to delete descriptions of the destruction of cyclotrons by the U.S. occupation forces. Other titles were censored only because of nationalistic and militaristic expressions.[135]

Sasamoto, then, suggests that maybe the Japanese media was not really keen on reporting on the damages to Hiroshima and Nagasaki, and maybe Japanese were not so much interested in knowing it.[136] Sasamoto's evidence is probably not enough to support his argument because if, as Yamamoto argues, the Japanese media were already used to censorship; they would rather practice self-restraints in order to avoid trouble with the GHQ. In that case, the Japanese media's unwillingness to report nuclear atrocities resulted not from their indifference but from the informal pressure of censorship. Yet Sasamoto's suggestion might actually be right. U.S. censorship might have helped to obscure gruesome images of atomic bombs, but without censorship, Japanese people might already have been quite willing to see atomic bombs in a much more favorable light. We have already seen some examples of cultural meanings of *atomu* in the previous section. Some contemporary testimonies corroborate this point more explicitly. For example, Taketani Mituo, a Marxist philosopher and physicist who was an intellectual hero in post-war Japan, criticized those who blamed the United States for her use of the atomic bombs.[137] Just as the atomic bomb was the tool of liberation for those who suffered under Japan's invasion, it was a righteous weapon even to many Japanese until the devastation in Hiroshima and Nagasaki dawned on them.

# Conclusion

Extreme optimism about science and technology has not necessarily continued to dominate Japan since World War II. Already in the mid 1950s, a counter-discourse began to rise. It was triggered by the nuclear experiments in the Bikini Islands and Japan's fishing vessel the *Lucky Dragon*'s exposure to its radioactive fallout in 1954. Later in the same year, the film *Godzilla* appeared. Another turning point was probably in the late 1960s and 1970s. The Vietnam War discredited American democratic values and the power of science and technology. Then, in the 1970s, environmental problems disillusioned the dream of technological utopia.

Tracing these developments is out of the scope of this paper. One thing, however, seems to be certain: images of robots and of science and technology were inscribed into popular science works and revived from time to time. They are like memory devices. Popular culture is in itself a factor that shapes public perceptions of science. Not only does it shape the public perception of science and technology, but also it is used and manipulated to do so.[138]

The popular images of robots in Japan underwent a dramatic change from the 1930s to the 1950s. In the 1930s, robots were threatening tools of the enemy. In the 1950s, robots became idealized friends. This change corresponds to changes in public perceptions of technology in Japan. In the 1930s, technology was a tool of military strengths that belonged to the enemy, and therefore a threat to the Japanese. In the 1950s, technology became an icon of justice and democracy, and Japan's future prosperity was deemed to depend upon advancing it.

Certainly, Astroboy or Mr. F are not the only things that reflect popular perceptions of technology. Nor are they the only cultural icons of technology. In addition, many other events contributed to the formation of public perceptions of technology. Moreover, people in one country never have a homogeneous perception of technology. Always, there are competing and contradictory images of technology, which accumulate over years. As a first step to entangle this complexity, however, studying popular cultural seems very promising.

Images of robots in popular culture, therefore, matter to historians of technology. More than that, as we have seen in the case of Astroboy's birthday in 2003, memories of the past continued to pay or to be engineered to exert forces to shape popular perceptions of science and technology. Contextualized against the historical background, fantasies of technology become an object of inquiry in their own right, providing historians and sociologists of science and technology with a tool to examine public perceptions of technology.

# Notes

1. This work is an expanded and heavily revised version of the paper published in *Japan Journal for Science, Technology & Society*, vol. 12 (2003): 39–63. I thank Professor Matsumoto Miwao at the University of Tokyo, the editor of *Japan Journal for Science, Technology & Society*, for allowing publication of this paper here. This chapter is based on a research project partially supported by the *grant-in-aid* for young scientist (B) No. 17700631, 2005–2006, of the Ministry of Education Science, Sports, and Culture of Japan, and Twentieth-Century Japan Research Awards of the University of Maryland. Japanese names are in the traditional order, except when they appear as authors of Western language publications.

2. In the first animation of Astroboy in English as well as in Frederik L. Schodt's translation of Astroboy, the name was presented as "Astro Boy." Yet, in the recent notation, "Astroboy" seems to be the official English name. In this paper, I use the latter notation regardless of the period of the work in question.

3. For more discussion of Astroboy's birthday, see Kenji Ito, "Astroboy's Birthday: Robotics and Culture in Contemporary Japanese Society" (paper presented at the Second East Asian Science, Technology, and Society Conference, Taipei, August 2007), sts.nthu .edu.tw/easts/2007/day1.htm (14 January, 2009); Kenji Ito, "Astroboy's Birthday: Theorizing Science, Technology, and Popular Culture in Contemporary Japan," unpublished manuscript, 2009.

4. The relation between science and technology is an issue I avoid discussing here. In the Japanese context, the word *kagakugijutsu* corresponds to "science and technology," but in the 1930s this word was employed to mean advanced technology or technological applications of science; hence it meant technology more than science. In many instances, Japanese write "science" when they mean technology. Given this complexity, I decided not to deal with this issue in this paper.

5. According to a prominent Japanese science fiction writer, Hoshi Shin'ichi. See Hoshi Shin'ichi, "Kagaku no hekichi nite," *Iwanami kôza gendai geppô*, no. 6 (Tokyo: Iwanami Shoten, November 1963), 3.

6. See also Ito, "Astroboy's Birthday" (2007); Ito, "Astroboy's Birthday" (2009).

7. For example, see: Tsurumi Shunsuke, *Genkai geijutsu ron* (Tokyo: Chikuma Shobō, 1967, 1999). For a discussion of Tsurumi and Fujikawa, see Uryu Yoshimitsu, "Manga-ron no keifugaku," *The Bulletin of the Institute of Socio-Information and Communication Studies*, University of Tokyo, No. 56 (1998): 135–53.

8. See, for example, Uryu (1998).

9. Ito Go, *Tezuka izu deddo: Hirakareta manga hyōgenron e* (Tokyo: NTT Shuppan, 2005), 11–12.

10. Inoue Haruki, *Robotto sōseki: 1920–1938* (Tokyo: NTT Shuppan, 1993). This is the most comprehensive book on the cultural situation in relation to imagery of robots in the interwar period.

11. *Shinseinen* Kenkyūkai, ed., *Shinseinen dokuhon: Shōwa gurafiti* (Tokyo: Sakuhinsha, 1988).

12. Translation is mine. Yumeno Kyūsaku, "Tantei shōsetsu no shinshimei," *Yumeno Kyūsaku zenshū*, vol. 7 (Tokyo: San'ichi Shobō, 1970), 366–67.

13. Yumeno Kyūsaku, "Kōga Saburō shi ni kotau," *Yumeno Kyūsaku zenshū*, vol. 7 (Tokyo: San'ichi Shobō, 1970), 371–72. As for an analysis of Yumeno's view of detective stories, see Horikiri Naoto, *Taishō genmetsu* (Tokyo: Riburopōto, 1992), 158–60. As for Yumeno in general, see, for example, Tsurumi Shunsuke, *Yumeno Kyūsaku to Haniwa Otaka* (Tokyo: Shin'ya Sōsho Sha, 2001), 1–105.

14. Yumeno Kyūsaku, *Dogura magura*, Yumeno Kyūsaku zenshū, vol. 7 (Tokyo: Chikuma Shobō, 1992).

15. As for relation between Oshikawa and Unno, see Ito Hideo, "Unno Jūza to Meiji tantei shōsetsu," *Unno Jūza zenshū*, vol. 1, *Unno Jūza zenshū geppō* (1988): 1–8.

16. Washida Koyata, "Unno Jūza no kagaku shōsetsu," *Ushio*, no. 367 (1989): 406–9.

17. All of them are in *Unno Jūza zenshū*.

18. Unno Jūza, "Kurogane Tengu," *Unno Jūza zenshū*, vol. 4, Tokyo: San'ichi Shobō, 1989, 115–25.

19. Jack London's *The Iron Heel* was published in 1908, Aldous Huxley's *Brave New World* in 1932, and George Orwell's *1984* in 1944.

20. Unno Jūza, "Jūhachiji no ongakuyoku," in *Unno Jūza zenshū*, vol. 4 (Tokyo: San'ichi Shobō, 1989), 195–227.

21. As for this point, see, Aizu Shingo, "Unno Jūza to senzen senchūno kagaku shōsetsu," in *Tanjō! Tezuka Osamu*, ed. Takanaka Shimotsuki (Tokyo: Asahi Sonorama, 1998), 198.

22. Unno Jūza, "Jinzō ningen efu-shi," in *Unno Jūza zenshū* (Tokyo: San'ichi Shobō, 1989), 229–93.

23. Similarities between Mr. F and Astroboy have been pointed out by Aizu Shingo. Aizu, however, does not discuss differences. See Aizu, "Unno Jūza to senzen senchūno kagaku shōsetsu."

24. Unno, "Jinzō ningen efu-shi."

25. Ibid., 283.

26. Ibid., 285.

27. Ibid., 292.

28. For newspaper reports of the time, see "Nomonhan jiken no zenbō: Kyōi! Waga shōhei no seishinryoku, sorengun no kikairyoku ni dōdō taikō," Irie Tokurō, ed., *Dainiji Taisen: Kurai Seishun*, Shimbun Shūsei Shōwashi no shōgen, vol. 13 (Shōwa 14-nen) (Hompō Shoseki, 1985), 451–52.

29. As for the Nomonhan Incident, see Alvin D. Coox, *Nomonhan: Japan against Russia, 1939* (Stanford, Calif.: Stanford University Press, 1985).

30. Jeffrey Herf, *Reactionary Modernism: Technology, Culture, and Politics in Weimar and the Third Reich* (Cambridge/New York: Cambridge University Press, 1984).

31. Hirosige Tetu, *Kgaku no shakaishi* (Tokyo: Chūō Kōron Sha, 1973).

32. Unno Jūza, *Unno Jūza zenshū. Bekkan*, vol. 2 (Tōkyō: San'ichi Shobō, 1993).

33. As for images of robots in Japan during this period, see Inoue's most comprehensive work: Inoue Haruki, *Nihon robotto sensōki, 1939–1945*, first ed. (Tokyo: NTT Shuppan, 2007).

34. For a catalogue of this collection, see: Murakami Hisayo and Tani Eiko, eds., *Guide to the Gordon W. Prange Children's Book Colletion: Occupation-Period Censored Children's Books, 1945–1949* (Ann Arbor: ProQuest Information and Learning, 2002).

35. There are exceptions, such as Tezuka Osamu's *Metropolis*, which I discuss later.

36. Sawada Ken, *Kyurī fujin: Jinrui no onjin* (Tokyo: Kabushikikaisha Gihōdō, 1948).

37. Kimura Fujio, *Chikyū no chichi Galilei* (Hokkaido: Genbunsha, 1947).

38. Hirota Yoshihiro, *Watashitachi no kagaku seikatsu* (Nara: Yamato Shoen, 1946).

39. Iida Yukisato, *Genshi bakudan* (Tokyo: Shōheisha, 1948).

40. Takeda Shimpei, *Genshi bōru* (Tokyo: Ohkawaya Shoten, 1949).

41. Tanaka Shin'ichi, *Chōjin Atomu kaikijō no maki* (Osaka: Tōkōdō, 1948).

42. Suzuki Hiroshi, *Fukakuteiseigenri: gendai butsurigaku no kotoba* (Kyoto: Tomi Shoten, 1948).

43. Ayukawa Tetsuya, *Maboroshi no tantei sakka o motomete* (Tokyo: Shōbundō, 1985).

44. Suzki Hiroshi, *Atomu-kun no bōken* (Osaka: Asahi Shimbunsha, 1951).

45. Miyachi Kenjirō, "Nō moa Hiroshimazu: sekai no heiwa undō," *Shūkan asahi* (7 August 1949): 8–9, on 8; Yasaka Seigekishi, "Atomu no susu Hiroshima no uta," *Kōha* (20 April 1949): 8.

46. S, "Dokusha ronpyō," *Shōtenkai* (1 October 1949): 28.

47. "Atomu jidai ni arawareta bakemono shū: tōzai ryōki kurabe," *Sekai gurafu* (20 August 1948): 20–23.

48. "Eigo kōza: visiting atom Hiroshima," *Rōen* (1 May 1948): 58–59.; "Heiwa no zenshin: atomu Hiroshima kyō yonshūnen," *Nishi-Nihon Shimbun* (6 August 1949): 2; Y-kisha, "Ippitsu keijō: Tōzai tsūshin: atomu Hiroshima no kyō konogoro," *Sand mainichi* (31 July1949): 20–21.; Yagi kisha, "Atomu Hiroshima to tennō gaijin kisha ni kiku," *Kyūshū taimuzu* (7 December 1947): 1; "Atomu no machimachi," *Sasebo jiji shimbun* (2 August 1948): 2; "Atomu Nagasaki ni Nagai hakase wo tazunete (ge)," *Kumamoto nichi-nichi shimbun* (10 August 1948): 2; "Onban ni noru atomu Nagasaki,"

*Nagasaki nichi-nichi shimbun* (21 July 1949): 2; Uehiro Tetsuhiko, "Megami no gotoki sono magokoro ni: Atomu no machi ni katsute atta futatsu no monogatari," *Shinsei* 1949: 21–24; Aoyama Kazuma, "Kaze kaoru atomu no machi," *Shinsei* (1 July 1949): 47; "Keizai saiken e no dai-ippo: Okiagatta atomu Hiroshima," *Keizai bukka gaido* (3 March 1949) ; Mishima-kisha, "Amaeru genbaku koji," *Kyushu taimuzu* (7 December 1947): 1.

49. Tanaka Giichi, "Nihon yakyū Hokkaido enseiki," *Bēsu bōru magajin* (1 October 1949): 59.

50. "Tokyo-sen: dai nijūsan-setsu," *Yakyū fan* (15 September 1949): 11.

51. "Ōru romansu hyakka jiten (a)," *Ōru romansu* (1 October 1948): 42.

52. "Shin seihin shōkai," *CQ ham radio* (1 April 1949): 43.

53. "Ton'yagai nyūsu," *Seizō ton'ya annai* (25 October 1948): 57.

54. *Nishi nihon shimbun* (11 August 1948).

55. Fukazawa, "Osaka chihō rōdō iinkai toriatsukai sōgi gaiyō," *Rōdō jihō* (25 December 1948): 21–22; Honda, "Osaka chihō rōdō iinkai toriatsukai sōgi gaiyō," *Rōdō jihō* (25 January 1949): 18.

56. *Nishi nihon shimbun* (30 September 1949): 2.

57. *Ehime shimbun* (13 January 1949): 2.

58. Yokoi Fukuzirō, "Atomu sensei to Bon-kun," *Kodomo kagaku kyōshitsu* (1 April 1948): 25; Yokoi Fukuzirō, "Atomu sensei to Bon-kun," *Kodomo kagaku kyōshitsu* (1 July 1948): 25; (1 May 1948): 22–23; (1 June 1948): 24–25; (1 April 1948): 20–21.

59. H. K. Sei, "Saiensu dorama: aru asa no Atomu hakase," *Kagaku shunjū* (20 September 1948): 11–14.

60. Nikkagiren 50-nenshi henshū iinkai, ed., *Zaidan hōjin nihon kagaku gijutsu renmei sōritsu 50-nen shi* (Tokyo: Zaidan hōjin Nihon Kagaku Gijutsu Renmei, 1997), 7.

61. Nishina Yoshio, Sagane Ryōkichi, Ōshima Bun'ichi, Yuasa Toshiko, and Mukaiyama Mikio, "Genshiryoku jidai wo kataru," *Atom* (1947): 22–28.

62. *Atomu* (20 September 1947): 1.

63. *Atomu* (14 June 1948): 1.

64. The term "science fiction" or SF became popular only in the 1950s and widely used in the 1960s. In this sense, the genre Unno started in Japan did not have a definitive name until later.

65. I do not pretend to follow all the studies and commentaries related to him. There are several biographies or biographical memoirs, including Tezuka's own: Tezuka Osamu, *Boku ha mangaka* (Tokyo: Mainichi Shimbunsha, 1969); two versions of memoirs by his wife: Tezuka Etsuko, *Otto Tezuka Osamu to tomoni: Komorebi ni ikiru* (Tokyo: Kodansha, 1995); Tezuka Etsuko, *Tezuka Osamu no shirarezaru tensai jinsei* (Tokyo: Kodansha, 1999); one by a daughter of Tezuka's: Tezuka Rumiko, *Osamushi ni tsutaete* (Tokyo: Ōtashuppan, 1994); and others: Ichiokunin no Tezuka Osamu henshū-iinkai, ed., *Ichiokunin no Tezuka Osamu* (Tokyo: JICC shuppankyoku, 1989); Nakao Akira, *Tezuka Osamu* (Tokyo: Kodansha, 1991); Oshita Eiji, *Tezuka Osamu: Roman dai uchū*, two vols. (Tokyo: Ushio Shuppansha, 1995); Imagawa Kiyoshi, *Sorawo koete: Tezuka Osamu den* (Tokyo: Sōgensha, 1996). Many of Tezuka's essays are autobiographical: Tezuka Osamu, *Tezuka Osamu totteoki no hanashi* (Tokyo: Shinnihon Shuppansha, 1990); Tezuka Osamu, *Mitari Tottari Utsushitari* (Tokyo: Kinema Junpōsha, 1987); Tezuka

Osamu, *Tezuka Osamu essei shū*, eight vols., Tezuka Osamu manga zenshū (Tokyo: Kodansha, 1996–1997). There are at least two commemorative volumes on Tezuka: Tezuka Production, ed., *Tezuka Osamu manga 40-nen* (Tokyo: Akita Shoten, 1984); Tezuka Production, ed., *Tezuka Osamu zenshi: Sonosugao to gyōseki* (Tokyo: Akita Shoten, 1998); Books on Tezuka include: Natsume Fusanosuke, *Tezuka Osamu no bouken: Sengo manga no kamigami* (Tokyo: Chikuma Shobō, 1995); Natsume Fusanosuke, *Tezuka Osamu wa dokoniiru* (Tokyo: Chikuma Shobō, 1992); Ishiko Jun, *Manga shijin Tezuka Osamu* (Tokyo: Shin Nihon Shuppansha, 1991); Mizuno Masashi, *Tezuka Osamu to Konan Doiru* (Tokyo: Seikyūsha, 2002); Otsuka Eiji, *Atomu no meidai: Tezuka Osamu to sengo manga no shudai* (Tokyo: Tokuma Shoten, 2003). There is a recent groundbreaking work on Japanese comics rather than Tezuka alone: Ito Go, *Tezuka izu deddo: Hirakareta manga hyōgenron e* (Tokyo: NTT Shuppan, 2005). Several works in English on Japanese manga and anime mention Tezuka: Frederik L. Schodt, *The Astro Boy Essays: Osamu Tezuka, Mighty Atom, Manga/Anime Revolution* (Berkeley, Calif.: Stone Bridge Press, 2007); Roland Kelts, *Japanamerica: How Japanese Pop Culture has Invaded the US* (New York: Palgrave Macmillan, 2006, 2007); Frederik L. Schodt, *Dreamland Japan: Writings on Modern Manga* (Berkeley, Calif.: Stone Bridge Press, 1996).

66. Ishiko Jun, *Sengo mangashi nōto* (Tokyo: Kinokuniya Shoten, 1975), 55.

67. Tezuka, *Boku wa mangaka*, 87–88.

68. Ibid., 130–31.

69. Yaguchi Takao, *Boku no Tezuka Osamu* (Tokyo: Kodansha, 1994).

70. Tezuka was trained as a physician and received a doctoral degree in medicine.

71. Yuasa Akira, "Kagakusha eno michi," *Syōnen* 1, no. 1 (1947): 16–21; Yuasa Akira, "Kagakusha e no michi: Yoku miru koto tameshite miru koto," *Syōnen* 1, no. 2 (1948): 22–27; Yuasa Akira, "Kagakusha e no michi: Jintai no fushigi," *Syōnen* 2, no. 1 (1948): 29–33.

72. Toki Yoshimaro, "Minasan wa naze rōmaji wo narauka," *Syōnen* 1, no. 1 (1947): 26–32.

73. Yokoi Fukuzirō, "Otenki bōya," *Syōnen* 1, no. 1 (1947), supplement. Yokoi was one of the most important comic authors of this period, who was well known for his *kagaku manga* (scientific comics), as I discuss below.

74. "Boku no sonkeisuru hito," *Syōnen* 6, no. 5 (1951): 63.

75. Ibid., 64.

76. Translation is mine.

77. "Boku no sonkeisuru hito," 64.

78. Tezuka Osamu, "Waga omoide no ki," in *Tezuka Osamu essei shū*, Tezuka Osamu manga zenshū 395 (Tokyo: Kodansha, 1997), 14; Tezuka Osamu, "Boku no shōnen jidai," in *Tezuka Osamu essei shū*, Tezuka Osamu manga zenshū, 394 (Tokyo, 1997), 22–24; Osamu Tezuka, "Watashi no Takarazuka," in *Tezuka Osamu essei shū*, Tezuka Osamu manga zenshū 395 (Tokyo, 1997), 52–54.

79. See Tezuka Minako's interview: Tezuka Minako, "Atomu no haha, Takarazuka kageki?," *Asahi Shimbun*, evening edition (4 April 2003): 11. Reprinted in Hirata Shōgo, Keisuke Nemoto, Yoshio Shirai, Eiichi Otsuka, and Hiroshi Sasakawa, eds. *Nihon no Reonarudo da Vinchi: Tezuka Osamu to rokunin* (Tokyo: Boutique Sha, 2005), 101.

80. Shimamoto Mitsuaki, "Tezuka Osamu wa Unno Jūza o dou miteitaka," *Unno Jūza kenkyū* no. 15 (1993): 1–4.

81. Aizu Manga Kyōkai, "Unno Jūza to Tezuka Osamu no sekai," in *Nihon no Reonarudo da Vinchi: Tezuka Osamu to rokunin*, ed. Hirata Shōgo et al. (Tokyo: Boutique Sha, 2005), 144–65; Aizu, "Unno Jūza to senzen senchūno kagaku shōsetsu"; Shiozaki Noboru, "Tetsuwan Atomu no rūtsu o saguru," in *Tanjō! Tezuka Osamu*, ed. Shimotsuki Takanaka (Tokyo: Asahi Sonorama, 1998), 153–80.

82. Tezuka, *Boku wa mangaka*. 56.

83. Quoted in: Aizu Manga Kyōkai, "Unno Jūza to Tezuka Osamu no sekai."

84. The title *Kitarubeki Sekai* is same as the Japanese title of the 1936 British movie, *Things to Come*, by William Cameron Menzies, based on H. G. Wells's novel: H. G. Wells, *The Shape of Things to Come, the Ultimate Revolution* (London: Hutchinson, 1933). The English title in the text, however, appears on the cover of the comic.

85. Tezuka Osamu, "Sengo SF manga dai ichigō," in *Tezuka Osamu essei shū*, Tezuka Osamu manga zenshū, 395 (Tokyo: Kodansha, 1997), 97.

86. Shimotsuki, ed., *Tanjō! Tezuka Osamu*.

87. Tezuka, "Sengo SF manga dai ichigō," 95; Tezuka, *Boku wa mangaka*, 102; see Tezuka Minako's interview: Tezuka, "Atomu no haha, Takarazuka kageki?"

88. Yokoi Fukuzirō, *Kanzenban fushigi na kuni no pucchā* (Tokyo: Tōgensha, 1975), 158.

89. As for Yokoi, see also: Shimizu Isao and Suzuki Satoo, *Sengo manga no toppu rannā Yokoi Fukuzirō: Tezuka Osam umo hirefushita tensaimangaka no kiseki* (Kyoto: Rinsen Shoten, 2007). Shimzu and Satoo recognize Yokoi's Pucchā as a precursor of Astroboy.

90. There is another magazine with the same name published by an organization called Osaka Seikatsu Kgaku Kenkyūkai (Association for Studies of Everyday Science in Osaka) established in 1948, led by educators in the Kansai region and business leaders such as Matsushita Kōnosuke, the founder of Panasonic. In the series of "Kūso seikatsu," Yokoi depicts life in future society and everyday conveniences made possible by future technology.

91. Yokoi, *Kanzenban fushigi na kuni no pucchā*, 3.

92. As I discuss later, Astroboy has one hundred thousand horsepower. However, in the original version, Astroboy's power was one hundred thousand dyne. It is not clear if Tezuka was directly influenced by Yokoi's work here.

93. Yokoi, *Kanzenban fushigi na kuni no pucchā*, 9.

94. Ibid. 129; Shiozaki also points out this expression: Shiozaki, "Tetsuwan Atomu no rūtsu o saguru."

95. Yokoi, *Kanzenban fushigi na kuni no pucchā*. 102.

96. Ibid. 29.

97. James Whale, dir. *The Invisible Man* (Los Angeles: Universal Studio, 1933).

98. Tezuka Osamu, *Metoroporisu*, Tezuka Osamu manga zenshū, 44 (Tokyo: Kodansha, 1979, 2002). 164–65.

99. Shimamoto, "Tezuka Osamu wa Unno Jūza wo dou miteitaka," 3.

100. Gaston Derreaux, "Honoo no jōō," in *Amējingu sutōrīzu* (Tokyo: Seibundō Shinkō Sha, 1950), 1–100.

101. Tezuka, *Boku wa mangaka*, 47–48.

102. Tezuka, *Mitari Tottari Utsushitari*, 156–58.

103. This is an example of how Tezuka's reminiscences cannot be trusted. Nuclear testing on Christmas Island (Kiritimati) started in 1957.

104. Tezuka, *Boku wa mangaka*, 138–40.

105. Tezuka Osamu, *Tetsuwan Atomu tanjō! taizen* (Tokyo: Kobunsha, 2003).

106. Various versions of Astroboy are not consistent concerning Astroboy's year of birth. In fact, in the original version of *Atomu Taishi*, the story is supposed to take place thousands of years in the future.

107. Tezuka, *Tetsuwan Atomu tanjō! taizen*.

108. Tezuka Osamu and Iwaya Kunio, "Taiwa nijuūseiki no inshō: Tezuka manga no hōhōishiki," *Yuriika* 15, no. 2 (1983): 97–127.

109. Tezuka Osamu, "Furankenshutain no maki," in *Tetsuwan Atomu*, vol. 1, Tezuka Osamu manga zenshū, 221 (Tokyo: Kodansha, 1979), 125–70.

110. Tezuka Osamu, "Yūrei seizōki no maki," in *Tetsuwan Atomu*, vol. 4, Tezuka Osamu manga zenshū, 224 (Tokyo: Kodansha, 1980), 65–150.

111. Tezuka Osamu, "Burakku Rukkusu no maki," in *Tetsuwan Atomu*, vol. 4, Tezuka Osamu manga zenshū, 224 (Tokyo: Kodansha, 1980): 65–150.

112. Tezuka Osamu, "Maddo mashīn no maki," in *Tetsuwan Atomu*, vol. 5, Tezuka Osamu manga zenshū, 225 (Tokyo: Kodansha, 1980): 159–78.

113. Tezuka Osamu, "Deddo Kurosu denka no maki," in *Tetsuwan Atomu*, vol. 8, Tezuka Osamu manga zenshū, 228 (Tokyo: Kodansha, 1980): 67–160.

114. Tezuka, *Metoroporisu*.

115. Tezuka, *Tetsuwan Atomu tanjō! taizen*. 7.

116. Susan J. Napier, *From Impressionism to Anime: Japan as Fantasy and Fan Cult in the Mind of the West* (New York: Palgrave Macmillan, 2007).

117. In one of his later long comics, Tezuka let the protagonist say: "[An air raid] struck me more as the end of the world than simply a disaster." See Tezuka Osamu, *Adorufu ni tsugu*, vol. 5, Tezuka Osamu manga zenshū, 376 (Tokyo: Kodansha, 1996). As for his war experience, see Tezuka, *Boku wa mangaka*.

118. Tezuka, *Tetsuwan Atomu tanjō! taizen*. 53–55.

119. Ibid. 84.

120. Ibid. 50–51.

121. John W. Dower, *Embracing Defeat: Japan in the Wake of World War II* (New York: W. W. Norton & Company, 1999), 493–95.

122. Hirosige Tetu, *Kagaku no shakaishi* (Tokyo: Chūō Kōron Sha, 1973).

123. Hideo Yoshikawa and Joanne Kauffman, *Science Has No National Borders: Harry C. Kelly and the Reconstruction of Science and Technology in Postwar Japan* (Cambridge, Mass.: MIT Press, 1994).

124. Shigeru Nakayama, Kunio Gotō, and Hitoshi Yoshioka, *A Social History of Science and Technology in Contemporary Japan*, Japanese Society Series, (Melbourn: Trans Pacific Press, 2001), 41–42.

125. United States Strategic Bombing Survey, *Effects of Strategic Bombing on Japanese Morale, Report on the Pacific War*, no. 14 (Washington, D.C.: U. S. Government Printing Office, 1947), 3, 91–97, quoted in note 4 of Sadao Asada, "The Mushroom Cloud

and National Psyches: Japanese and American Perceptions of the Atomic Bomb Decision, 1945–1995," in *Living with the Bomb: American and Japanese Cultural Conflicts in the Nuclear Age*, ed. Laura Elizabeth Hein and Mark Selden (Armonk, N.Y.: M. E. Sharpe Inc., 1997), 173–201.

126. See ibid., 174–75.

127. As for the memory practices of Hiroshima as an A-bombed city, see Lisa Yoneyama, *Hiroshima Traces: Time, Space, and the Dialectics of Memory* (Berkeley: University of California Press, 1999).

128. Monica Braw, *The Atomic Bomb Suppressed: American Censorship in Occupied Japan* (Armonk, N.Y.: M. E. Sharpe Inc., 1991).

129. Etō Jun, *Tozasareta gengo kūkan Senryōgun no ken'etsu to sengo Nihon* (Tokyo: Bungei Shunjū, 1989).

130. Kai Yuzuru, *GHQ ken'etsukan* (Fukuoka-shi: Ashi Shobō, 1995).

131. Yamamoto Taketoshi, *Senryōki media bunseki* (Tokyo: Hōsei Daigaku Shuppankyoku, 1996).

132. Yukio Sasamoto, "Reporting on the Atomic Bomb and the Press Code," in *A Social History of Science and Technology in Contemporary Japan*, ed. Shigeru Nakayama, Kunio Gotō, and Hitoshi Yoshioka (Melbourne: Trans Pacific Press, 2001), 437–69.

133. Horiba Kiyoko, *Genbaku hyōgen to ken'etsu: Nihonjin wa dō taiōshita ka* (Tokyo: Asahi Shimbunsha, 1995). According to Horiba, in contrast to 227 cases where expressions failed to pass censorship because of nationalism or militarism, only seven cases did not pass censorship because of A-bomb-related expressions.

134. Tsuboi Sakae, *Jūgoya no tsuki* (Tokyo: Aiikusha, 1947).

135. Tani Eiko, *Senryōka no jidōsho ken'etsu shiryōhen purange bunko jidō yomimono ni saguru* (Tokyo: Shin Dokusho sha, 2004).

136. Sasamoto, "Reporting on the Atomic Bomb and the Press Code."

137. Matsuura Shōzō, *Senryōka no genron dan'atsu* (1969), 123–24.

138. See Ito, "Astroboy's birthday."

*Mani: whimsical (in spite of oneself)*
*ga: picture*

# CHAPTER 4  *Manga = whimsical picture*

# The Day the Sun Was Lost

## FROM THE FILM *TAIYO WO NAKUSHITA HI*

*Minoru Maeda*

The following chapter is taken from the animated film *Taiyo wo Nakushita Hi* by animator Minoru Maeda. Maeda is a Hiroshima native whose father is a hibakusha (survivor of the atomic bombing). Maeda made this movie about his father's experiences as a seven-year-old victim of the bombing. It has been converted into manga format for this volume.

Maeda's film is important to this book for several reasons. It is art that was created in direct response to the actual experience of atomic bombing. He meticulously researched the appearance of Hiroshima prior to the bombing in order to make his depiction of his father's days just before the bombing as accurate as possible. As a son of Hiroshima, he has drawn a loving tribute to his hometown and the loss of its architectural heritage.

But the work is also important because it is the work of the second generation after the atomic attack. It is not only a work about loss—it is a work about inheriting loss. As the son of a hibakusha, Maeda has created a work that honors something very important that his father lost on that day when he was seven—his childhood. His father's life, and that of countless other children, altered on that day from one of typical childhood playfulness (albeit in the shadow of wartime deprivations), to one of survival. Maeda's film spends a significant amount of time depicting his father and his friends at play, before Hiroshima was bombed. As the son of a hibakusha, he is trying to give back to his father that most precious thing—a lost childhood, a world in which play was central.

*Robert Jacobs*

STREETSCAPE BEFORE THE BOMBING

A BOY STOPS IN FRONT OF A SCHOOL

HE FLASHES BACK TO BEFORE THE WAR INTENSIFIED

CHILDREN PLAYING IN THE SCHOOLYARD

HE REMEMBERS THE PHOTO WHEN SCHOOL STARTED

NOW THE SCHOOLYARD IS FOR MILITARY TRAINING

HOUSEWIVES ARE CALLED TOGETHER

THE LOCAL COMMUNITY LEADER
ANNOUNCES
THE START OF THE FIRE DRILL

WAR TIME POSTERS

WHILE THE HOUSEWIVES ARE
ENGAGED IN THE FIRE DRILL...

THE CHILDREN ARE PLAYING

TRYING TO CATCH CICADAS

A FIRE DRILL

THROWING WATER ON A MOCK FIRE

GIRLS PLAYING RUBBER-BAND JUMP ROPE          A BOY DROPS A LEAF IN A STREAM OF WATER

THEY GET A KICK OUT OF

CHASING THE LEAF

THEY OPEN COVERS OF THE GUTTER DRAIN

DRAINAGE COVERS LEFT SCATTERED

THE BOYS RUN AWAY FROM AN ANGRY MAN

HOUSES ARE DELIBERATELY DEMOLISHED
TO AVOID SPREADING FIRE IN
THE EVENT OF AN AIR-RAID

WOODEN HOUSES ARE PULLED DOWN WITH A ROPE

SUNSET CASTS LONG SHADOWS

BROTHERS ARE ARM WRESTLING

WHEN A FATHER GETS HOME THE WHOLE FAMILY IS GATHERED

THE NEXT MORNING

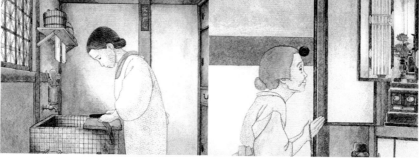

A MOTHER IN THE KITCHEN PREPARES BREAKFAST

THE BOYS HEAD TO A TEMPLE

THE TEMPLE HAS BEEN USED AS A TEMPORARY SCHOOL

GIRLS PRACTICE JUGGLING

SOME OF THE CHILDREN PREPARE FOR CLASS

AIRPLANES GLITTER IN THE SKY

A BOY SPOTS A LIZARD

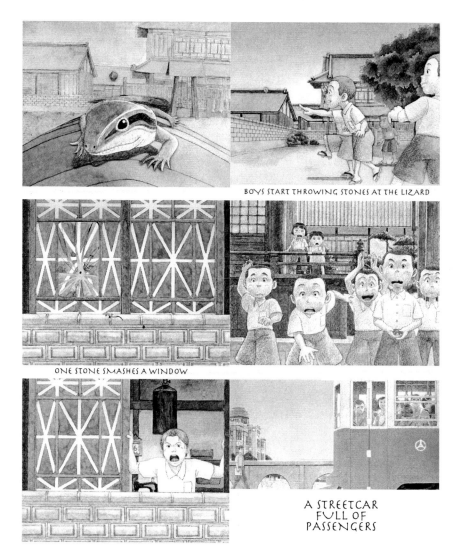

BOYS START THROWING STONES AT THE LIZARD

ONE STONE SMASHES A WINDOW

A STREETCAR
FULL OF
PASSENGERS

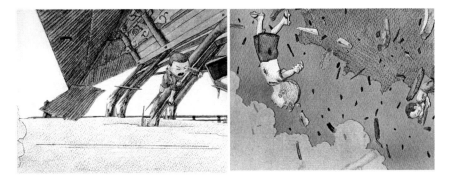

# IN AN INSTANT...

...EVERYTHING HAS CHANGED

PEOPLE CROUCHING FOR SHELTER

THE BOY ASKS HIS FRIEND TO COME WITH HIM

BUT THE FRIEND DRIFTS AWAY IN A DIFFERENT DIRECTION

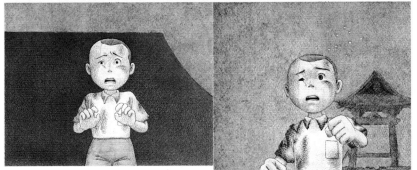

THE BOY RUNS TOWARDS AN EVACUATION TRUCK

AND IS PULLED UP ON THE BACK OF THE TRUCK

THE BOY WATCHES
THE TOWN HE WAS
BORN AND RAISED IN
AS IT BURNS...

...AND HE WONDERS
IF HE WILL SURVIVE...

# CHAPTER 5

# The Summer You Can't Go Back To

## FROM THE MANGA *KAERANAI NATSU*

*Naoko Maeda*

Translated by Atsuko Shigesawa

Naoko Maeda is the sister of Minoru Maeda, author of the previous chapter. This chapter is excerpted from a longer manga that Naoko Maeda has made about her experiences and the journey of her family as her brother Minoru made his animation *Taiyo wo Nakushita Hi.* It is a work that is engaged in the same task as this book, examining how art centered on atomic themes is made. In this case, how it is negotiated inside a family for whom the experience of atomic bombing is central to the family's identity.

When Minoru Maeda set out to make his animation, he made a critical editorial decision to focus the film on the period before the atomic bombing of Hiroshima. This is very unusual for a film about Hiroshima. As we have seen in the previous chapter, his film focuses on what was lost, rather than on what happened on August 6, 1945. For their father, whose story is being told in the film, the idea of focusing on him and his friends at play rather than on the horrors of the bombing seemed wrong-headed. There was a significant amount of discussion/argument around the Maeda family kitchen table through the process of planning and completing the animated film. Here we can see the negotiation between the experience of the atomic bomb, and the inheritance of that experience by the next generation being negotiated in art form. Naoko Maeda's manga is quite long and nuanced, and this short selection from the larger work only begins to hint at the power and complexity of the original. But it does give us a glimpse of the process of the inheritance of trauma.

*Robert Jacobs*

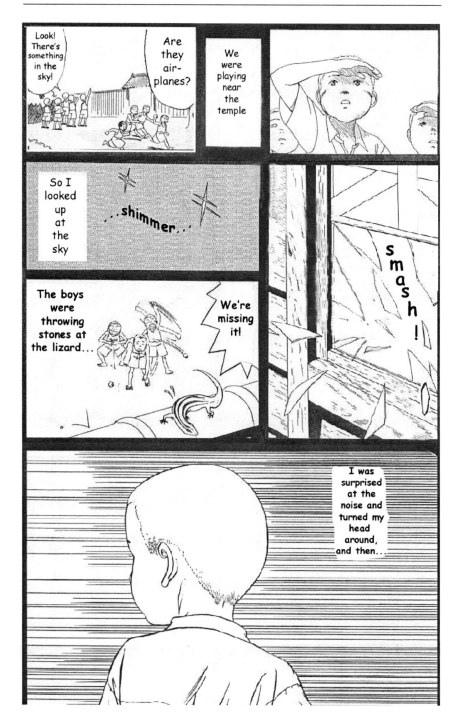

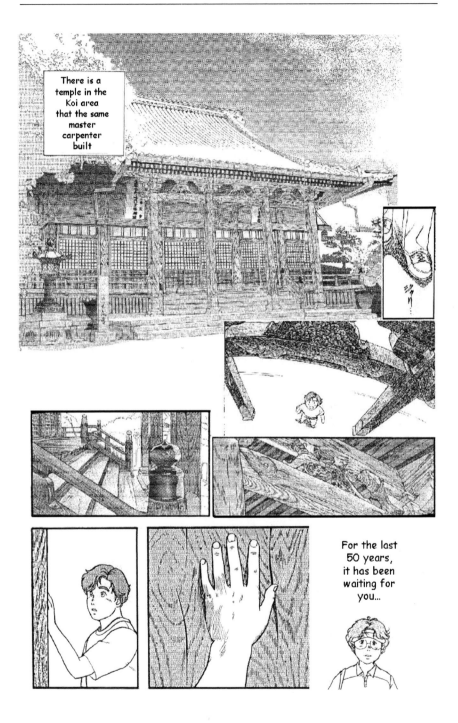

# "The Buck Stops Here"

## HIROSHIMA REVISIONISM IN THE TRUMAN YEARS

*Mick Broderick*

This chapter explores the relationship between the Truman administration and MGM concerning the 1945–1947 production of *The Beginning or the End*, the official Hollywood history of the Manhattan Project. In order to unravel the events and personalities involved, a chronological exploration is presented here to establish the roles of major players and demonstrate historical continuity.

The film is historically significant as a Hollywood entertainment product that was deliberately aligned with the political agenda of the White House where the studio bowed to presidential pressure to alter the script, replace an actor, and gloss over multiple historical inaccuracies in order to perpetuate the myth of the atomic bombing of Hiroshima as being the sole instrument of ending the Pacific war.

## Development

On August 6, 1945, the first atomic bomb, the uranium gun "Little Boy," was dropped on the city of Hiroshima (7:15 pm, August 5, Washington time) with approximately seventy thousand residents dying instantly and a further seventy thousand fatally wounded.[1] Three days later on August 9, a second A-bomb, the plutonium implosion "Fat Man," was dropped on Nagasaki (10:02 pm, August 8, Washington time), killing forty thousand outright and another thirty thousand by year's end. That same day Metro Goldwyn Mayer's Washington representative, Carter T. Barron, rang Major Stuart Palmer, chief of the Feature Film Section of the Pentagon's Bureau of Public Relations, to discuss the possibility of MGM making an A-bomb movie project, ostensibly based on the life of physicist Dr. Lise Meitner.[2]

On the day Japan officially surrendered (August 14, Washington time), MGM's Barron wrote Major Palmer a follow-up letter to "confirm our telephone conversation of August 9th"

> regarding our studio's interest in producing a picture based on the life history of Dr. Lise Meitner, the physicist connected with the atom bomb experimentation

with the project "tentatively titled 'ATOMIC BOMB, The Life of Dr. Lise Meitner.'"[3] Barron informed Palmer that MGM's research department was "now working on this" and would appreciate any useful "information or material."

Hence, it is clear that within seventy-two hours of the Hiroshima announcement in the media, MGM was in direct negotiation with the Pentagon to film an A-bomb story. However, this timing is curious. Either MGM had already developed a story on Meitner and quickly and expediently repurposed it to post-Hiroshima, or they wanted to "get in first" with the War Department to eliminate potential competition from other studios. It is important to recall that the war in the Pacific was still raging, and the second A-bomb (Fat Man) had only just been dropped on Nagasaki when Barron makes his first Pentagon call. It is possible that MGM worked up some kind of a "spec" pitch in the two days after the Hiroshima bombing, delivered verbally over the telephone, but there is reason for suspicion on at least two grounds.

Firstly, the incredible secrecy surrounding the Manhattan Project was not totally watertight, particularly in the arts. Some fiction stories were suppressed and comics censored.[4] In Hollywood, Alfred Hitchcock maintained that he heard an atomic bomb was being worked on in 1944 and his first post-war film, *Notorious* (1946), had as its narrative "Macguffin" Nazis in South America clandestinely stockpiling U-235 to avenge the fascist defeat.[5] So it is possible that MGM somehow became aware of the A-bomb program and immediately put into action their treatment upon learning "officially" of the Manhattan Project.

Secondly, the studio's own press kit for *The Beginning or the End*, released in 1947, recounted the script origins completely differently. According to the MGM publicity booklet, after President Truman's Hiroshima announcement, actress Donna Reed corresponded with a former high school chemistry teacher, Dr. Edward Tompkins, who she realized had been at Oak Ridge working on the bomb. Tompkins's reply, dated October 23, suggested to Reed that the atomic work would make a powerful motion picture. The press kit paraphrased Tompkins's letter, explaining:

> As a member of the Association of Oak Ridge Scientists, he was anxious to acquaint the people with the potentialities of the weapon

they had helped create. This understanding was necessary for a quick and sure control of the bomb, they felt.

Then quoting Tompkins's letter to Reed, the scientist suggested:

> Do you think a movie could be planned and produced to impress, upon the public, the horrors of atomic warfare, the fact that other countries can produce atomic explosives and the vulnerability of civilization to attack by these explosives?

The MGM press kit next described how Reed's husband and former Hollywood agent, Tony Owen, rang producer Samuel Marx at the studio pitching the idea. The media promotion continues:

> Thus did a high school friendship . . . result in a motion picture being filmed that has been labeled by government officials, military leaders and scientists as the *most important undertaking in Hollywood history* [my emphasis].

It is essential to not simply dismiss or disregard the studio's self-aggrandizing hyperbole here. This PR document tries to argue historical parity with the very project it is seeking to dramatically realize. Anticipating Francis Ford Coppola's mantra thirty years later that *Apocalypse Now* wasn't "a film *about* the Vietnam War—it *was* the Vietnam war," MGM was constantly at pains to demonstrate how its *The Beginning or the End* was Hollywood's equivalent to the Manhattan Project.

The rhetoric is further emphasized in the studio's description of unheralded secrecy surrounding the movie's production, as if MGM's studio lots had been annexed by the Manhattan Engineering District:

> the sets for "The Beginning or the End" were tightly closed to visitors. Only working press were allowed entrance, and then only on designated days. A sign on the stage door announced the rescinding of all regular studio passes, and a studio police officer was on hand to make it stick.
>
> This "security measure," installed by the studio, served a double purpose. Although the script had been approved by the White House and the War Department, it still was required that the completed picture be shown to government officials in Washington, D.C., before being released.

But the rest, so they say, is history. Or is it? The question remains, why did the studio bother to rewrite the genesis of this movie in its promotional literature some eighteen months later? Certainly the Reed-Tompkins story adds human interest; it's a cute angle that the press could adopt while talking up an otherwise conventional and potentially somber film development chronology. Yet Reed was ultimately not associated with the film in any way.

It is interesting to speculate, however, that MGM knew something about the Manhattan Project prior to Truman's public revelation and that this knowledge was at least enough to give the studio a competitive edge to initiate and fast-track their project long before anyone else had a chance. This does not necessarily imply any major national security breaches, but reflects the entertainment industry's data-mining through scuttlebutt and extrapolation—just as the movie's President Truman says later in *The Beginning or the End*: "Those newspapermen are shrewd guessers." Indeed, much of Hollywood's research and development process mirrors classic intelligence gathering by carefully scouring magazines, newspapers and other media for interesting story leads. It's part of their business *modus operandi*.

Of course, this is mere conjecture but since the initial MGM project "ATOMIC BOMB, The Life of Lise Meitner," officially registered with the Pentagon, bears absolutely no resemblance to the project hastily undertaken and ultimately realized, it suggests a significant reorientation of approach. Lise Meitner, for instance, appears nowhere in the film, nor is she ever mentioned.[6]

Nearly three months later on November 3, the War Department's Liaison Branch Chief, Lt. Colonel Gordon F. Swarthout, cleared a proposed visit to Oak Ridge by MGM producer Sam Marx and his assistant "for the purpose of obtaining background material and doing research on a projected atomic bomb motion picture." The only restriction for the visit came from General Groves, who dictated that the nuclear material production factories could not be visited and that any studio publicity regarding the trip be submitted to him personally for review.

One week later, though unaware of MGM's accelerated development process, Alfred A. Cohn, a former journalist, bestselling author, and then-member of the Board of Police Commissioners in Los Angeles, wrote to his friend in high places, Mathew J. Connelly, secretary to President Truman, about *his* plans for a motion picture dealing with the history of the atom bomb. Cohn enquired about any extant footage of Truman's announcement of the A-bomb.

> Dear Matt:
>
> If it isn't too much trouble can you find out for me if any motion picture was taken of the Boss when he broadcast that atomic bomb announcement while en route home from Potsdam; and if it would be available for a picture to be made showing the history of the bomb project from its inception to its initial reception at Hiroshima. I don't know whether I mentioned it to you or not when I was at the White House. Anyhow I conceived the idea while lunching with . . .

some of the scientists involved during my last trip and Hal Wallis, Paramount's leading producer is going to make the picture which I fully expect will be one of the greatest moving pictures ever made. My own idea would be to open the picture with a shot of President Truman making that momentous announcement, then tell the whole thrilling story—and it is a thriller as you know. Naturally we won't go into any technical stuff or anything esle [*sic*] involving security— just tell a story packed with drama and adventure and world shaking significance and import. . . . We have assurances that Dr. Bush and General Groves will co-operate and of course we are giving them veto power over anything that goes into the picture.

But what is going on here? If Groves gave "assurances" to Cohn, while at the same time directing his staff to arrange a visit by MGM to Oak Ridge, there is some duplicity. Groves was paid $10,000—a significant figure in 1945—for his official consultancy and cooperation with MGM, while employed as a two-star general.[7] It would seem that the general was having his cake and eating it too.

On November 14, Connelly replied to Cohn with details of the Paramount-shot footage showing Truman announcing the A-bomb taken en route from the Potsdam conference, but with the caveat that Truman's White House press secretary, Charlie Ross, would need to approve any use of the president in such a motion picture. Only a few days later on November 19, MGM's Samuel Marx, Tom Owens, and Carter T. Barron meet Harry Truman at the White house for thirty minutes. As the president's secretary, Connelly would have been intimately involved in such scheduling. The official presidential appointment entry states: "(re atomic bomb—OFF RECORD)."[8]

Back in Los Angeles, an eager Al Cohn wrote Connelly the next day, asking about "others" working on such a project. Little did he realize that Truman was in a conference with MGM honchos less than twenty-four hours earlier and discussing just such a film.

The following day Carter Barron wrote President Truman a gushing letter as a postscript to their meeting two days prior, presumably both as a *record* of their "off-record" discussions, and perhaps a reminder to Truman of MGM's commitment to the subject and its realization as "entertainment." Barron informs the president that alongside the political players and scientists, the filmmakers have been in fruitful negotiation with the principal military representatives of the Manhattan Project over the "past few months," naming General Groves among others:

all believed the motion picture industry could do a great service to civilization at large if the *right kind* of film could be made about this new element in our daily lives [my emphasis]. They were anxious to see if a film could be made, although always within the bounds of government approval.

Rhetorically this suggests that the military *hoped* MGM would get it "right." Significantly, Barron paraphrased Groves, suggesting that both the A-bomb and atomic energy had indeed affected the way the world went about its daily business.

Barron also reminds Truman, diplomatically, but oddly invoking Judeo-Christian authority, that MGM producer Sam Marx had deliberated with the conservative archbishop of New York, Cardinal Spellman, who similarly concurred "that this motion picture is almost necessary." The conservative Catholic cleric who had personally visited Hiroshima and had seen the bomb's effects firsthand, according to Barron, "was wholeheartedly in favor" of the project. Barron also adds the "congressional view," supplied by Senator Brian McMahon, who supported the film proposal observing: "that anyone acquainted with the facts relative to the release of atomic energy can only feel that it is the greatest event on the earth since the birth of Christ."

MGM's Washington representative concludes by reiterating the Studio's dramatic and didactic approach, while the prose waxes portentous:

> Following our discussion with you this morning, Mr. Marx, Mr. Owen, and I wanted to reaffirm to you that we will enter into this with only *the most solemn intention* of *performing a great service*. We are, of course, *anxious to put entertainment into this film*, rather than concentrate on its documentary phases, for it is our belief that only for solid entertainment does the world sit in theatres and listen. They go to school for education and to churches for sermons. We want them to come into theatres and to be entertained, but in a film of this nature, we are certainly going far deeper than ordinary entertainment. This film will have a great deal to say—*the things that you said* this morning supplied a theme and a message. . . .
>
> It was with considerable thrill that *we heard from you* some of the events *of your participation* in this historic event. We sincerely trust that we can portray some of these events. They are scenes of drama and excitement, *but always with dignity*. We are *very grateful to you* for giving us an insight into these scenes and in gratitude we sincerely promise to do our best to let the world know that it stands *as you said* at the beginning or the end [my emphasis].

Now the studio never missed an opportunity to milk the fact that President Truman concluded their meeting with words, quoted in the studio's publicity, "as near as [Producer Marx] can remember it":

> Make a good picture. One that will tell the people that the decision is theirs to make . . . this is the beginning or the end.

Truman's November 26 reply to Barron was terse but cordial. The president relays that he "very much appreciated" the letter and that "it was a pleasure to discuss the Atomic energy program." At this point Truman, not one to mince words, certainly had the opportunity to officially dispute the record of their meeting as outlined in Barron's letter but he does not, implying concurrence with MGM's version of events.

A few days later and still intent on pitching his A-bomb movie, Cohn again wrote to Connelly from L.A., not discouraged at having discovered MGM's intervention at the White House:

> Looks like everything is pretty well set for my atom bomb picture, despite the efforts of MGM of which I am now fully informed. I doubt that they will go through with their project. Anyhow it doesn't make any difference to me if they do.

Having received Truman's letter of November 26, which takes no offense at paraphrasing the president, Barron immediately wrote Col. Swarthout at the Pentagon on December 1, advising that the MGM A-bomb project now had a new title: "THE BEGINNING OR THE END," adding:

> It will interest you to know—and this, of course, should remain off the record until propriety dictates otherwise—that this title was suggested by The President during our conversation with him on the subject a few weeks ago.

It is clear from this correspondence that Barron sought to implicate the president as a catalyst for, and supporter of, MGM's project now with a title bearing Truman's personal imprimatur. Reading between the lines, it seems that Barron was also making it clear to the colonel, as the Pentagon's official film liaison officer, that the U.S. commander-in-chief was solidly behind the project.

Barron's letter to Col. Swarthout, however, seems to have had little impact on Pentagon bureaucracy. Nearly three months later, on March 19, 1946, Major Dallas Halerstadt wrote MGM's Silas F. Seadler in New York advising that his request for a copy of the Army's documentary film *The Atom Strikes* would *not* be made available to screen to studio executives in Los Angeles until the MGM A-bomb movie was granted *official* approval by the Pentagon, which was contingent upon reviewing the script which, at that point, had not been completed, nor submitted.

According to *The Hollywood Reporter*, in the background during December 1945 and January 1946, three competing studios (MGM, Twentieth-Century Fox, and Paramount) were in a race to produce the first feature on the atomic bomb.[9] On March 20, 1946, *Variety* reported that MGM and Hal Wallis Productions had agreed to pool their resources, mirroring the wartime Manhattan Project cooperation of the Allies, in the making of *The Beginning or the End*:

> Under terms of the agreement, which is without precedent in the film industry, Wallis Productions will transfer all story material and research information to Metro, which will produce and release the film. . . . Metro will finance the film entirely on its own, but Wallis Productions will receive an undisclosed share of the gross. . . .
>
> Almost simultaneous announcements by Metro and Wallis in December that they both planned to film atom bomb stories early this year caused considerable furore in the industry. It appeared that both would race to get their respective films first on the screen, with the further possibility that crews of both would conflict with each other in shooting schedules at Oak Ridge Tenn.; Los Alamos N.M., and Hanford, Wash. . . . Wallis, who announced his film would be titled "Top Secret," had already set out his production cost at about $2,000,000.

Considering the box-office flop *The Beginning or the End* became, perhaps Wallis would have been wiser to accept a larger, flat fee.[10]

# The White House Whitewash

Significant involvement by the White House began on April 19, 1946, with Truman's press secretary, Charles Ross informing MGM's Carter Barron: "The President has read the script of your proposed movie, 'The Beginning Or the End,' and, subject to the changes noted on the script, has no objection to its production as a motion picture film."

In return the same day, having previously congratulated the president on his epigrammatic turn of phrase (and parading this before the Pentagon), Barron replied that they had deleted the relevant opening lines of the script "which refer to the fact that the phrase 'The Beginning or the End' was taken from spoken words of the President." Other references to Senator Truman and the Truman Investigation Committee are removed, confirming that the Senator "will be in no way depicted." This later qualification referred to the potentially embarrassing revelation that the then-Senator Truman and his congressional Committee to Investigate the National Defense Program had tried to obtain details concerning a mysterious and expensive government project in Tennessee which, unbeknownst to him, was the giant Oak Ridge Manhattan Project facility. Truman's investigation gave General Groves significant security concerns, and was no doubt an embarrassing episode that the president wished erased from the public record.[11]

Complying with the White House request Barron also reinforced his agreement with Ross, confirming presidential protocol by adding:

> the President will be depicted only from the rear or from the side in such a way as not to show his countenance in any way.

Also on April 19, the Pentagon wrote to Barron issuing War Department approval for "limited cooperation" to be extended to the production with several standard legal caveats. Following General Groves's earlier memo, changes to the script were outlined "for security reasons." These included eliminating mention of "pure U-235" and "plutonium" in certain scenes; deleting any mention of the city "Kokura" from the target list, substituting Nagasaki; and the altitude of the Hiroshima detonation.

A month later Dr. Vannevar Bush, Director of the Office of Scientific Research and Development who had been present at the Trinity test, wrote to Charles Ross, complaining about the script, and explaining his refusal to sign a release form authorizing his representation in the movie. Worried about historical inaccuracies, he quizzed Ross concerning the White House position on the drafts since hearsay had it Truman approved the movie:

> It seems to me to be pretty important that a film which will fix a pattern of history in the minds of the American people, ought to be as accurate as possible.[12]

Regardless of this missive, Bush *does* feature in a number of scenes (played by Jonathan Hale), so presumably he preferred to be part of that cinematic history, rather than abstain. Like Lifton and Mitchell before her, Joyce Evans has adroitly suggested, confirming Bush's concerns:

> in the years since its release, *The Beginning or the End?* has reached a large audience, particularly as part of the MGM archive collection aired on Ted Turner's cable television movie channel. Due to its documentary style, this carefully constructed film view of history has probably come to be accepted as an accurate version of the events for most viewers. . . . Few viewers question the deliberate falsifications in the film or the motivations of the producers.[13]

The next day Ross replied to Bush clearly, but expediently, distancing himself and the White House from the broader agenda of the movie, suggesting that he had "passed upon the project only in so far as it brought in the president. The original script called for representation of the President on the Screen. In conformation with a long-standing White House rule against such representation, permission to depict the President was denied." This is disingenuous since Truman is depicted, albeit in silhouette and shot from behind a desk. Similarly, Ross implies that the project came to him as a *fait accompli*, with Groves and "a majority, if not all, of the others concerned" already granting their approval.

> The White House neither approved nor disapproved the film, but stated simply that with the changes we directed, as to the President, we had no objection to its production. . . .
> To repeat, the White House neither approves nor disapproves the film and certainly does not want to seem to be persuading anybody to sign such a release. . . . This is a matter in which each individual concerned must exert his own judgment.

Yet the White House did exert interest in the president's representation, as the production history and documentation attests.

# Production

Well into the film's production schedule, on September 30, 1946, Carter Barron contacted Colonel D. R. Kerr, chief of the pictorial section, War Department Bureau of Public Relations, advising him that MGM executives had previewed *The Beginning or the End* and that "Mr. Mayer has one suggestion which he thought would add greater value and world impact to the finish. He has suggested a closing sequence which would vividly show the destructive force of the bomb on Hiroshima." Barron appended the relevant script scenes adding that "General Groves read the sequence last Saturday and raised no objection."

It is difficult to imagine that some realization of the Hiroshima bombing and its effect was not planned by MGM all along. The eleventh-hour suggestion by Louis Mayer seems somewhat mendacious since six months earlier, as demonstrated, the studio was trying (unsuccessfully at that point) to obtain military footage of the Hiroshima attack. Indeed, initial drafts of the script, with significant input from concerned atomic scientists, featured a sequence at ground zero where Americans and Japanese encountered the "dead" city.[14]

In fact, Groves had written to Barron three days earlier referring to the specific script segment sent to him which depicted the destructive effect of the Hiroshima bombing, saying, "I feel that there is nothing in this portion of the script which in any way reflects discredit to the Army or in any way impairs security." And the following day the War Department concurred with Groves's assessment of the bombing scenes, officially stating that "no discredit to the Army" will be shown.

Considering the fabrications, distortions and dramatic license of the scene, there is little wonder that the military supported its inclusion. In the immediate lead-up to the Hiroshima bomb run, the film sequence inside the *Enola Gay* has enemy flak continuously buffeting the plane for well over two minutes of elapsed screen-time. The crew is shown nervously watching the onboard Geiger counter click menacingly amid the sustained high altitude barrage, with frequent concerned glances back at the armed bomb tethered precariously inside the bomb bay. This, however, is a total fabrication since Truman's published memoirs cites secret cables sent to him confirming that "there was no fighter opposition and no flak."[15]

Hence, this lengthy treatment of the *Enola Gay* under attack was clearly aimed at creating a dramatic tension while suggesting a palpable threat to both the plane's mission and men which did not exist. As Lifton and Mitchell suggest, the scene "makes the attack more contested, the airmen more courageous."[16]

## Rewrites, Retakes, and Revisionism

Finally, in late October 1946, MGM screened *The Beginning or the End* at the White House with Truman and key presidential staff in attendance. On October 29, Charles Ross wrote Carter Barron:

> All of us enjoyed very much the showing of "The Beginning or the End." This is a thrilling picture. The story is beautifully worked out, and the acting is fine. As I told you, I have only one quarrel with it: something needs to be done about the sequence in which President Truman appears. I think you agreed with the rest of us on this point.

The disputed scene, cut from the final release, showed a fabricated meeting between Groves, Secretary of War Henry Stimpson, and the novice President Truman shortly after Roosevelt's death. The two advisers inform Truman about the Manhattan Project and the atomic bomb, with Groves warning that without the American use of the atomic bomb against Japan at its earliest disposal, the enemy might be using their *own* A-bombs against a later American invasion force. Groves warns, "The minimum estimates of our losses is half a million men."[17] Truman ponders for a moment then promptly agrees to the bomb's deployment, saying: "This is the most difficult decision any man had to make. I think more of our American boys than I do of all our enemies. If the bomb test is successful . . . *you will take it to the Marianas and use it*" [original emphasis].[18]

However, as Lifton and Mitchell point out, it was not the audacious and fallacious misrepresentations which unsettled the White House viewers at the advance screening but rather "[t]hey objected to the president deciding, after only a brief reflection, that the U.S. would use the weapon against Japan."[19]

Within days of Press Secretary Ross raising the White House concerns over the Truman scene, MGM script doctor James K. McGuinness sent Ross copies of the revised Truman sequence, suggesting "This seems to me to incorporate all the matters we talked about, but it is, of course, tentative and I am eager to discuss it with you and incorporate anything else you deem advisable."

The "New Scene" is replaced by a note explaining the setting—a move from the post-Roosevelt presidential succession scenario to a newly concocted one in the Little White House at the Allies' July 1945 Postdam meeting. The text is rigorous in its set direction and proposed *mise-en-scene*:

> Lighting should be so contrived that the President is always in shadow. The intent is to establish his presence, but—in keeping with precedent—not to photograph him clearly at any time. Photographic emphasis in the scene must be away from the actor who plays the President and never towards him. He must never be photographed full face, or straight on. There must be no close angle on the President. Changes of angle necessary for dramatic progression of the scene must be so contrived that they are from the President's point of view, shooting over the shoulders. In longer shots, he must figure in shadowed profile.
>
> In the re-casting, it must be emphasized that the President is a man of upright and military bearing; that is he is physically trim, alive and alert, and that his actions are brisk and certain.
>
> The President wears in his lapel the bronze star discharge button of World War I.[20]

Clearly, from this rejoinder, Truman and his White House minders were less than impressed by the choice of actor and the previous scene in which he was depicted.

The revised sequence, reshot with a new actor playing Truman, opens with a title indicating the location as "the Little White House" at Potsdam, Germany, and depicts the president at his desk viewing a top secret file showing images of the successful atomic detonation "Trinity" at Alamagordo in New Mexico on July 16. An intercom interrupts, advising of Press Secretary Ross's arrival. At Truman's request, Ross enters Truman's study.

> Ross: (standing) I have just distributed to the press the text of the Potsdam Declaration—the ultimatum to Japan.
>
> Truman: (seated) What was their reaction?
>
> Ross: Great approval—and some curiosity.

Truman: Why the curiosity? Why shouldn't we and Great Britain and China call on Japan for immediate surrender, now Germany is beaten?

Ross: That last sentence, Mr. President. (reads) "The alternative for Japan is prompt and utter destruction." That word "prompt" struck them. Some of the men are guessing that it means we've got more B-29s than anybody knows. Some of the others think we've got some mysterious new weapon.

Truman: Those newspapermen are shrewd guessers.

Ross: (startled) Sir?

Truman: Sit down Charlie. (Ross sits.) I want to tell you our nation's top secret. It must remain just that—top secret.

Ross: Of course!

Truman: We have developed the most fearful weapon ever forged by man—an atomic bomb.

Ross: (Ross jolts backwards in his seat.) Even the *word* is frightening.

Truman: It has been tested—and it works. It's a harnessing of the basic power of the universe. In peacetime, atomic energy can be used to bring about a golden age—such an age of prosperity and well-being as the world has never known. In war, this same energy has destructive power almost beyond the comprehension of man.

In this revised draft text the following material was cut from the final version, rejected by Ross and the White House. After describing the consultation process surrounding the bomb's development and potential use the actor playing Ross asked the president, if anyone "disagreed," to which Truman replied:

Truman: Nobody, actually. Some scientists who worked on the project think we should drop it on an uninhabited area as a warning. But the staff is sure the Japanese militarists would never let their people learn about it.

Ross: I go along with that completely.

The scene was ultimately revised to have Ross say:

Ross: It's clear now what those words "prompt and utter destruction" mean. Thank God we have the bomb and not the Japanese! If they had it, they would surely have used it on us.

Truman: That's one argument for using it, Charlie, but it's not the decisive argument.

> Ross: The whole thing is terrifying. You must have spent some sleepless nights over it.

And here is further excised text, which is significant since its *removal* conforms precisely with Truman's later, repeated claims that he did not hesitate, nor lose a moment's sleep over the decision:

> Truman: Yes, it cost me some sleep. I have had to make a tremendous decision.

Now, the fact that these sentences were cut by the White House illuminates the conflict of historical and artistic agendas between the filmmakers/screenwriters and the Truman Administration. The MGM scenarists preferred to portray a compassionate, moral president anguished by his cataclysmic choice, whereas Truman wanted to instill the mythology that there was, in reality, no choice given the circumstances and consensus—and, equally important for the president, nothing which gave rise to moral anguish or ethical uncertainty. As the film's final version portrays the fictitious conversation, Ross concurs gravely: "As President of the United States, sir, you could make no other decision," to which Truman replies somberly, "As President, I could not."

However, as with the majority of contemporary historians who have had the benefit of access to primary documentation accumulating over the past decades conclude, J. Samuel Walker's exhaustive historical survey of scholarly attitudes to Truman's decision would beg to differ:

> The scholarly consensus holds that the war would have ended within a relatively short time without the atomic attacks and that an invasion of the Japanese islands was an unlikely possibility. It further maintains that several alternatives to ending the war without an invasion were available and that Truman and his close advisers were well aware of the options.[21]

And here, ultimately, is what Truman had to say in his published memoirs:

> It was the [Interim Committee's] recommendation that the bomb be used against the enemy as soon as it could be done. They recommended further that it should *be used without specific warning* and against a target that would clearly show its devastating strength [emphasis mine]. I had realized, of course, that an atomic bomb explosion would inflict damage and casualties beyond imagination. . . . The final decision of where and when to use the atomic bomb was

up to me. Let there be no mistake about it. I regarded the bomb as a military weapon and never had any doubt that it should be used.[22]

So, not much room here for presidential equivocation, agonizing doubt or sleepless nights.

Ironically, however, this White House–approved sequence in *The Beginning or the End* is a deliberate distortion of fact in order to enhance Truman's public persona as a humane president. Also in the final approved scene, Truman tells Ross about the sole military rationale for the Japanese cities' target selection, adding: "We're going to shower these places for ten days with leaflets telling the populations to leave—telling them what is coming. We hope these warnings will save lives." Ross concurs resolutely with "They should."

This is nonsense. It didn't happen. It plays into the popular mythos that America would never launch a "sneak attack" equivalent to Roosevelt's rhetorical "day of infamy" by Japanese forces attacking Pearl Harbor. The distortion is further recounted in a later sequence aboard the Enola Gay, when the A-bomb crew is fallaciously shown being buffeted by enemy flack, while Captain Deak Parsons (who arms the bomb in flight) says dismissively to a fictional colleague aboard the *Enola Gay*: "We've been dropping warning leaflets on them for ten days. That's ten days more notice than we got at Pearl Harbor."[23] Again, the distortion emphasizes atomic payback as morally justified by the fabrication of explicit warnings.

In fact, it was only *after* Hiroshima's attack, and the absence of an immediate unconditional surrender that millions of leaflets were printed explicitly detailing the A-bomb's power. Unfortunately, the thousands destined for Nagasaki were only printed and available the day *after* it was obliterated by Fat Man (bombed August 9, with leaflets ready August 10).[24] Presumably, had a third bomb been required for the remaining reserved targets (either Kokura or Niigita), these leaflets may have been air-dropped over the city.[25] But best intentions are no substitute for historical fact.

Not surprisingly, neither Groves nor the Pentagon objected to *these* inaccuracies when they vetted the film for its historical veracity.

More significantly, this Potsdam briefing of Ross by Truman, revised and reshot according to explicit White House instruction, is essentially a *retrospective* justification for the bombing-without-warning. Further, the unintended subtext of the sequence strongly suggests that this aspect of the Potsdam declaration is so *vague* as to be of no real worth as a diplomatic or strategic warning whatsoever. What this scene clearly establishes is that even the president's press secretary (Ross), responsible for promulgating the text, has no idea what "The alternative for Japan is *prompt and utter destruction*" actually means. It only makes sense *after* Truman tells Ross about "our nation's top secret," the atomic bomb, and its immense destructive power. At this point the penny drops and Ross surmises, "It's clear *now* what those words 'prompt and utter destruction' mean" [my emphasis].

Well, precisely. Only *after* being briefed about the A-bomb can the declaration be fully understood. Without this knowledge, according to the film, even someone as well versed in the communication of diplomatic and political rhetoric as Truman's press secretary is confused. Hence, the new film sequence reads as a *revisionist* justification for the bombing on the basis that the enemy was specifically forewarned about the atomic bomb headed for Hiroshima—a complete fabrication which, as discussed, is repeated again towards the film's conclusion.[26] And, as demonstrated above, Truman's script revisions comply with the manufacturing of a popular Hiroshima mythology yet are clearly contradicted in his later published memoirs, in which he states categorically that he complied with the Interim Committee's recommendation that the first A-bomb "should be used without specific warning."

The other significant distortion by the Administration afforded from nearly eighteen months of historical revision after the Hiroshima attack is the film's stated justification that the bombing would mean, according to the president, "life for three hundred thousand—maybe half a million—of America's finest youth." Now there is no doubt that Truman's decision to use the bomb "against the enemy as soon as it could be used" saved American lives. Casualties continued to mount in the Pacific theatre, and each day between the Hiroshima bombing on August 6 and the Japanese surrender on August 15, American and Allied troops continued to suffer losses (to say nothing of the higher Japanese casualties and ongoing U.S. campaign of firebombing cities).

But it is the size of potential casualties and their increasing inflation, according to scholars such as Gar Alperovitz and Barton Bernstein, which was magnified over the years in order to combat increasing domestic and international criticism about the decision to drop the bomb. As Alperovitz has convincingly demonstrated, from August 9, 1945, to late 1946, the time of *The Beginning or the End*'s script approval, Truman's statements on the public record increase anticipated American invasion casualties from "thousands of American lives" to "a quarter of a million" on December 15, 1945, to the movie's articulated three hundred thousand to a half million. By 1953, the president claimed, "as much as a million, on the American side alone," and finally in 1959 Truman announced "the dropping of the atomic bombs stopped the war, saved millions of lives."[27]

J. Samuel Walker concludes his impressive and extensive overview of historical and contemporary scholarship on this very matter:

According to the scholarly consensus, the United States did not drop the bomb to save hundreds of thousands of American lives. Although scholars generally agree that Truman used the bomb primarily to shorten the war, the number of American lives saved, *even in the worst case*, would have been in the range of tens of thousands rather than hundreds of thousands [my emphasis].[28]

Walker, citing David Lowenthal, credits this "discrepancy" of "collective memory" arising from the "rich array of books, articles, pamphlets, documentary collections, films, docudramas, and television programs" as the primary sources, rather than educative and scholarly texts. Clearly, Truman and his administration saw in MGM's movie *The Beginning or the End* a unique opportunity to mould public opinion on the Hiroshima decision in order to complement and strengthen the series of favorable revisionist articles being simultaneously written by friends of the administration in late 1946 and early 1947.

Space does not permit a thorough examination of all the key issues *The Beginning or the End* evades—selected omissions such as the strategic deployment of the atomic weapons prior to the agreed declaration of war and invasion of Manchuria by the Soviets; the ultra-secret Quebec agreement excluding Stalin from participation in or sharing of atomic secrets; the complete failure to depict the Nagasaki bombing; the petition by Manhattan Project scientists, and Einstein's second letter; the deliberate saving of key "virgin" cities in Japan from conventional bombing earlier in the war to test the physical and psychological effects of the nuclear detonations; and so on.[29]

Needless to say, these strategic omissions from the final film reveal as much as what was chosen propagandistically for inclusion. In this manner the agenda to inculcate a sympathetic view of the Administration was abetted by the studio and the Pentagon through careful excision and skillfully crafted narrative falsifications.


# Look Back in Anger

Perhaps the most bizarre episode in the Truman-MGM saga comes from an exchange of correspondence between the president and the original actor chosen to play him, Roman Bohnen, a small part character actor who cofounded the Actors Laboratory and is best known for his roles as Candy in *Of Mice and Men* (1939) and Pat Derry in *The Best Years of Our Lives* (1946). As discussed previously, Truman and Ross suggested Bohnen be dumped after the October 1946 White House preview screening. The relevant scene was subsequently rewritten and reshot using a new actor, Art Baker, with revised White House–approved dialogue. It is worth considering these two short letters in full:

ROMAN BOHNEN
10537 VALLEY SPRING LANE
NORTH HOLLYWOOD, CALIFORNIA

December 2, 1946

Hon. President Truman
The White House
Washington, D.C.

Dear Mr. President:

When you privately previewed M.G.M's atom bomb picture "The Beginning or the End," the actor playing you, was me.

I understand [from the press] that you first approved, but now have rejected the scene which depicts you making the decision to send the atom bomb thundering into this troubled world. And I can well imagine the emotional torture you must have experienced in giving that fateful order, torture not only then, but now—perhaps even more so.

Although I have spent half a lifetime aspiring to a documentary sincerity and simplicity in my work, and was probably cast for that reason only, (since I certainly do not look like you) I can nevertheless understand your wish that the scene be re-filmed in order to do fuller justice to your anguished deliberation in that historic moment,

So I have a suggestion to offer; and I respectfully offer it in light of the fact that posterity will inherit this motion picture, and posterity will be talking about your "instant of decision" for a hundred years to come, and posterity is quite apt to be a little rough on you in any case for not having ordered that very first atom bomb to be dropped *outside* of Hiroshima with other bombs poised to follow, but praise God never to be used.

This is my suggestion: that you *yourself* re-enact that historic moment of decision before the camera. Why not? Why shouldn't you be photographed saying exactly whatever you said? If I were in your difficult position I would insist on so doing. Unprecedented, yes—but so is the entire circumstance, including the unholy power of that monopoly weapon.

I am taking the liberty of sending a copy of this letter to Mr. Mayer at M.G.M. in the sincere hope that he will invite you to play yourself in the retakes.

Respectfully,
Roman Bohnen

THE WHITE HOUSE
Washington D.C.

December 12, 1946

My dear Mr. Bohnen:

I appreciated very much your letter of December second and thank you for suggesting to Mr. Mayer of M.G.M. that I become a movie star. In the first place I haven't the talent to be a movie star and, in the second place, I am sure you will do the part creditably.

The only objection to the film, as it was, was that it appeared to have been a snap judgment program. It was anything but that—the use of the atomic bomb was deliberated for long hours and many days and weeks, and it was discussed with the Secretary of State, The Secretary of War, the Secretary of the Navy and the General Staff of the Allied Armies, as well as with Mr. Churchill and Mr. Attlee.

When it was finally demonstrated in New Mexico that the operation of the bomb was a successful one, it was decided to give the Japanese ample warning before the bomb was dropped. I have no qualms about it whatever for the simple reason that it was believed that the dropping of not more than two of these bombs would bring the war to a close. The Japanese in their conduct of the war had been vicious and cruel savages and I came to the conclusion that if two hundred and fifty thousand young Americans could be saved from slaughter the bomb should be dropped, and it was.

As I said before, the only objection to the film was that I was made to appear as if no consideration had been given to the effects or result of dropping the bomb—and that is an absolutely wrong impression.

Sincerely yours,
HARRY S. TRUMAN

*why would be respont.???*
*This is beginning of power of visual media*

At first, Bohnen's letter to Truman comes across as penned by some petulant thespian who doesn't much appreciate the interference of amateurs, even if those amateurs include the president and White House staff. Superficially, it could also be read as a serious and helpful suggestion from a theatrical professional to the president—and Louis Mayer—that, regardless of precedent, President Truman should add a documentary authenticity by appearing in the film himself. But Bohnen's *tone* is deeply sarcastic, hostile, and accusatory. Essentially he chides Truman for his cowardice, directing the reshoots from afar, in the same way he subtly evokes his cowardice in the dispatch of the "unholy . . . monopoly weapon" against a city, rather than first demonstrating its power.

However, what is so strange and compelling about this exchange is that there is indeed any exchange at all. For Harry S. Truman to give the letter consideration and to be bothered to reply ten days later, in a considered way, suggests to two things. Either Truman (mis)read it superficially and he replied cordially in kind (which is how Lifton and Mitchell interpret this in *Hiroshima in America*), or, not wanting to get into a "pissing match" with a fellow American, he carefully avoids returning invective by stating what he regards to be objective facts.

Interestingly, though, Truman's hand in the script rewrite is further apparent from this correspondence since he cites systematically: the saving of a quarter of a million men; the lengthy process of advice and consensus; the dehumanizing of the enemy as "vicious and cruel savages"; that "it was decided to give the Japanese ample warning before the bomb was dropped"; and that cities selected were "devoted almost exclusively to the manufacture of ammunition and weapons of destruction." All of these points remain controversial more than sixty years later, and continue to be the subject of debate and analysis.

Suffice to say, once Louis Mayer received Bohnen's letter, his contribution to *The Beginning or the End* (and MGM) was sealed. The actor only appeared in one more MGM film, that same year, and never worked for the studio again.

A month later Truman's second cinematic simulacrum, actor Art Baker, wrote to Charlie Ross on January 7, 1947: "I'm the fellow who was picked to play the part of President Truman in 'The Beginning or the End,'" and he enclosed a *fan* letter to Harry S. No sly reproaches here. A few days later on January 13, Ross replied warmly to Baker, inviting him to ring the presidential press secretary if ever he visited Washington adding, for the record, under the title "PERSONAL AND CONFIDENTIAL":

> I suppose you know that the first sequence on President Truman was, as we thought here, pretty bad because it gave the impression that he made a snap decision to drop the bomb on Hiroshima. The new scene puts over the idea—the true idea—that this decision *was only taken after the most prayerful decision* [my emphasis] and upon the advice of all his leading military advisers. You and Edward Earle [the actor who impersonates Ross] bring out this fact very clearly, and for this I feel personally indebted to both of you.

This letter clearly suggests that Ross felt the need to perpetuate and inculcate a mythos that the Hiroshima bombing, in fact, *did* weigh heavily on the president, since "this decision was only taken after the most prayerful decision."

But this sentiment is precisely one that Truman was at pains to publicly reject for the rest of his life.[30]

military: wanted it to be a thoughtful decision
For LARRY

Truman: Maintained it was an easy decision.

# Notes

1. Three weeks earlier on July 16, 1945, a tower-mounted plutonium device (nicknamed "The Gadget") was secretly detonated in New Mexico—the first atomic explosion. See also Rhodes 1986, 711.

2. Dr. Lise Meitner was a famous pre-war physicist and an Austrian Jew who fled Hitler's annexation to work with Nhils Bohr in Sweden and later for the Manhattan Engineering District on the A-bomb program. Unofficially, she worked with Otto Hahn and Fritz Straussmann on the proof that uranium atoms could be split (fission) via neutron bombardment.

3. All correspondence and quotation from Pentagon files and Truman Presidential Library Papers. My thanks to Laurence Suid for access to the military correspondence.

4. Peter Nichols (ed), *Encyclopaedia of Science Fiction*, Granada, Sydney, 1979, 432. One recently discovered comic that bypassed censorship was the July 1942 issue *of Bill Barnes, America's Air Ace*, featuring a story of a U-235 atomic bomb dropped near Japan, which is graphically shown destroyed by a massive tsunami and related undersea volcanic eruptions. My thanks to Paul Brians.

5. Hitchcock recounts how he described the use of such materials for the development of an atomic bomb to disbelieving producers in 1944. See Albert J. LaValley (ed), *Focus on Hitchcock*, Prentice-Hall, Englewood Cliffs, New Jersey, 1972, 44. A fine, detailed analysis of *Notorious* can be found in Sam P. Simone's *Hitchcock as Activist: Politics and the War Films*, University of Michigan Press, Ann Arbor, 1985, 121–60

6. According to Kim Newman in *Millennium Movies*, "a last-minute change of mind on the part of [a] scientist meant Agnes Moorehead's role had to be cut from the picture" (Newman, 37)—presumably this was to be Meitner's characterization.

7. Dr. Vannevar Bush, director of the Office of Scientific Research and Development (who would later expressed his concerns to the White House over the film), along with Robert Oppenheimer and Leo Szilard, also received a significant fee (Evans, 29).

8. Presumably the appointment must have been diarized some days earlier, but I could find no record of when. The MGM press kit suggests, however, that the meeting lasted "a full hour" uninterrupted.

9. See "Notes for The Beginning or the End (1947)," at www.tcm.com/tcmdb/title .jsp?stid=1531&category=Notes, accessed June 1, 2009.

A December 1945 *Hollywood Reporter* news item noted that M-G-M stars Spencer Tracy, Clark Gable and Van Johnson were "being groomed for roles" in the film. According to various *Hollywood Reporter* news items in June 1946, a controversy erupted when former First Lady Eleanor Roosevelt objected to the casting of Lionel Barrymore as Franklin D. Roosevelt, alleging that the actor had made disparaging remarks about the late president. Production on the film had already begun when the studio decided to hold up Barrymore's scenes until Mrs. Roosevelt had the opportunity to respond to a letter from Barrymore, in which he explained his political statements. Though Barrymore claimed that his remarks were misinterpreted, the Roosevelt family continued to disapprove of the casting and M-G-M replaced him with Godfrey Tearle.

10. According to Evans (42-43), "At least seventy-five films grossed more at the box office in 1947."

11. See Rhodes (617).

12. Letter dated May 20, 1947.

13. Evans, 43.

14. Lifton and Mitchell, 360.

15. Truman, 465.

16. Lifton and Mitchell, 361.

17. In fairness to Groves, in his April 15, 1946 letter to Barron approving the script, with noted revisions, the general explicitly requested MGM to remove the lines about Japanese A-bombs:

> Groves's last speech. Eliminate the words "atomic weapons" and substitute "suicide planes." This change is desirable because it has been repeatedly emphasized that we always knew that Japan could not produce an atomic bomb and we made such statements repeatedly throughout the war to higher authority. (82-163 [F])

Groves's notation "(F)" for these script scenes was a specific directive to MGM: "Doesn't seems right. I would very much prefer to see it written as suggested but would not object if you find it essential to dramatization." Regardless of these deliberate falsifications, Groves still agreed officially to the extant script, later attesting that it "did not bring discredit" to the Armed services nor encroach upon security concerns.

18. Scene #161 penciled as "rejected" in the Charles Ross papers, Truman Library.

19. Lifton and Mitchell, 362-363.

20. This is an odd request, since Ross later makes it clear that the president should be filmed from behind, so Truman's military button will not be visible in any case.

21. Walker, 190.

22. The Interim Committee was comprised of Truman's most respected advisors and included Robert Oppenhiemer, and was created specifically to recommend to the President a decisive course of action for the bomb's use. Truman, 462.

23. Parsons also vetted the script, but there is no record of his objecting to this particular, deliberate falsification mouthed by his screen persona, even though he was upset by other technical inconsistencies in the film.

24. Rhodes, 736–37.

25. According to Rhodes, with no sign of surrender after the second A-bombing of Nagasaki on August 9, "Strategic Air Forces commander Carl Spaatz cabled Lauris Norstad on August 10 proposing 'placing [the] third atomic bomb . . . on Tokyo,' where he thought it would have a salutary 'psychological effect on government officials'" (Rhodes, 744).

26. This general point is well argued by Lifton and Mitchell who implicate a White House campaign to win back public opinion on the Hiroshima decision by orchestrating strategic media commentary as official history in late 1946 and early 1947, such as the famous Stimpson *Harpers* article of February 1947, which appeared shortly before the movie's release. Actually Stimpson appears to have been a "beard" with James Conant,

General Groves, McGeorge Bundy, Harvey Bundy, George Harrison, Gordon Arneson, and Rudolph Winnacker all providing complete drafts, rewrites or major contributions to the "official narrative" (Lifton and Mitchell, 91–109).

27. Alperovitz, 515–17. See also Robert H. Ferrell, "Truman and the Bomb, a Documentary History, Chapter 18: Selected White House Memoranda, 1952–1953," at www.trumanlibrary.org/whistlestop/study_collections/bomb/ferrell_book/ferrell_book_chap18.htm, accessed June 1, 2009.

28. Walker, 190.

29. Many of these debates can be found in the historical literature. For instance, the movie's failure to mention Nagasaki is important since only two bombs were immediately ready for use in early August prior to the agreed Soviet entry into the war, but the *intention* was clearly to use *both*, regardless of an early surrender (see Groves memoirs in Rhodes, 676). Correspondingly, there is no mention of the Truman administration's accelerated efforts to A-bomb the Japanese into unconditional surrender *before* the agreed Soviet declaration of war which was set for, on or about, August 15 (Alperovitz, 227, 231).

30. In a letter dated August 4, 1964, Truman wrote to Mr. Haydon Kline (Attalla, Alabama), explaining that "I have never worried about dropping the bomb. It was just a means to end the war and this is what was accomplished," at www.trumanlibrary.org/whistlestop/study_collections/bomb/large/documents/index.php?documentdate=1964-08-04&documentid=9-16&studycollectionid=&pagenumber=1, accessed June 1, 2009.

# Bibliography

Gar Alperovitz, *The Decision to Use the Atomic Bomb*, Vintage Books, New York, 1985.

Barton J. Bernstein, "Understanding the Atomic Bomb and the Japanese Surrender: Missed Opportunities, Little-Known and Near Disasters, and Modern Memory," in Michael J. Hogan (ed) *Hiroshima in History and Memory*, Cambridge University Press, Cambridge, 1996, 187–99.

Joyce A. Evans, *Celluloid Mushrooms Clouds: Hollywood and the Atom Bomb*, Westview Press, Boulder, Colorado, 1998.

Albert J. LaValley (ed), *Focus on Hitchcock*, Prentice-Hall, Englewood Cliffs, New Jersey, 1972.

Robert Jay Lifton and Greg Mitchell, *Hiroshima in America: Fifty years of Denial*, Grosset/Putnam, New York, 1995.

Kim Newman, *Millennium Movies: End of the World Cinema*, Titan Books, London, 1998.

Turner Classic Movies, "Notes for The Beginning or the End (1947)," at www.tcm.com/tcmdb/title.jsp?stid=1531&category=Notes, accessed June 1, 2009.

Peter Nichols (ed), *Encyclopaedia of Science Fiction*, Granada, Sydney, 1979.

Richard Rhodes, *The Making of the Atomic Bomb*, Simon & Shuster, New York, 1986.

Harry S. Truman, *Years of Decision, Volume I*, Signet, New York, 1964.

J. Samuel Walker, "The Decision to Use the Bomb: A Historiographical Update," in Michael J. Hogan (ed.), *Hiroshima in History and Memory*, Cambridge University Press, Cambridge, 1996, 11–39.

——. "History, Collective Memory, and the Decision to use the Bomb," in Michael J. Hogan (ed.), *Hiroshima in History and Memory*, Cambridge University Press, Cambridge, 1996, 187–99.

CHAPTER 7

# Godzilla and the Bravo Shot

## WHO CREATED AND KILLED THE MONSTER?[*]

*Yuki Tanaka*

## The Creation of Godzilla

The original Godzilla film was produced in 1954 and released in November that year, only nine years after the end of the Pacific War. The same production team produced a sequence of twenty-two Godzilla films between 1954 and 1995, and six more films were created in the years 1995 to 2004 by a different production team. The original Godzilla film, *Godzilla*, and its first sequel, *Godzilla Raids Again* (produced in 1955), were the result of close cooperation between producer Tomoyuki Tanaka, director Ishiro Honda, special effects director Eiji Tsuburaya, and scriptwriter Shigeru Koyama.

In 1953, Tanaka, who was a young film producer working for Toho Film Corporation, was assigned to the production of a film entitled *In the Shadow of Honor*, a Japanese-Indonesian coproduction. The film was to be a story about a former Japanese soldier who participated in the Indonesian independence movement right after the Pacific War. However, due to rising diplomatic tensions between the Japanese and Indonesian governments, the project was cancelled before filming began. As a substantial sum of money had been allocated for this project, Tanaka suddenly had to find an alternative film project to utilize this budget to make an attractive popular film. Tanaka was a visionary producer who later produced some of Akira Kurosawa's best films such as *Yojimbo*, *Sanjuro*, and *Aka-hige* (Red Beard). Facing this unexpected crisis, he decided to take advantage of a recent horrific incident that was capturing the popular imagination. That was the hydrogen bomb test, Bravo shot, that the United States conducted on Rongelap (or Bikini) Atoll in the Marshall Islands in March 1954 and the

[*] Courtesy of The Asia-Pacific Journal: Japan Focus, japanfocus.org/-Yuki-TANAKA/1652.

159

fallout of radioactive dust from this nuclear test onto a Japanese fishing boat called the *Fifth Lucky Dragon.* He wanted a giant monster film like *The Beast From 20,000 Fathoms*, an American film produced in 1953 and distributed worldwide. In 1952, the 1933 classic film *King Kong* was rereleased, and Tanaka knew that Japanese audiences were fond of this kind of monster film.

Thus he asked a mystery storywriter Shigeru Koyama to write a script based on Tanaka's original idea that a dinosaur sleeping in the Southern Hemisphere had been awakened and transformed into a giant monster by the hydrogen bomb, and eventually attacked Tokyo. He asked Ishiro Honda to direct the film. Honda was a close friend of Kurosawa's and often acted as an assistant director for Kurosawa. During the war Honda was a soldier in the Japanese Imperial Army stationed in China. On his repatriation to Japan he landed at Kure port and then passed through Hiroshima, the city devastated by the A-bomb. Shocked by the devastation of the A-bomb, he had wanted to make a film to illuminate the horrors of nuclear war. It was largely due to Honda's anti-nuclear sentiments that the strong message of the evil of nuclear weapons and nuclear tests made their way into the film *Godzilla*. Eiji Tsuburaya had been involved in making models of war ships, naval ports, military bases, and the like, which were used in war films produced during the Asia-Pacific War. *The War at Sea from Hawaii to Malaya* was one of the films highlighting Tsuburaya's rare talent in special effects. He was creative, skillful and meticulous in making miniature models.

Takashi Shimura, who enjoyed a reputation as one of the best Japanese actors at the time, played Dr. Yamane, one of the main characters in the first two Godzilla films. He played the major role of a samurai leader in Kurosawa's *Seven Samurai*, which was also produced in the same year as *Godzilla*. 1954 must have been an extremely busy year for Shimura. In the second Godzilla film, *Godzilla Raids Again*, actors such as Minoru Chiaki and Takao Tsuchiya, who also acted in Kurosawa's *Seven Samurai* and *The Hidden Fortress*, played important parts. Thus, in the choice of cast, the Godzilla films were certainly not cheap productions.

*The Beast From 20,000 Fathoms* was a film about a large dinosaur of about thirty meters long and five hundred tons in weight. In this story, a dinosaur, which began hibernating in the Ice Age, thaws out as icebergs melt due to an American nuclear test conducted at a secret site somewhere in the Arctic Circle. Unlike Godzilla, this nameless beast—simply called beast, monster, or dinosaur—does not emit radiation from his body. It is simply a super-large dinosaur. The beast travels south carried by an ocean current in the North Sea and appears in New York. Eventually, however, this monster is killed by a deadly radioactive isotope launched by U.S. soldiers, which is firmly embedded in its neck. The film explores the doubts scientists held about eyewitness accounts by people who actually saw the monster as well as the process through which existing scientific analysis proved to be invalid. The monster embodies a contradiction between scientific knowledge and the unknown power of nuclear weapons. Yet the *power of radiation* (i.e., a new scientific knowledge) resolves this contradiction. In this way the story unfolds in a scientific and logical manner—typically American in style—and ends with the victory of nuclear science over the monster.

Godzilla is a dinosaur that survived from the Cretaceous Period and lives around a fictitious southern Japanese island called Otojima. Godzilla is a legendary monster who is deified by the islanders and even used in *kagura* or local sacred music and dance. In some sense it is similar to Oni (devil) and Daija (big snake), both of which are legendary creatures in Japan and China. It is a giant monster fifty meters long (one hundred meters long, including its thick tail) and twenty thousand tons in weight. It appears at the same time as a typhoon and travels a similar course to that usually taken by typhoons to attack Japan. In other words, the emergence of Godzilla is seen as a kind of "natural phenomenon" similar to a typhoon or "an act of God" that human beings cannot control. Unlike the dinosaur in *The Beast From 20,000 Fathoms*, Godzilla is a malevolent deity or genie. *Gojira*, the Japanese original name, is a word derived from the combination of *gorira* (Japanese for gorilla) and *kujira* (meaning whale). When the original film was about to be exported to the United States, Toho Film Corporation came up with the new spelling, "Godzilla," believing that this word evokes an image that is the amalgamation of god, lizard, and gorilla.

Unlike *The Beast From 20,000 Fathoms*, the main theme of the original film Godzilla is not the victory of science over nature. Rather, it implies that human beings are destroyed by the impact of science on nature.

In Kōyama's original draft script, the film would have started with the following narration:

> X day of November, 1952, was a crucial day for mankind as the entire world had to live under the immense fear of nuclear tests from that day on. The first H-bomb test can be called "liquidation" rather than "test." Does the H-bomb test remain within the limits of an experiment? No, absolutely No![1]

Eventually this narration was not used. Nor did the film include the actual scene of the blast of the H-bomb. It was not necessary to give such a direct message nor to show any picture of a nuclear test, as the Japanese audience clearly knew the horrific impact of nuclear arms. In the film people only talk about the H-bomb test. Hearsay without an actual picture of the nuclear blast, an implied link between the unknown monster and the nuclear test, was far more effective in conjuring the mysterious and fearful affect of radiation caused by the nuclear test.

# Destruction of the City

## THE BEAST FROM 20,000 FATHOMS

In this film the beast walks the street, smashing cars or picking them up in its mouth when they get in its way. It destroys only one building, and this by accident when the beast leans heavily against a building, trying to avoid shots fired by police. People flee, crying that this is war, as the city turns into a battlefield. The film appears to portray all out war between the beast and the city population. Yet the battlefield is confined to several wide streets in New York City. The beast appears in the city in broad daylight, so everyone knows where it is. It attacks people, although only policemen try to shoot it. A woman screams as she watches a policeman being eaten by the beast. Yet the beast does not attack the woman. In other words, the attack by the beast is not a random, indiscriminate assault. It is a "precision attack" on those who try to harm it. It is clear that this film has been produced by people who have no experience of "total war," in particular indiscriminate aerial bombing. The same can be said of other American monster films such as *Alien* and the Hollywood production *Godzilla* in 1998 in which the main target of the attack by Godzilla is again the people, not the city itself, and the monster and its babies are carnivorous dinosaurs.

## THE JAPANESE ORIGINAL *GODZILLA*

Godzilla neither chases nor eats people, but simply attempts to destroy the city completely and thereby kill its inhabitants. Attacking indiscriminately at night, Godzilla not only smashes everything, but also breathes radioactive fire. The city is not only demolished, but also burned by fire. The time spent on the scene where Godzilla destroys Tokyo is more than ten times longer than the scene in which the city is attacked in the film of *The Beast From 20,000 Fathoms*. Tokyo citizens try to escape as far from the metropolitan area as possible, carrying as many personal belongings as they can.

Many scenes in the film thus reminded the audience of aerial bombing of Japanese cities by B-29 bombers in the final months of the Pacific War. For example, on March 10, 1945, about one hundred thousand people in the Tokyo metropolitan area were burned to death within a few hours by 237,000 firebombs dropped from 334 B-29 bombers. An estimated one million lost their homes and were driven from the city.

Godzilla prefers darkness and intensely dislikes light. This behavior resembles B-29 bombers, which flew at night and sought to avoid the beams of searchlights. From the raid on Tokyo on March 10, 1945, Brigadier General

Curtis LeMay, the commander of the XXI Bomber Command, changed the bombing strategy from precision bombing during the day to carpet bombing with napalm bombs at night. The United States carried out "saturation bombing," using napalm until the end of the war in August 1945, repeatedly attacking cities from Hokkaido to Okinawa, including Tokyo, Kawasaki, Nagoya, Osaka, Kobe, Fukuoka, and Naha. More than one hundred cities were destroyed, causing one million casualties, including more than half a million deaths, the majority being civilians, in particular women and children. Indiscriminate bombing reached its peak with the use of atomic weapons at Hiroshima and Nagasaki in August 1945. It must be remembered that many Japanese people who saw the original Godzilla film had firsthand experience of aerial bombing and had lost relatives and friends as a result.

In one scene, a boy cries "Chikusho ("Damn it," or "You brute"), watching Godzilla walking away towards the ocean from Tokyo Bay after a rampage. This scene also vividly reminded the audience of B-29 bombers flying away after dropping tens of thousands of bombs on their urban target. The film includes scenes of people trying to escape carrying household goods, of a burning city, of injured people being brought into a safe shelter, and of screaming children. These horrible pictures could be seen as reproductions of what actually happened in cities throughout Japan in napalm attacks.[2]

There is also a scene in which a homeless mother tells her small children that they will soon join Daddy in heaven as they look up at the ferocious Godzilla breaking down the building of Matsuzakaya Department Store in Ginza. This indicates that the woman is a widow who lost her husband in the war and subsequently became homeless. In reality it was not possible for a war widow to have had four- or five-year-old children in 1954. Yet there were many homeless war widows. According to a survey conducted by the Ministry of Welfare in 1952, for example, the total number of widows in Japan that year was 1,883,890, and 88.4 percent of these women had children under eighteen years of age. Seventy thousand such households were jobless, leaving women struggling to survive day by day, many doing odd jobs as day laborers or peddlers. Thus the film clearly reflects the deep scars of war on Japanese society.

It must have been very difficult to watch serious films that directly portrayed the horrors of war, reminding Japanese of their own wartime agony nine years earlier. Yet *Godzilla* allowed Japanese to heal their pain through watching an entertaining film, which at the same time indirectly reflected tormenting wartime experiences.

From 1955, another series of popular comedy films called *Nitohei Monogatari* (The Story of A Soldier Private) began to be produced. This series was immensely successful, too, as each film ridiculed the military system and ideology of the Japanese imperial forces. It was necessary for former soldiers to laugh at their own wartime conduct before they could reflect upon it. Japanese people needed more time to be able to watch serious war films such as *Ningen no Joken* (The Human Condition), produced in 1959.

There are almost no scenes in which people are actually killed by Godzilla, although the film makes the audience imagine that many people die under the collapsed buildings, in the burning houses or in the train carriages that Godzilla holds up and crunches in his mouth. This suggests that the Japanese audience in those days could not bear to watch even fictitious pictures of dying people, as they were too close to the recent experience of deaths by aerial bombings. Instead, the film concentrates on the destruction of famous buildings in Tokyo such as the clock tower of the Hattori Corporation, Nichigeki Theatre, Kachi-dokibashi Bridge, the Metropolitan Police Department, and the Diet building. The audience clapped joyously when Godzilla destroyed the Diet and the Metropolitan Police Department—both symbols of state authority. I presume that many at the time felt that the state and politicians had dragged them into a disastrous war culminating in the U.S. aerial bombardment. In actual fact, the Diet and the Metropolitan Police Department were hardly damaged by the aerial bombing mainly because they were close to the Imperial Palace. For political reasons, the Imperial Palace was removed from the target list of aerial attacks. Thus it seems quite natural that the audience was delighted to see those buildings attacked by the monster in the film.

# Godzilla as Both Victim and Perpetrator of Nuclear Weapons

On March 1, 1954, the United States conducted a hydrogen bomb test called Bravo shot at Rongelap Atoll in the Marshall Islands. The H-bomb used was a fifteen megaton bomb (i.e., one thousand times bigger than the one dropped on Hiroshima). As a result of this nuclear test radioactive dust fell not only on many Marshall Islanders but famously on a Japanese tuna fishing boat called the *Fifth Lucky Dragon*, irradiating all twenty-three fishermen on board, including Captain Aikichi Kuboyama. Kuboyama died on September 23 that year. Since then thirteen other members of the crew have died from various types of cancer, and those who are still alive are also suffering from the disease. The United States conducted four more nuclear tests at Rongelap Atoll until May 14 that year. Consequently, 856 Japanese fishing boats were contaminated with radioactive materials, and 486,000 tons of tuna and other fish had to be disposed of.

Because of these nuclear tests and their effects upon Japanese people who had previously experienced the atomic bombing of Hiroshima and Nagasaki, anti-nuclear sentiments were further strengthened and the movement against nuclear tests quickly spread throughout Japan. Thus, in August of that year, the first Conference Against Atomic and Hydrogen Bombs was held in Hiroshima. It was natural, therefore, that the film reflected these strong anti-nuclear sentiments and used the *Fifth Lucky Dragon* as a model for the boat called *Eiko Maru* attacked by Godzilla. In fact, one of the many boats that was showered with radioactive dust in the Marshall Islands was called the *Thirteenth Koei Maru*. The name *Eiko Maru* was undoubtedly taken from the name of this real boat. In the film, popular expressions widely used at the time such as "Genshi maguro" (atomic tuna) meaning "irradiated tuna" and "hoshano" (radio active fallout) were also used.

For example, three office workers—a woman and two men—on their way to work are conversing in the train. The woman says "It's terrible, isn't it? Irradiated tuna and radioactive fallout, and now this Godzilla to top it all off! What will happen if he appears out of Tokyo Bay? Oh awful. I survived the bombing of Nagasaki at great pains, yet I have to go through this again." One of the men says, "I guess I'll have to find a place where I can be evacuated again. It stinks, ha!" Thus the fear of radioactive fallout is directly linked to the bombing of Hiroshima and Nagasaki, and the appearance of Godzilla is closely related to the U.S air raids and wartime evacuations.

In short, the original Godzilla film clearly conveyed anti-nuclear messages. Yet, somehow, the fear of radiation does not really stand out in this film. When Godzilla lands in Tokyo, he burns down buildings and drives away civilians by breathing radioactive fire. Nevertheless, there is little explanation of the effects of radiation. We, in the audience, expect that the places Godzilla passes must be heavily contaminated by radioactivity, although the main reason that the *Fifth Lucky Dragon* incident shocked so many Japanese people was neither the thermal rays nor the blast, but the radioactive dust. In the film, radioactivity is not seriously addressed, but in a few scenes a Geiger counter is used to detect radioactivity. "Geiger counter" had become a familiar term in Japan at the time.

Posters touted "the H-bomb monster" and "the Super monster that breathes radioactive fire." So why wasn't radiation highlighted? The young manager of Nankai Salvage Boat Company, Ogata, confronts the paleontologist, Dr. Yamane, saying, "Isn't Godzilla a product of the A-bomb that still haunts many of us Japanese?" The film as a whole, however, portrays Godzilla as a victim of the H-bomb test rather than the radioactive perpetrator. For example, at the Parliamentary Investigation Committee Dr. Yamane describes Godzilla with certain sympathy, saying:

> Godzilla probably quietly survived by eating deep sea organisms occupying a specific niche. Yet, repeated H-bomb tests may have destroyed his environment completely. To put it plainly, it can be said that Godzilla was forced out of his peaceful living place by H-bombs.

In this manner, Godzilla is described as a creature that is forced to bear the double burden of both victim and assailant. Indeed, Godzilla is a sad monster that mirrors human beings, who produce nuclear weapons and at the same time victimize fellow human beings by using them. In particular, the ugly Godzilla symbolically represents the Japanese who were victimized by A-bombs and H-bombs, yet still support the possession of nuclear arms by the United States and directly supported the U.S. war in Korea. In the end, Godzilla appears more victim than assailant. In other words, his propensity to emit radioactivity is not overtly shown. This characteristic seems to be closely intertwined with the weakness in Japanese people who fail to see themselves simultaneously as perpetrators and victims of war. Indiscriminate aerial bombing of many Japanese cities including Hiroshima and Nagasaki doubtlessly contributed to the strong image the Japanese have of themselves as victims of war, despite the fact that the Japanese imperial forces invaded China and conducted indiscriminate bombing of civilians on many Chinese cites such as Shanghai, Nanjing, Wuhan, and Chongqing during the Asia Pacific War.

Nevertheless, due to this double characteristic, Godzilla is not simply a dinosaur. He is a heretic or a rebel, like some of us, who violently struggles to solve the contradiction of duality. Although only a small child when I first saw the original Godzilla film, I clearly remember feeling sad seeing Godzilla finally die in agony. This emotion was quite different from that I had two years later in 1956 when I watched another film called *Radon*, about a flying monster that leaped out of a lake. I was so scared of *Radon* that I could not have a bath for some time afterward, as I could not forget that frightening scene.

The Godzilla film highlights the fact that as producers of nuclear arms we human beings are the assailants of Godzilla (i.e., ravagers of the natural environment). In other words, the film tells us that nature will exact revenge on human beings who have unlocked the brutal power of science.

In the original Godzilla film there are many other scenes which reflect contemporary political problems such as the Cold War, the Korean War, and the remilitarization of Japan, as well as the fear Japanese people have of being dragged into war again in the near future. Thus the film evokes not only anti-nuclear sentiments but also strong anti-war feelings.

# Problems with the American Godzilla Films

The first Godzilla film produced in the United States was *Godzilla: King of the Monsters*. This 1956 production used many clips from the original Japanese film and combined them with inserts made by producer Joe Levine and director

Terry Morse. Raymond Burr starred as Steve Martin, an American newspaper journalist who reports on Godzilla.

This film does not, however, explain how the radioactive Godzilla was created. The American audience never learns that this monster is in fact the byproduct of an H-bomb test conducted in the Pacific by their own country. Moreover, many scenes considered unsuitable for an American audience were revised or omitted. The following are some such examples.

1. In the Japanese original, Dr. Yamane is intrigued by Godzilla's extraordinary strength and ability to survive the H-bomb test and sets out to find a reason for this. In the American version, however, Dr. Yamane simply wants to investigate Godzilla as a rare monster.
2. There is a scene in the original in which a Geiger counter is used to measure the level of radioactivity of injured people. This scene naturally led the Japanese audience to visualize the harrowing situation immediately after the bombing of Hiroshima and Nagasaki and the firebombing of other cities. In the American version, however, the narration simply explains that people died from strange burns.
3. In the original film, a Geiger counter is used to locate Godzilla, whereas in the American version, sonar (i.e., sonic depth finder counter) is used.
4. The American version omitted the conversation among the office workers on the train, which includes the woman's statement, "I survived the bombing of Nagasaki at great pains."
5. In the original film, the last words of Dr. Yamane are "I cannot believe that Godzilla was the only surviving member of its species. If we keep conducting nuclear tests, it's possible that another Godzilla might appear somewhere in the world, again!" The American version replaces these words by Steve Martin's statement: "The menace is gone. The world can wake up and live again!"

In this way, producer Joe Levine and director Terry Morse avoid dealing with the nuclear issue. In this film Godzilla is a mysterious monster whose origins are unknown. The film suggests that when the monster dies, it is best to forget about it as quickly as possible. When Dr. Yamane's daughter, Emiko, asks Steve why they have to face such a dreadful problem, he responds simply, "I don't know, Emiko, I don't know."

In the original Japanese film, the story flows naturally without narration. By contrast, the American version is framed entirely by the newspaper correspondent, Steve Martin. For the observer, Steve Martin, Japan is simply the source of a mysterious news item. He observes the events there without any real concern and makes no effort to help the Japanese people struggling with the problem of Godzilla. Basically, he is uninterested in the crisis facing the Japanese nation. He simply reports superficially on what is happening. Steve is said to be a friend of Dr. Serizawa, who graduated from the same American university. Yet he smokes a pipe dispassionately, observing his friend and other Japanese people with indifference.

The second American Godzilla film, simply entitled *Godzilla* and produced in 1998, is the story of an iguana which was irradiated by a French nuclear test at Muraroa Atoll and somehow appears in New York as Godzilla. For Americans, monsters like Godzilla and King Kong must come from an uncivilized world far away from the United States. As far as American film studios are concerned, it would seem that Godzilla must not, or should not, be created by *American* nuclear tests. This film opens with a scene in which an American scientist, Dr. Niko Tatopulos, is investigating giant earthworms, deformed by a high dosage of radioactivity leaked from the Chernobyl accident. It is well known that there have been many cases of cancer and leukemia among people living in areas adjacent to the Chernobyl power plant. Dr. Tatopulos, however, seems unaware or uninterested in the human problems caused by the nuclear power plant accident at Chernobyl. Still less is he interested in the effects of the nuclear disaster much closer to home at Three Mile Island in Pennsylvania, where many deformed flowers and leaves were found in areas close to the power plant.

Unlike the Japanese Godzilla, the American Godzilla is simply a giant dinosaur that looks exactly like a reptile. It eats huge quantities of fish and lays many eggs and its babies attack and cannibalize human beings. Godzilla runs around the streets of New York, chasing people in a car who had tried to destroy its eggs. As mentioned earlier, monsters that appear in New York do not randomly destroy buildings and commit mass killings. The American Godzilla does not breathe radioactive fire, and is eventually killed not by nuclear arms but by conventional weapons. Apart from a few early scenes, this film does not refer to nuclear issues at all. It is more appropriate to call it an expanded version of *Jurassic Park* rather than *Godzilla*. In other words, the Hollywood production of Godzilla in 1998 depoliticized, denuclearized, and de-Japanized Godzilla, at the same time corrupting Godzilla by changing it into a giant reptile simply controlled by animal instincts. The American Godzilla has been stripped of its vital elements of rebellion, contradiction, heterodoxy, and social criticism.

The American Godzilla films lack another crucial theme present in the Japanese original, the moral dilemma that faced top scientists. In the original Japanese film, Dr. Serizawa accidentally comes across an unknown form of energy in the course of his research on oxygen. Eventually, he invents a lethal device called the oxygen destroyer. Even a small baseball-sized oxygen destroyer can kill the entire population of sea organisms in Tokyo Bay by depriving them of oxygen. In other words, this is potentially a weapon as powerful as the H-bomb. This places Dr. Serizawa in an agonizing moral dilemma. On the one hand he knows he could use it to annihilate Godzilla, but there is also the danger that the weapon could subsequently be abused by others. Should he therefore keep it a secret? Eventually he decides to use it against Godzilla, but plans to commit suicide immediately after destroying Godzilla so that knowledge of oxygen destroyers would not survive. In this sense, he shares Godzilla's fate of duality as both victim and perpetrator. Incidentally, Dr. Serizawa wears a black eyepatch on his right eye and his right cheek has a big burn scar, indicating that he was a victim of a napalm bomb or atomic bomb attack by the U.S. forces during the war. Many Japanese emerged from the war with keloidal scars on various parts of the body as a result of aerial bombing.

In summary, the original Japanese film contains a powerful and thought-provoking critique of the development and deployment of nuclear weapons. It is also worthwhile to note, that it was not military forces like the U.S. Air Force or Japan's Self-Defense Forces that finally killed the original Godzilla. The person who killed Godzilla was a scientist who also chose to kill himself in an effort to save humanity from the dangers of his discovery.

# Conclusion

Many other versions of Godzilla have been produced in Japan since 1954, but from the 1960s Godzilla rapidly lost its power of social realism. (An important exception is *Godzilla vs. Hedra* of 1971, which explores Japan's pollution problems like Minamata Disease.) Godzilla became a good guy who wrestles against bad monsters and always wins. In other words, it became a pet Godzilla. Yet a pet Godzilla is no longer a monster. A monster is only entitled to be a monster because of an unpredictability that surpasses our imagination. A monster should have a future that includes the possibility that it will rebel against the corrupt and wretched world. Failing that, it should be terminated. For me a pet Godzilla is the product of Japanese parents—i.e., kyoiku mama and papa (educationally ambitious mothers and fathers)—as well as of the Japanese school system that moulds children, making them obedient and depriving them of imagination. The taming of Godzilla could account for why Japanese adults are losing their imaginative and creative powers.

In more recent Godzilla films, the main character is no longer Godzilla. For example, in films such as *Godzilla vs. Mecha-Godzilla*, *Godzilla vs. Space-Godzilla*, and *Godzilla vs. Destroyer*, it is the so-called G Force (said to be the Self-Defense Forces) that drives the story. The G Force builds military robots to fight against Godzilla, or creates a device to control Godzilla's nerve system by shooting into Godzilla's body. It is not surprising that this kind of film is produced as the SDF now demands that their own ideas be included in the script in return for providing tanks, jet fighters, and the like for the filming. Is this not a product of an age in which the SDF sallies forth in support of U.S. forces in Iraq, and Article 9, the peace provision of the Constitution, is left in tatters? I find this kind of Godzilla film really sad.

Well, who killed Godzilla? My answer is that it is we Japanese who appear to have lost the will to confront injustice and inhumanity and to recognize the ambiguities inherent in the new technologies of destruction. Let us revive the real Godzilla in our minds!

# Notes

1. This is cited in the book, *Gojira ga Kuru Yoru ni* (The Night Godzilla Appears), Toshio Takahashi (Shuei-sha, Tokyo, 1993), 42.

2. All the script quotes used in this article were taken when viewing the films.

# CHAPTER 8

# Thank You, Mr. Avedon[*]

*Carole Gallagher*

Martin Luther King once remarked that there can be no great disappointment where there is no great love.

And who would argue that for an artist, there is nothing deeper in feeling, or closer to love, than the urge to create that drives each day, every day?

It might be a bit peculiar to say that there was much to love while I lived downwind of the Nevada test site, the site of 128 atmospheric detonations of nuclear bombs during the Cold War. Here was one of the few places on earth that experienced true catastrophe, surrendering to radioactive fallout comparable to that of Chernobyl time and time again, yet never did my heart beat truer than when I lived for almost a decade in Utah. I had diverted the river of my life from the wily, ambitious canyons of Manhattan, fertile culture capital of the country, to the secret slickrock canyons of Moab, Cedar City, and other desert towns, living in the basement of a home owned by two polygamous widows in St. George. It was, to quote a great writer and a dissimilar situation somewhat askew, "the best of times and the worst of times." (My years in Utah were not so dramatically Dickensian, since the limitations and discomforts of acute poverty were cured by the landscape I saw before my eyes. There was a wealth of beauty in my life thanks to the various parts of Utah and the West where I photographed. That beauty, access to those places, provided the best aesthetic opportunities and emotions of my life. My encounters with certain emotionally dishonest, bigoted, or narrow-minded individuals, however, tempered what beauty I encountered with a sense of shock.)

Driven by a force I didn't understand, while working on this book I was utterly transformed. A powerful motivation once again took hold of me much like that I had experienced as a child while cowering in the basement of the peaceful, cloistered monastery where I attended grammar school, during infamous "duck-and-cover" exercises in Bay Ridge, Borough of Brooklyn, New York City, a Ground Zero if there ever was one. The crucible of living among human beings who had witnessed the explosion of nuclear weapons, and were living with them and dying from them for most of their lives, held within it the transformative power of love and the urge to create something permanent to honor their suffering.

Such a drastic personal exodus from all I had known, as a New Yorker by birth and by conviction, had not exactly happened by accident. In 1981, in my early thirties, two phrases I came upon in my readings made a fortuitous connection that changed the direction of my life, and just in time: under President Ronald Reagan's administration, a decade of unprecedented American greed and political duplicity was in its infancy. While studying a biography of the American photographer Dorothea Lange, who incidentally had photographed Mormon life in Utah in the 1950s, I discovered she had always pinned to her darkroom door a thought by Francis Bacon:

> The contemplation of things as they are,
> without error or confusion,
> without substitution or imposture,
> is in itself a nobler thing
> than a whole harvest of invention.[1]

By then I had been researching for many years the entity that President Eisenhower had warned could destroy our democracy, the military-industrial complex. I had also found recently declassified Atomic Energy Commission documents from the 1950s both riveting and deeply disturbing. In one "top secret" AEC memo, the people living downwind of the Nevada test site during the atmospheric atomic testing era were described as "a low-use segment of the population." The shock at such callous bigotry fused with the ideal of clear seeing expressed by Bacon and lived by Lange through her photographic work. It was that illuminating moment which brought me to Utah to research, investigate, contemplate, and document the effects of exploding a thousand nuclear devices above and below the land of the Shoshone Nation, and the effect of those detonations on three groups of people: those who lived closest to the test site, as far north as South Dakota, the workers at the site, and the soldiers exposed to the bomb at close range by military fiat, as an experiment to see what a soldier could endure on the atomic battlefield.

And so I surrendered to the bomb, and dropped out of life as I had known it.

Dorothea Lange had much good advice for documentarians, all of which I followed, but my most useful adaptation was to wear what she called "the cloak of invisibility." I, too, had hoped to become a blank slate upon which the stories and imagery could be written, but to do so it was necessary to lose my own needs and habits, particularly those deeply engraved upon my brain by years of living in the ruthlessly self-serving art world of New York. From that moment on, I clothed my life in "the cloak of invisibility" which had helped Lange become an instrument without ego. When doing field work, it is also best to realize how ignorant you are—you have traveled to a new place because you want to learn something. It soon became apparent that in listening to and photographing the downwinders and other radiation survivors, it would be more respectful to stop thinking as an artist or photojournalist. Thus, I had hoped to avoid the pitfalls of exploitation while recording their oral histories and making portraits.

Of course, this insight worked against me in terms of professional success for the next decades, after *American Ground Zero* was published and the companion exhibition traveled the world, in ways I would never have guessed. My refusal to photograph anyone who had endured breast cancer by showing the scars of her mastectomy, as I was told over and over by photojournalists, was an indicator of my lack of courage or talent. I was aware of the aggressive, macho culture of journalism, but I had thought better of this, since devout Mormons always wear "garments," a type of holy underclothing that is never completely removed even when bathing. I had many a laugh with some of the more straightforward Mormons in conversations about these ritual garments, how an inch of material was kept touching the skin while changing from soiled to clean garments, so that they were always modest in the eyes of God. It struck me as a poignant act of dedication and commitment to a life of the spirit, such as I had not seen since my monastic days.

Who was I to act disrespectfully in the face of such religious ritual? I would photograph each person simply, in the places where they worked and lived, without artifice. There would be no room for artistic grandstanding in this documentary.

There was not quite so much respect, I found, in a few of the downwinders, and hence my great disappointment. There were at least two who understood that they could make a living by promoting themselves as advocates for downwinder issues on a national scale. In a rural state such as Utah, where adequate employment was scarce, particularly for those with barely a high school education, I could sense the desperation of those who were ill-suited to exhausting farm and ranch labor or construction work, the sole venues for work other than clerking robotically at the local K-Mart for a pittance of wages.

In trying to work with two such advocates for downwinder issues, I found myself wasting a lot of emotion and time seeking to find people to interview through them. One activist thought that there should be a *quid pro quo*: she would reveal names of appropriate people to interview in return for my working *gratis* for her organization, full time. By linking up with other advocacy groups in Washington and New York, she and one other advocate in a separate organization had managed to pull in piles of money by seeking funds from well-meaning foundations located too far away on the East and West Coasts to comprehend the significant difference between fabrication and fact in activists' funding proposals. These foundations sent no on-site investigators, and money flowed freely, often used not to advocate but to buy new cars and other items I thought unrelated to the serious downwind issues, like liquor and drugs. I called these two downwinders PVs: professional victims. They made quite a living from it, and after a few years became territorial and arrogant, thinking no one could speak about living downwind of a nuclear test site but them, particularly an outsider from New York. They also hated each other, a deep loathing based on competition for funds and fame, and soon I was unwittingly entangled in their trite drama, based on the maxim, "The enemy of my enemy is my friend."

In this environment of farce, I soon understood that there would be no networking possible with either of these venues, but maintained good relations nonetheless, speaking not a bad word about them when foundations would ask me my opinion of their work. "Straight from the grass roots," I would say to foundation directors who sought my advice, "the only act in town." I wanted to get myself off the hook by telling the truth but also keeping my shirt clean. Blaming the victims in any way would have been bad form. I received no such courtesy from them, however, when tables were turned, yet I lived with it, peeved but hanging on to discretion, silence at all costs, while lying quietly on their exquisite beds of competitive nails.

My association with some downwinders was problematic from the outset, particularly those who expected to speak for everyone exposed to the nuclear tests. Despite the battering of my idealistic naïveté about these matters, I eventually found many people to interview thanks to the lawyers who were representing thousands of downwinders, atomic veterans, and test site workers. These were believable people, many with credible documentation. Each person I interviewed told me of a dozen more with the same health problems, the same work history, or the same service on the atomic battlefield, and so I felt no need to rely on the fraudulent PVs any longer to get work done.

This didn't mean I wasn't observing them closely for many years, even though they knew I had their number. Thus I may tell you my best story of the twisted, if laughable, way that the art world, from afar, and these PVs, up close and personal, helped me to take the most beautiful portrait in my book, an improbable photograph and the one that I love the most.

One year into my Utah sojourn, I hitched a ride with PV#1 from Cedar City to Salt Lake City, in her spanking new car, to attend a meeting of the "board of directors" of her tiny, tax-exempt organization, hoping to make some work connections. Years previously, I had seen PV#1 on a Phil Donahue show concerning the downwinders, and she spoke of having thyroid disease from the fallout from atomic tests as well as the death of her brother from pancreatic cancer, another radiogenic illness, when he was a very young man. She was, and had been for some years, morbidly obese, perhaps 350 pounds or more, which she attributed to the thyroid disease slowing down her metabolism.

What PV#1 didn't know was that I had suffered thyroid disease as a child, 1962–1965, beginning in the year when the last of the atmospheric bombs were tested at least once a week, until the years after the Partial Test Ban Treaty, when tests went underground but were still releasing substantial radiation downwind, even as far as the agricultural areas of New York state where our milk was produced. I knew there was medication and treatment for hypothyroidism, just a daily dose of Thyroxin to mimic the thyroid hormone that the organ itself had stopped producing. Hypothyroidism can create serious weight gain and also clinical depression, and in some cases there is also severe, burning body pain in muscles and joints that makes exercise unlikely. When I looked at PV#1, I tended to give her the benefit of the doubt, "believing the best of people until one learns otherwise," as my beloved avatar Charles Kuralt would say on his cross-country interviewing trips. But why would she not have gone to a doctor, and taken Thyroxin to return her life to normal? My thyroid illness had changed my life for the better: to lose the weight I started cycling, running, and hoops. How much more pleasant it would be to run the line of multicolored mesas in southern Utah for daily exercise! But some downwinders would prefer to be victims of the bomb, not survivors. I learned this all too often in the decade I spent downwind: there was political capital to be earned by these self-styled victims, particularly by the activists, and emotional and financial capital as well.

I said nothing to her about my own thyroid disease. It's always better to listen, not to contaminate personal truths with outside influence from one's own biography. We stopped in Delta, Utah, preferring to explore the back roads rather than take the interstate, because, she explained, there was a cheese factory there, and she wanted to buy some gifts for her board members. The aroma of the factory was sickening, perceptible miles away. Once we parked, I stayed in the car to make some notes about the landscape, the factory being truly in the middle of nowhere. Out she waddled from the factory store with a five-pound bag of "cheese curd," an orange mass of what looked like predigested lumps, which she plopped between us in the car. I opened my window, settled in with my notebook and pen to begin more of my information pursuit about her, her brother, the family, and we took off for Salt Lake City, still at least three stinky hours away.

Somehow I forgot to mention that I had actually seen her on the Phil Donahue program, but I asked her about her own health, and she revealed, once again, that she had thyroid disease, like so many other downwinders, particularly because she just could not lose any weight. Expressionless, I asked who were the local doctors who had diagnosed thyroid problems locally in Cedar City and St. George, and though she could not name one in particular, she did mention that there were a few federally funded cancers studies at the University of Utah in Salt Lake City that had been tracking both thyroid disease and leukemia since the 1950s.

*(In 2007, a scientist working with Dr. Joseph Lyon, director of these studies, would write in an email to a survivor of thyroid cancer that he finally had come to a point of conscience, and revealed that these studies were fraudulent, that the statistics were manipulated for the decades that the studies had been funded. Thus many millions of taxpayer dollars had been wasted on more big lies, many thyroid disease patients dying in the process because although they were examined and interrogated, they were rarely given medical treatment. The scientists only wished to observe "the natural progression" of exposure to radioactive iodine from these atmospheric atomic bomb detonations.)*

As PV#1 and I talked, the five-pound bag of cheese curd was quickly disappearing, though I had only managed to eat a few morsels out of politeness at her urging. I asked her who had diagnosed her thyroid disease, had she any nodules, or, God forbid, cancer?

PV#1 replied that she had never seen a doctor about it, not one, ever.

Despite "the cloak of invisibility," I was only thirty-four and had still not earned many stripes when it came to keeping a blank stare in the face of absurdity. Nor could I keep my mouth shut at this point, either. I asked how she had the courage to state on national television that she had thyroid disease from bomb exposure when she had never been diagnosed by a doctor. I had even remembered her stroking her throat lasciviously as she described her thyroid problems to the quite handsome Phil Donahue. She turned sullen, so I looked away, and through the windshield I caught sight of my very first magpie, a western bird of the corbid family, majestic in its deep blue and bright white colors with a very long tail, notable in its habits for stealing the eggs out of other birds' nests and eating them. I had the good sense to keep my cackling silent, the irony of it all, and PV#1 was silent for a while too. She knew she had made a mistake and was working on it, red-faced, chewing on the remaining curds.

We toured through a very small town south of Delta, once the Mormon capitol named Deseret, full of modest homes built of typically orange brick from local clay. I learned that the University of Utah was also doing a study on these bricks to judge how much radioactive decay they could demonstrate. I looked past one of these homes to see a catalpa tree in the yard, unusual in such a desert environment; its branches were heavily laden with dark, sleeping birds. Trusty binoculars in hand, I jumped out of the car to identify them. Heads tucked under their wings, crowded into this one tree, were hundreds of nighthawks, members of the nightjar clan, birds that stalk their prey only under cover of night. I was delighted. By the time I got back to the car, the bag of cheese curd was close to empty, and we had only, I guessed, backtracked fifteen miles from the cheese factory to Deseret.

"There's another photographer from New York here in Utah, and he's doing a book about downwinders too," PV#1 remarked snidely as I shut the car door. I felt my deepest, most raw emotions finally being manipulated. She was grinning like a Cheshire Cat. My heart sank. I'm not a person who ever enjoyed the competitive, beat-'em-down journalistic races to the finish, perhaps one good reason I'm a documentarian and not a photojournalist; I need the gift of time to research a story in depth. Neither was it in my nature to kneecap the competition to break a story, perhaps the reason I had always chosen topics which others would be unlikely to have the time and fortitude to cover.

But now, apparently, after some years of working on my research and this book, I was about to enter a race with the type of competitor for whom I was totally unprepared, a rich and very famous one. The irony of PV#1's consumption of five pounds of cheese in less than an hour was in direct contrast to my own experience in previous weeks, being hospitalized for the effects of starvation, blood pressure sinking to 60/40, thus causing frequent *grand mal* seizures from lack of blood to the brain. And I had recently relocated to Cedar City from St. George because the polygamists had asked me to leave. After being visited and surveyed by the local Mormon bishop at the request of my polygamous landlords, I was deemed less than righteous. I was "working against the government," federal agencies such as the Atomic Energy Commission being considered by Mormons to be "divinely enlightened," much as our Constitution is "divinely inspired," and so I was evicted forthwith. Despite my tears and questions, I was told, "Don't worry, sweetie, you'll get your book done." I had read enough Mormon history to remember how many towns and communities in the East and Midwest had evicted LDS settlers because of their odd beliefs, including polygamy. Now the tables were turned. The widows were intransigent, though kindly, but they had a look of fear in their eyes. Clearly, their instructions had come from "on high"—in this case, the ward bishop who had inspected me and found me morally deficient.

For many months after moving an hour north to Cedar City, I had been surviving on one bowl of Total a day, with water not milk, having so little money to buy film and gas that I usually walked to my interviews, carrying all my heavy photo equipment and tape recorder, no matter how far away they lived in town. There was just no extra money for the frivolity of personal sustenance. And in order to keep myself from succumbing to depression, which was keeping me from sleeping for weeks on end, I was also running a few miles a day into the

Cedar Valley to a local ranch to breathe in the distinctive aroma of their horses and their colts, the perfume of the sage, in the hope of a brief reprieve from my mood via endorphins and the beauty of these new equine lives.

In a fit of gallows humor, I noted in my research that Mormons were obliged to keep a year's worth of food in their pantries, and prepare their large families to withstand an upcoming, and much hoped for, Armageddon, when proof of their faith and righteousness could be witnessed by all the world. I was surrounded by chosen people who were darned certain to be raptured into heaven. Clearly I would remain forever as a green-gray heap of sinful misery on the crust of the earth when the end times came. All of this was very disorienting, given that I had been raised as an American to work hard, play by the rules, and succeed in whatever endeavor would be my bliss, even though I was female. That was the New York Way of Life.

I wasn't sure why the chosen people disliked me so much, but learned later that I wasn't anything special as an outsider when I learned the history of the Mountain Meadows Massacre, which occurred on September 11, 1857, quite close to where I was living. Modern life had blessed me; Utah now allegedly observed modern law with an old-fashioned twist, as I would find when dragged into court in Salt Lake City in 2008 under a "long arm of Utah law" statute—for "stalking" a downwinder hundreds of miles away from my home. This stalking slander was her legal contrivance to keep at bay a plagiarism and defamation lawsuit against her. She had written a play based without attribution or permission on my copyrighted book *American Ground Zero*, with my persona, a character in it, played with the grace of a Mafia moll in *The Sopranos*, despite my begging her not to do so. My begging was reinvented as stalking by her lawyer—much the same tactic used at Mountain Meadows, that the emigrants passing through were intent on killing the local Mormons and stealing their land, and should thus be massacred, women, children, all.

*(A film based on historical research of the Mountain Meadows Massacre, "September Dawn" (2007) starring Jon Voight, with Terence Stamp as Brigham Young, is highly recommended for its realistic revelation of hardships endured by pioneers who passed through Utah on the way to California.)*

Here I was, living downwind of the Nevada test site, where 128 nuclear bombs were exploded in the cool morning air, many detonations rendering fallout downwind comparable to Chernobyl, but twenty-five years later these gentle, faithful people were still awaiting Armageddon? I thought this through. We drove out of Deseret slowly down the main street at twenty miles per hour, the limit for the town.

"Who is this photographer? Do you know?" I asked.

"Richard Avedon," she replied. She pronounced it "Av-ee-don" with a French inflection.

Alrighty, then, I was finished. Project over, just go home.

Money, and thus class status, was key. It always is. As Robert Adams writes in "Why People Photograph":

> Money is important. It allows you the power over yourself—your time, your energy, the place you live, the tools you have, to be yourself, to get the job done.

I had already spent all my savings, had cast my bread upon the waters, and had sent out hundreds of funding applications for four years to no avail. I was living above Bradshaw Home & Auto on Main Street in Cedar City, where the previous tenant had left a mattress with a huge hole burned in the middle, which I had stuffed with newspapers and covered over with plastic before sheeting it, as well as a ripped black Naugahyde couch belching forth wads of puffy filler, which I was told had served as a haven for his two pet ferrets, their waste pellets awaiting me as malodorous proof. There were bats in the hallway, but I rather enjoyed them. I could see redrock cliffs from my bed, and PV#1 had lent me a broken old kitchen table to work on. My world was complete, or at least functional, until I heard the name Richard Av-ee-don.

She described his customary, sizeable entourage of a dozen assistants which supported him in photographing what would become his rather mean-spirited book which he thought would portray various representational "types" of the people of the West for New Yorkers, Manhattan natives, really, whose idea of anything west of the Hudson River was grossly, perversely ill-informed and pitiably condescending. He would give them precisely the book they needed to remain chauvinistic.

PV#1 was mistaken about the actual content of Av-ee-don's book; he was just cherry-picking the freakish entities of the Old West gone modern, much as Diane Arbus, another New Yorker who documented the non-*glitterati*, portrayed in photographs what other urban sophisticates might consider the dark side of the moon, in purportedly human terms.

I was becoming outraged. PV#1's sullen mood began to elevate, sensing, perhaps, my unnatural rise in blood pressure. Anyone could have seen my confusion and abject consternation. Apparently she enjoyed having "won," giving me a good shot to the knees. I knew I would lose everything I had worked for to the wealthy, estimable competition. When you're thirty-four, spending five years on a project that another photographer with a big signature and bigger bucks could take away in an instant, there can be no adequate sense of proportion when facing the loss of that much time and effort. Worse still, I had the feeling that Mr. Avedon could never have developed, in just a few luxurious, well-insulated trips from his Manhattan kingdom, the kind of emotion, even love, such as I was experiencing in my life downwind.

I was so young. So very young and *so very dumb*. Some years passed, and when Mr. Avedon's book was published, I looked through it with sadness. Of course, there were no downwinders in it, because downwinders are not "freaks," nor are they bleeding to the naked eye, or otherwise interesting enough to journalism, a world where "if it bleeds, it leads (Ledes)." Nor would they be notable to the art world, a milieu interested only in people as self important as it is. Downwinders were salt of the earth, hardworking citizens who were in the wrong place at the wrong time, no more or less. They were you and I at our most sweaty and sincere, untarnished, at least at that time, by the American craving for fame and celebrity. They worked hard, loved their families, BIG families, and played by the rules, BIG rules. And so it turned out that I had nothing to fear from Mr. Av-ee-don and his cadre of fawning assistants, so long as I kept both journalism and the art world far from mind. I understood within months of living in Utah that it is much easier to succeed at ignoring the art world once you leave Manhattan, a gift of psychic and intellectual freedom that I had not known before, my only nourishment.

About five years after that memorable trip to Salt Lake with PV#1, I made an appointment to photograph one of the subjects of the federal study conducted at the University of Utah of downwinders for thyroid disease, and met Della Truman from West Jordan, Utah, then a southern suburb of Salt Lake City. Years of "thyroid storms," as her son, Jay, described them, had accelerated her metabolism to the point where her life was unbearable. The nodules on her thyroid had thus created chronic heart problems due to her chaotic metabolism, and other health difficulties. Despite periodic checkups at the University of Utah Medical Center scheduled by the doctors conducting the federally funded studies, she was clinically inspected but never helped in any palliative way. Her face told the story of her life: there was not a millimeter of it that was not heavily creased, crosshatched in deep furrows from her years of excruciating pain. Never had I seen a face so distorted by suffering in a woman so young.

Previously, while living in Enterprise, Utah, a tiny, spartan town on the Nevada border directly downwind of the test site, she had also suffered many miscarriages, so prevalent in downwind communities. To look into Della Truman's eyes was to know just what a life of suffering and betrayal could do to the human spirit.

*(Her son, now officially known as "Preston" Truman, and PV#2, was born in this hardscrabble town where the fallout clouds burned the tops of the trees as they passed through. He had, as a teen, developed a type of lymphoma, Walderstrom's disease, thyroid problems, and the emotional armor and ruthless sense of overentitlement that I had seen in many victims who used their situation for personal gain. This psychological reconfiguring of downwinders and the effect it had on their emotional*

*lives and stability was worthy of more research, but that would have to be postponed for another book, the one that I am writing now. The bomb had created its own distinct paranoia, it seemed, because those betrayed in the downwind areas had believed so blindly in their government, thought of themselves as more patriotic than anyone, and the cognitive dissonance of being both "chosen people" and murdered by a God-inspired entity seemed an entirely new demographic to me, worthy of its own book, minus photographs, and more anonymous. I would not be naming names, to spare those I interviewed any embarrassment.)*

**"Preston Jay Truman,"** from *American Ground Zero: The Secret Nuclear War* (© Carole Gallagher 1993–2009)

Truth stranger than fiction, Mr. Avedon had also come to visit Della Truman, hoping to photograph a "stereotypical downwinder" for his book. He almost had his way with her, I was told by her son, until Mrs. Truman heard snide whispers among the assistants and Mr. Av-ee-don about photographing "that old prune." Dignity intact despite years of suffering and betrayal, Della Truman decided that she would never again in her lifetime allow anyone to photograph her. While visiting her, and hearing this from her son while she sat stone cold before me, I decided that Della Truman deserved all the respect from me that she had not received from either Mr. Av-ee-don's photo circus or her government. I visited her again and again over the next few years, hoping to hear more about her life "under the cloud," but never would ask to take her portrait. I had finally understood in the most profound way the ancient maxim, that to take a photograph was to steal a person's spirit.

The human heart can only endure so much, physically and emotionally—this was the lesson learned best from the downwinders during my years living in Utah. When Jay Truman called me one morning to tell me that his mother had died, I knew instinctively that her heart had failed during one last "thyroid storm." True enough, he said, and he invited me to her funeral, the first and last I would attend while living downwind. I was honored to be included, but also extremely anxious, in deep conflict. Propriety and kindness dictated that I attend this Mormon religious service as a human being who had come to love this family, but professionalism demanded that I bring my cameras, while remembering the shame of Mr. Av-ee-don's insult.

Thus the joy of being a documentarian: the gift of time. Shortly after I accepted the invitation to the funeral and burial, Jay asked me, as a favor to him and to his family, to photograph his mother as she lay in her casket. I packed all kinds of cameras, even my heavy studio 4 × 5 view camera, yet I felt, as I always do, that bringing studio lights or using a strobe would be too disrespectful, attracting unwanted attention in the mortuary. This limited the possibilities but, as ever, the true problem would lie deep within me, making an image of a woman so humiliated in her own lifetime as to forbid any photographs to be taken of her. Would she appear mangled by her life's last struggle? Would there be any possibility at all for me to portray her with respect, without exploitation, somehow capturing the spirit of the person she had been before the bomb's fallout had transformed her, body and soul?

I have since learned that anxieties such as these are purely neurotic fantasies, and the reality of making an image is actually quite simple. Della Truman was laid to rest in traditional Mormon garb, a simple white wedding garment with a thin veil over her face and body. Beneath this I observed a kind of apron, sewn and embroidered by her closest female relatives, of green fig leaves, the emblem of innocence and virtue to which all Mormon women aspired. In this quaint and lovely clothing Della Truman would meet her heavenly father, at long last.

In all my anxiety, however, I had set up my camera on the tripod before even looking into Della Truman's casket. It was very dark in the mortuary, with no additional lighting possible. The white of her bridal gown against the white satin of the casket created a bright aura, blending all the tones into a harmony of whites and grays that seemed to glisten. No technical issues to disturb me, I finally prepared myself to look at her face, but what I saw astonished me. In life, her face had been chaotic, riven with deep lines, leaving not a single smooth patch of skin. Now, at peace in death, her skin was luminous, entirely free of wrinkles, smooth as that of a young girl.

In a lifetime, any photographer not totally asleep at the wheel will take tens of thousands of photographs, maybe more. Many of these will have a backstory never told. Some images will be much beloved, others will never be printed larger than a contact sheet, and for good reason! Being a photographer is a gamble, and a life in photography is by its nature absolutely against all odds.

My photograph of Della Truman at her final rest will always be my favorite, not only because of the lessons I learned in obtaining it, technical and personal, over many years, but also because it taught me to appreciate so many things about a photographer's life: the harsh leavening of uncertainty, the foolishness of professional competitiveness, and the power of perseverance and love even in a culture, as our own today, where the banality of evil is our daily bread. And had I been as aggressive and as rude, or as rich and famous, as Mr. Av-ee-don had allegedly been, this image of Mrs. Truman would never have been created.

Near the end of my time downwind, I experienced an uptick of the harassment—professional, physical, and emotional—that had made my seven years in Utah so impossible. In the middle of the night for about three months, my phone would ring numerous times, and I would pick up the call because my father was becoming increasingly ill and frail back home in New York. Sometimes muffled voices threatened me, sometimes it would be just a hang-up and then a few more calls; it was enormously distressing, and the insomnia it created was ruinous to my work and health. I asked the police to help me and in late 1989, they did. I was told I could have my phone tapped to see who was calling me, and then get a civil stalking injunction to make it stop.

1988 was the year that the MacArthur Foundation awarded funding to finish my project, and while I finally had the financial freedom to finish the book, the jealousy and outright harassment from other artists, activists, PVs, and particularly the men where I was teaching at the University of Utah, was palpable and devastating. Yet never would I have guessed, thanks to the Salt Lake City police, that the perpetrators of this nightly agenda of phone calls and threats lay

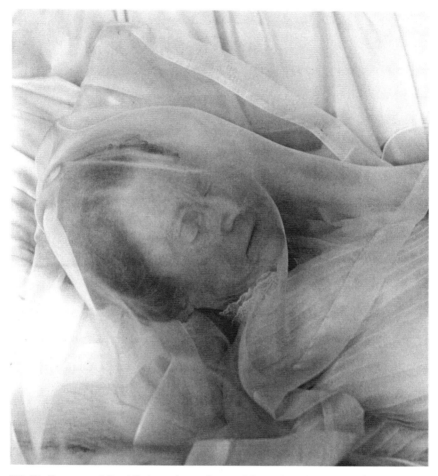

**"Della Truman at Rest,"** *American Ground Zero: The Secret Nuclear War* **(©
Carole Gallagher 1993–2009)**

at the feet of Preston Truman and his trusty sidekick and lifelong companion,
Monte Bright. I knew I had to go home to New York to be safe, peaceful, and
productive now, but I still had so much work to finish in the downwind states.
It would be professionally tricky to use the legal system against any downwinder,
and even a restraining order would cause hard feelings. I didn't know how I
could finish my field work and survive emotionally, and the idea of commuting
from New York to Utah a few times a year also felt stifling and inadequate—and
expensive! But it was my only alternative, a 2,300-mile commute, one-way, work
for a month while living in a safe place with friends, and another 2,300 mile

commute home. Nevertheless I was absolutely resistant to the idea of leaving Utah before my work was done. It felt like such a cop-out.

After photographing Della Truman, and years later discovering a darker truth about her son than I might have imagined, I had a beautiful early morning dream while sleeping on the floor of my North Main Street apartment in Salt Lake City. I had become accustomed to falling asleep in the living room on a yoga mat in front of an enormous picture window which faced west to the Great Salt Lake, a view I had come to cherish over the years. I could see tremendous storms approaching from fifty miles to the west, and often watched a pale yellow moon set in the early morning hours behind the peaks of Antelope Island. That was the bright side of being an insomniac, watching the night sky. I kept hummingbird feeders hanging outside the other open window, where I could hear the birds buzz and trill as they fed while the sun rose from behind the Wasatch Mountains and whistles blew at the nearby train yards. That morning I dreamed that a strong wind blew me back home to New York, and I could feel the force of that warm wind on my face in the moments before awakening. I opened my eyes to see a hummingbird hovering a few inches above my nose, watching me, perhaps attracted to the color of my pink nightgown or red duvet cover. I don't know why Della Truman came immediately to mind, such a very tiny woman in her shining white casket, as I gazed at that hummingbird, but I thanked both of them for what I hoped was a reprieve from seven years of trauma and local ill will in Utah, a return to my home on Mercer Street, my fieldwork almost done. She knew her son better than I did, and it seemed that she released me from him, and all the other professional victims, whose slander and emotional dishonesty had created such turmoil, such distress requiring so much of my energy to keep an aura of false calm while I worked in "the cloak of invisibility" to document their secret nuclear war all those years.

Many years later, I learned from a reporter from one of the local television stations in Salt Lake City, Michael Rawson, that Jay Truman had told him and many others that I "hated Mormons," and that I was an operative for the CIA or the FBI. He was also fond of telling anyone who would listen that I had encouraged every foundation *not* to fund him, and thus, "Nobody has done more to harm the cause of downwinders than Carole Gallagher." Small wonder I was so reviled! None of it was true, yet I had lived for seven years in a state with the highest statistics for fraud in the country, highest level of prescribed anti-depressants and sedatives, the highest levels of child sexual abuse, and plenty of pretty creepy paranoia to go around. I supposed that people would believe just about anything if this kind of place represented itself as the Promised Land, filled to the gills with "white and delightsome unto the Lord" chosen people. If I wasn't blonde or blue-eyed enough, fine. If I was a brown-eyed brunette and looked

Jewish enough to have people come uncomfortably close to me many times, look at my nose, scrunch up their faces in disdain and ask, "Are you Gee-you-ish?" then I had learned all I wanted to know about ignorant bigotry and developed a thicker skin. Rural Utahns still called African Americans "niggers" completely without guile—reason enough for me to join the Salt Lake City chapter of the NAACP. But I was no war correspondent, and I didn't want any more war-level bigotry, hatred, physical assaults, office break-ins, threats and petty slander as my daily bread. One morning I discovered a bullet placed just outside the door of my apartment, reminiscent of sleazy Mafioso death threats. I packed up the entire three tons of paperwork, negatives, and research I had collected and put it in a moving van. The next day I headed home to Manhattan in my truck, K. D. Lang singing a song of solace about "western skies" on the stereo, and told almost no one I was leaving. The hummingbirds and Della Truman were on my side, and I trusted their message as I've never trusted anything in my life. The message was: Get the hell out! You've got the book you came for! Go home!

Much as I may try, eighteen years later, at fifty-eight, I am content that I may never again do anything in my life so well or so deeply moving and trans-formative as that book, but somehow I feel I have Della Truman's blessing on my life to "keep on keepin' on," as they say in the Marines, her encouraging, generous spirit hovering above my head like that tiny, whirring hummingbird, its fragrant breeze of unrequited love on my face.

"There can be no great disappointment where there is no great love."

So thank you, Mr. Av-ee-don. I could never have done this without you. And Mrs. Truman . . . I cannot thank you enough.

# Note

1. This quotation is a modern paraphrase of what Bacon wrote in Latin in his 1620 work *Novum Organum,* Book I, Section CXXIX. A convenient version of the original is in James Spedding, et al., eds., *The Works of Francis Bacon*, vol. I (London: Longman's & Company, 1872), 222. For a slightly different modern translation, see Hugh C. Dick, ed., *Selected Writings of Francis Bacon* (New York: The Modern Library, 1955), 539. The version that Lange favored I found in Milton Meltzer, *Dorothea Lange: A Photographer's Life* (New York: Farrar, Straus, and Giroux, 1978), 79.

# CHAPTER 9

# Target Earth

## THE ATOMIC BOMB AND THE WHOLE EARTH

*Robert Jacobs*

> Once a photograph of the Earth, taken from outside, is available—once the sheer isolation of the Earth becomes known—a new idea as powerful as any in history will be let loose.
>
> Fred Hoyle, 1950[1]

# Introduction

The image of the whole Earth is one of the most ubiquitous visual icons of the late twentieth century. It is everywhere, on books, posters, advertisements, packaging, and all over the World Wide Web. It is the descendent of such essential early tools of human imagining as the map and the globe. But the whole Earth is a radical reformulation of those older tools. It is a new tool that opens modern humans to a new perspective about the relationship of the individual to the planet, and to all of the other creatures living on the planet, especially the other people.

The history of the modern visual image of the whole Earth derives from photographs taken of the Earth from space. Much as our ability to see deeply into space has completely revised our ideas about the nature of the universe around us, our ability to see our home planet from space has fundamentally revised our concepts of the nature of the planet on which we live.

Photographs of the whole Earth entered culture in the late 1960s as a result of the development of satellites and manned space travel. But in this chapter I will argue that the visual content of the icon of the whole Earth actually emerged several decades earlier. Before there were color photographs of the Earth from space, the visual image of the Earth as whole was first expressed in a manner we

**Figure 9.1.   The Whole Earth, Taken by Apollo 17 (December 7, 1972)²**

would come to associate with this icon by editorial cartoonists in direct and immediate response to the use of atomic bombs on the Japanese cities of Hiroshima
and Nagasaki in 1945.

These cartoonists grasped, as did others, that the threat posed to human
civilization by the invention and manufacture of nuclear weapons threatened the
people of the Earth in a holistic way. That it threatened the very existence of life
on Earth. In December 1945, Harlow Shapley, director of the Harvard College
Observatory, wrote in *Parent's Magazine*:

> We must educate ourselves and our children to the facts that science
> and commerce suddenly have brought to us the One World epoch
> . . . let us thoroughly understand that we cannot buy our way to

political security for ourselves and our children with money. The medium of exchange is not dollars, pounds or rubbles, but units of planet-wide understanding, coins of good will. . . . But this Golden Age will come only if we can become good neighbors all over the surface of this small but attractive planet.[3]

Here in December 1945, Shapley recognized, as did many others at the time, that the threat posed by these new weapons was a holistic threat, and the response to them must also be holistic. Among the most holistic responses to the advent of nuclear weapons was the emergence of the image of the whole Earth, an icon that could convey these complex ideas about the nature of the modern atomic dilemma (and the later environmental crisis) in an instant. I believe that the first articulation of this idea as a visual icon did not have to wait for photographs of the Earth from space; they were already in the minds, and then in the published works of a broad range of editorial cartoonists by the end of the first week of the Atomic Age. While the image of the whole Earth had to wait for cameras to be sent up into space on rockets, the content of the icon blew in on the wind along with the fallout from Hiroshima and Nagasaki.

# Whole Earth Image Content

As a visual icon, the image of the whole Earth as seen from space communicates a very complicated set of ideas in a very simple image. This iconography centers on the way in which the image unifies many of the complexities of human society through the idea of wholeness. Let's examine the most important of these iconographic statements.

The image of the whole Earth shows a world without the political borders that have for so long defined the way most people envision the world. This old model is of a world of divisions: divisions between countries, religions, races and ethnicity, economic philosophies, and political systems. In the image of the whole Earth there are no visible borders on the landmasses. The only real division visible on the Earth's surface is between land and sea. It reinforces the idea that the borders we have envisioned between our societies are largely artificial and of human construction. It tells a story about us all being from the same place.

The other border that comes into sharp relief in this image is the separation between the beautiful blue planet and the cold darkness of space. This aspect of the image emphasizes the fragility of life on Earth. The Earth is seen as a small outpost, a delicate planet enveloped by a thin atmosphere in which all of life exists; this is cast against the immensity and emptiness of space. It almost seems as if the iciness of space could swallow the Earth up if we are not lucky, and careful.

Rather than an eternal sense of timelessness, the Earth appears to be precarious when cast against such emptiness, giving it a sense of vulnerability. The maintenance of life on this planet would appear to take constant vigilance against much more powerful forces. It suggests the need for the careful balancing of complex factors as necessary for continued life here.

What these other values combine to ultimately suggest is that all of the creatures alive on Earth share a single common destiny. Apart from our individual destinies, when one considers the long-term welfare of this fragile planet in the darkness of space, either the planet will survive, along with its inhabitants, or it will perish. This is perhaps the most powerful and profound aspect of the iconography of the whole Earth. If a nuclear war were to break out, the borders so important to humans, between the two sides of the conflict, between combatant and noncombatants, are seen to be illusory. The contamination of radioactive fallout would not stop at the borders that humans draw on maps: the planet as a whole would be affected. And in this sense, the victims of the nuclear war would be all of the inhabitants of Earth. The *victim* of a nuclear war would be the Earth itself.

Another significant thing to emerge out of such a perspective is the sense of the Earth as a single ecosystem. Whereas previously people may have thought of themselves as living in the mountains, or on an island, or on the plains, consideration of the whole Earth makes one realize that the problems that affect one segment of the ecosystem may affect all the others. An enlargement of the sense of self accompanies this realization—whereas previously may identify as a citizen of a certain country, tribe, or religion, looking at the image of the whole Earth can work to change one's social calibration to a more global perspective. Such a perspective is at the root of the debate about global warming. People are aware that their efforts to make changes will not succeed if some countries work against those changes. The solutions must be holistic, systemic, and not restricted by the artificial borders of human mapmaking or voting.

# History of the Whole Earth as a Visual Icon

The image of the whole Earth is taken from photographs of the Earth as seen from space. These photographic images have a specific history, but first, let's look at the roots of our concept of the Earth from space.

The first rendering of images of the Earth was in the form of globes and maps. Early philosophers in classical Greek society envisioned the cosmos as a celestial sphere surrounding the Earth, which was borne on the shoulders of the Titan, Atlas. In the Middle Ages, the era of exploration heralded by Columbus's landing in the Americas led to a burst of globe manufacturing in

Europe. "The period of the great discoveries produced a tremendous upsurge of interest in geography, which went hand in hand with making globes," writes Dutch cartographer P. C. J. van der Krogt, "Terrestrial globes and world-maps with accompanying descriptions were *the* means of making the results of these discoveries known."[4]

This era was marked by the production of two styles of globes, the celestial globe (like the one on Atlas's shoulders) that was used by astronomers, and the terrestrial globe, which turned the gaze back from space and looked towards the Earth. The terrestrial globes of this period along with those produced over the next several centuries were a constantly changing tableau that reflected current knowledge about the structure of the Earth's surface. But once the basics of the Earth's geophysical structure were established, globes continued to undergo frequent changes: the primary role of globes focused on the display of current political boundaries between human nations. "Every time world boundaries change, one of the biggest little businesses in the country gets a boost," asserted a 1951 article in *Business Week*.[5] That was because shifting political borders meant that globes must be updated to reflect and to emphasize the current divisions. Globes would have different colors for nations that bordered each other so that the border might stand out more dramatically. There were always bold black lines to define those borders, and, in the case of globes made in the United States, thinner lines to divide the nation into states, so that even minor political boundaries were highlighted.

This model of the Earth first began to change with the advent of rocket technology. Not long after humans launched rockets into space, they began to attach cameras to them in order to photograph the Earth. This was done primarily to study weather patterns on Earth, and assist weather prediction and military reconnaissance.

Some of the earlier manned and unmanned space rockets took photographs of the Earth that were published in popular magazines. Typically these were taken too close to the Earth to show the whole blue ball that is familiar to us now. Often these early pictures would show the curvature of the Earth in the grainy black and white photographs. The image below shows a still photograph from the very first television pictures taken in space on April 1, 1960, by a satellite for TIROS-1 (Television Infrared Observation Satellite Program), an early NASA effort to gage the usefulness of satellite observations of the Earth.

Photography was an afterthought on the early manned space missions. John Glenn was the first American astronaut to bring a camera into space on his historic first orbit of the Earth on Mercury 6 (February 20, 1962). This was an Ansco Autoset 35mm camera (made by Minolta) that was purchased at a drug store near the launch site at Cape Canaveral in Florida not long before take off.[6]

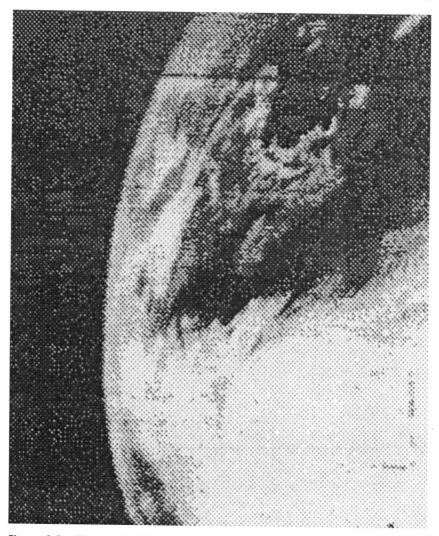

**Figure 9.2.   Figure #X, TIROS-1 (April 1, 1960)[7]**

Subsequent to this, photos of the Earth from space became more common, yet tended to focus on showing familiar landmasses from space. Such photographs might show the horn of Africa, or the Florida peninsula; features familiar to readers from a lifetime of seeing maps and globes, now seen as actual photographs from above. This perspective tended to reinforce previously held images about the nature of the Earth rather than to challenge them, as Fred Hoyle's 1950 statement in the opening quote encouraged.

Hoyle's idea sprouted one day in the mind of a counterculture visionary (though the Hoyle quote was unknown to him at the time). Stewart Brand had been a member of the legendary 1960s crew the Merry Pranksters led by Ken Kesey and Ken Babbs, and had been an organizer of the Trips Festivals, held in 1965–1966. Brand recounts that in February of 1966, he was doing LSD and sitting on the roof of his apartment building in San Francisco's North Beach and looking at the San Francisco skyline. Dwelling on a point made at a Buckminster Fuller lecture that he had recently attended in Santa Fe, New Mexico, Brand noticed that the buildings were not parallel, because the Earth beneath them was curved. Brand remembered that Fuller claimed that, "people perceived the Earth as flat and infinite, and that that was the root of all their misbehavior. Now, from my altitude of three stories and one hundred miles, I could *see* that it was curved, think it, and finally feel it."[8] Brand expanded his initial vision from that seed-point, realizing that "the more altitude I got, the more I would see that curvature until the curvature closed and you saw the whole thing."[9]

Still tripping, Brand conceived of making buttons to promote this vision. At first he phrased his statement, "Take a photograph of the entire Earth." But this didn't feel right. He didn't like the word "entire." Then the phrase came to him, "Why haven't we seen a photograph of the whole Earth yet?" Thus coining the term that would have almost as much cultural clout as the image it described. Brand had several hundred of the buttons manufactured and he put them on a sandwich board and began to sell them at Sather Gate of the University of California at Berkeley. He sent them to NASA administrators, members of Congress, Soviet scientists and diplomats, Buckminster Fuller, Marshall McLuhan, and UN officials. He eventually brought his sandwich board to other college campuses, selling his buttons at Stanford, Harvard, Columbia, and MIT.

The very first photographs that show the whole Earth as we now recognize it were taken during the historic Apollo 8 mission in December of 1968. This was the first rocket that circled the Moon and returned to Earth. When it passed behind the Moon, it was cut off from radio contact with the Earth for four minutes, a tense time for NASA scientists and for the huge television audience watching at home.

After the third revolution, a historic moment occurred. It was early evening on Christmas Eve Day. The astronauts showed the television audience what they could see from their window, a half Earth rising above the lunar surface. Then the three astronauts made one of the most historic readings in modern history, "For all the people on Earth," started astronaut William A. Anders, "the crew of Apollo 8 has a message we would like to send you." The three astronauts then took turns reading the first eight verses of the book of Genesis, and when they had finished, crew commander Frank Borman concluded, "And from the crew

**Figure 9.3. Stewart Brand's Whole Earth Button, 1966[10]**

of Apollo 8, we close with good night, good luck, a Merry Christmas, and God bless all of you—all of you on the good Earth."[11]

Poet Archibald MacLeish wrote about the color images coming back from Apollo 8 on the front page of the *New York Times* the next day, Christmas 1968: "To see the earth as it truly is: small and blue and beautiful in that eternal silence where it floats, is to see ourselves as riders on the earth together, brothers on that bright loveliness in the eternal cold. Brothers who know they are truly brothers."[12]

Among the most widely reprinted photographs from that historic space mission was one known as the "Earthrise" photograph taken with the Moon in the foreground. This was important, according to Brand, because it showed the "clearly living Earth over the edge of a clearly dead planet."[13]

**Figure 9.4. "Earthrise" Photo from Apollo 8 (December 1969)**

This image was virtually ever-present for Americans in the next few years as it was reprinted on a U.S. postage stamp, and was also used by CBS new anchor Walter Cronkite as the backdrop to his set for several years.

Among the first artists to use the image of the whole Earth as a powerful visual iconic tool was Stanley Kubrick in his 1968 masterpiece, *2001: A Space Odyssey*.[14] This film, among the most philosophically speculative and visually striking movies ever made, has several scenes that feature the partial images of the whole Earth that were available to Kubrick at the time of production. For many of the viewers who saw *2001* in the theaters, this was their first exposure to this powerful visual icon.

Kubrick uses the image of the whole Earth as a backdrop to scenes set on the Moon early in the movie, but the most dramatic use of the icon was in the film's conclusion.[15] In this scene, astronaut Dave Bowman has gone through the abstract series of moments that follow his attempts to land on the "monolith" orbiting Jupiter, and sending radio signals to some unknown distant destination. Bowman's journey into the monolith takes him through a series of time and space distorting changes, including a journey through his own life from infancy to old age and death. Bowman is then reborn as the Star Child, which appears to be the next step in the evolution of human consciousness. The Star Child is depicted as a fetus floating in space in an amniotic sack. The Star Child turns to consider the whole Earth floating in front of it, both glowing a bright blue-white. The two appear as newborn versions of Man and Earth, face-to-face, ready to be born into a future of unthinkable possibilities.[16]

*2001* was widely heralded as a film about "the future of humanity," and among the visual tools that informed viewers that they were looking at the future was the image of the whole Earth as seen from space.

Also in 1968, Stewart Brand would publish his counterculture classic, *The Whole Earth Catalog*.[17] This virtual guide to the counterculture lifestyle of the 1960s would go through several editions (selling 2.5 million copies for all editions combined), and win the National Book Award for its 1972 edition. In his 2005 commencement speech at Stanford University, Apple Computer cofounder Steve Jobs said of the *Whole Earth Catalog*, "It was sort of like Google in paperback form, thirty-five years before Google came along."[18] *The Whole Earth Catalog* put a photograph taken by a satellite in 1967 on its cover, and also put the phrase "whole Earth" into public discourse. It began with the statement, "We are as gods and might as well get used to it."[19]

One of the immediate impacts of the entry of the image and concept of the whole Earth into popular culture was Earth Day. The first Earth Day was celebrated on April 22, 1970, in many different cities in the United States and several other countries. This was a day intended to heighten awareness of environmental issues in the public mind, and also to "celebrate the Earth." Twenty million Americans took part in the first Earth Day, on hundreds of college campuses, high schools, and city parks.[20]

Stewart Brand had gotten many of his ideas, and much of his inspiration for the *Whole Earth Catalog* from the work of Buckminster Fuller. Fuller was a technologist, and a visionary who held many patents, had invented the geodesic dome, and had a knack for reframing traditional concepts. Fuller had spoken for years of what he called "Spaceship Earth." British economist Barbara Ward paraphrased Fuller's ideas in her presentation at the sixth series of the George B. Pegram Lectures at Columbia University in 1965. Ward titled her lecture series "Spaceship Earth," after Fuller's phrase, and explained his perspective that:

> The most rational way of considering the whole human race today is to see it as a ship's crew of a single spaceship on which all of us, with a remarkable combination of security and vulnerability, are making our pilgrimage through infinity. Our planet is not much more than the capsule within which we have to live as human beings if we are to survive the vast space voyage upon which we have been engaged for hundreds of millennia—but without yet noticing our condition.[21]

Fuller himself added another critical perspective to the spaceship concept: "Spaceship Earth was so extraordinarily well invented and designed that to our knowledge humans have been on board it for two million years not even knowing that they were on board a ship. And our spaceship is so superbly designed as to be able to keep life regenerating on board despite the phenomenon, entropy, by which all local physical systems lose energy."[22]

Here Fuller was foreshadowing the theory that would come to provide much of the intellectual framework for the ideas encoded in the content of the whole Earth icon; the "Gaia hypothesis" of James Lovelock. A consultant at the Jet Propulsion Laboratories of the California Institute of Technology in Pasadena during the early and mid 1960s, Lovelock was working on the problem of formulating methods to determine if there was life on Mars. The method that Lovelock and others designed involved the use of atmospheric analysis as a means of life-detection. This theory was based on the idea that a key outward sign of the presence of life on a planet would be a local reduction of entropy:

> The design of a universal life-detection experiment based on entropy reduction seemed at this time to be a somewhat unpromising exercise. However, assuming that life on any planet would be bound to use fluid media—oceans, atmosphere, or both—as conveyor belts for raw materials and waste products, it occurred to me that some of the activity associated with concentrated entropy reduction within a living system might spill over into the conveyor belt regions and alter their composition. The atmosphere of a life-bearing planet would thus become recognizably different from that of a dead planet.[23]

Lovelock and his colleague Dian Hitchcock then proceeded to use the Earth as a model to test the theory: "Our results convinced us that the only feasible explanation of the Earth's highly improbable atmosphere was that it was being manipulated on a day-to-day basis from the surface, and the manipulator was life itself."[24]

Turning this technique to an analysis of Mars, it was easy to conclude from a simple atmospheric analysis performed from Earth, that there was no life currently on Mars. But what interested Lovelock was no longer Mars, but the Earth. Lovelock began to focus on this problem in 1966 while on a grant from Shell Research Limited. Lovelock's work led him to the:

> development of the hypothesis that the entire range of living matter on Earth, from whales to viruses, and from oaks to algae, could be regarded as constituting a single living entity, capable of manipulating the Earth's atmosphere to suit its overall needs and endowed with faculties and powers far beyond those of its constituent parts . . . that

the Earth's atmosphere is actively maintained and regulated by life on the surface, that is, by the biosphere.[25]

Lovelock felt that this single entity (life, the biosphere) needed a name. His neighbor in Wiltshire the Nobel Prize–winning novelist William Golding, "recommended that the creature be called Gaia, after the Greek Earth goddess also known as Ge, from which root the sciences of geography and geology derive their names. . . . By now a planet-sized entity, albeit hypothetical, had been born."[26]

Lovelock's Gaia hypothesis caught the fascination of the public during the 1980s, and by the 1990s it had become a common name in the American environmental movement for the Earth. While few could cite the basis for the theory, many could sum up its implications as describing "mother Earth," or the "Earth goddess." The implications of the Gaia hypothesis gave seeming scientific grounding to the wholeness many had perceived in looking at the image of the whole Earth. Certainly of the many books published each year with the word "Gaia" in the title, few do not have the image of the whole Earth on their cover (although Lovelock's book did not).

# The Cartoons

On Sunday August 12, 1945, the *New York Times* published the following three editorial cartoons together, just as they are reprinted below.

All three cartoons, by three different cartoonists, offer visions of the impact of the new atomic bomb on human civilization. The first one is by cartoonist Lute Pease, who would win the Pulitzer Prize for editorial cartoons in 1949. It shows a devilish character named "Future Threat of War" being restrained from

**Figure 9.5.** *The New York Times* **(August 12, 1945)**[27]

hammering the Earth by a hand named "Control of Atomic Power"; the caption reads, "For a perfect earth." The statement here is that the future of war threatens the Earth as a whole, and that only control of atomic power can keep that threat in check.

The second one is by Sir David Cecil Low, originally of New Zealand, who worked in England. His cartoons were reprinted in the *New York Times* for almost a decade during the 1940s. This cartoon shows a man dressed as a scientist standing astride the Earth; he has a paper in his pocket titled "The Atom," and he is addressing a baby named "Humanity," and offering the baby a ball named "Life or Death." He tempts the baby with the question, "Baby play with nice ball?" The implication of this cartoon is clear; playing with "the atom" is a life or death game for immature humanity.

In the third cartoon a heavenly hand is striking the Earth with a lightning bolt named "Atomic Power." Here, the caption reads, "A new era in man's understanding." The cartoonist, Daniel Fitzpatrick, had won the Pulitzer Prize for editorial cartoons in 1926 and would win it again the year that this cartoon was printed, 1945.

Two pages further into that Sunday's *New York Times*, the first Sunday issue after the bombings of Hiroshima and Nagasaki, is another cartoon reprinted from *The Philadelphia Record*, drawn by cartoonist Jerry Doyle, among the most prolific cartoonists of the New Deal era. Here we see the giant hand named "Science" holding the Earth, which is named "The Future of Civilization," which Science is holding; the caption reads, "In the palm of his hand."[28] Much like in the iconography of the whole Earth, the fate of human civilization appears to be a collective one.

While the specific focus of the cartoons differs some, a striking continuity is their depiction of the Earth in all four cartoons. All of the cartoons show the Earth exhibiting visual content that perfectly foreshadows the later icon of the whole Earth. The emphasis on the Earth as a place of separate nations is gone. In each cartoon, the Earth is present as a single entity that is being forced to deal with the advent of atomic weapons. It is clear that in each, the destiny of all the people in the world is a common destiny. Even in the one cartoon in which landforms are depicted ("Baby play with nice ball"), the baby does not appear to be located in one specific country; there are no political borders seen, only the division between land and sea. In all of the cartoons, the Earth is a whole planet with a grid, a traditional means of establishing three-dimensionality in a two-dimensional image, but which also emphasized the continuity and equality of the different locations.

In early October of 1945 the *St. Louis Post-Dispatch* printed another cartoon by Daniel Fitzpatrick, in which the Earth hangs in space facing an equally large, and menacing sphere named "Atomic Bomb." The worried Earth looks at the

**Figure 9.6. "In the Palm of His Hand," Reprinted in the *New York Times* (August 12, 1945)[29]**

atomic bomb and asks it, "Well?" The Earth is seeking to determine its destiny at the hands of this new threat, which is as large and powerful as the whole planet itself. Again the planet is shown as having a grid, no individual nations, and in this case, it is depicted as a single being.

**Figure 9.7.   Cartoon by Daniel Fitzpatrick, Appeared in _St. Louis Post-Dispatch_ (October 10, 1945, 2C) (courtesy of the _St. Louis Post-Dispatch_ Editorial Cartoon Collection, the State Historical Society of Missouri)**[30]

As the world moved into the Atomic Age, such depictions became more common. The cartoonist Roy Justus originally published a cartoon in the _Minneapolis Star Journal_, which was reprinted in a March 1946 review of the booklet _One World or None_ in _The Saturday Review of Literature_ which shows the world depicted as a dog. This dog/world is named "World Politics" and seems helplessly under the control of its tail that is named "Atomic Bomb." The caption advises, "The tail does wag the dog."[31] Again the world has a grid and no borders between nations. It is a single being and the fate of all world politics is clearly a collective one.

Perhaps no Cold War cartoonist went further with this new visual construct of the world than did Herbert Block, better known as Herblock of the _Washington Post_. In a cartoon from 1949, a character that Block would use repeatedly (_Atom_), is seen as far bigger and more powerful than the puny Earth. Atom is holding the Earth, which has four birthday candles on it to symbolize the number of years since the bombing of Hiroshima, and is speaking to an Everyman who hangs his head while holding a newspaper that reports the United Nations as having given up on atomic control. Atom has a downright menacing look to his face as he asks the human, "Want to see me blow out everything with one puff?"[32]

The theme of nuclear weapons holding the world's collective fate in its hands was a continual theme in Herblock's work. A 1953 cartoon shows a hand, far bigger than the Earth, and far bigger than Atom's hands, named "H-bomb." This hand is tossing the world up and down in its hand like a ball. Again, the Earth is a globe with a grid rather than nations, and it would be hard to imagine that the fate of any part of it would be different than the fate of any other part in the hands of such a threat.[33]

There were political movements contemporary to these cartoons that helped to inform and give substance to their iconography. Not long after the bombing of Hiroshima and Nagasaki the world government movement emerged as a direct response to the new weapons. Many social leaders, and especially scientific leaders, believed that a single world government was the only way to avoid an arms race and eventual nuclear war between two or more competing nations.

An example of this advocacy can be seen in the 1946 booklet, *One World or None*. This booklet, published through the Federation of American Scientists, included contributions from Shapley, Eintein, Leo Szilard, and many others who had become well known with the publicity following the news from Hiroshima. Part of the piece written by the "Father of the Atomic Bomb," J. Robert Oppenheimer, amply illustrates the arguments of the book:

> The vastly increased powers of destructions that atomic weapons give us have brought with them a profound change in the balance between national and international interests. The common interest of all in the prevention of atomic warfare would seem immensely to overshadow any purely national interest, whether of welfare or of security. At the same time it would seem of most doubtful value in any long term to rely on purely national methods of defense for insuring security. . . . The true security of this nation, as of any other will be found, if at all, only in the collective efforts of all.[34]

But while such efforts as the drive towards one world government crumbled under the political and military realities of the Cold War, the icon of the whole Earth continued to grow and be nurtured in American culture until it burst, in full bloom, onto the televisions, the postage stamps, and into the minds of Americans everywhere in the late 1960s, and people all over the world through the end of the century.

# Conclusions: Target Earth

I have so far collected dozens of such editorial cartoons printed between August of 1945 and 1959, all of them pre-dating even the oldest of the photographs of the Earth from space. In these cartoons, the Earth is depicted, not as the whole Earth we would recognize, with all of its attributes of life—the "blue bubble of air" that Archibald MacLeish spoke of on the front page of the *New York Times* on Christmas Day of 1968, the mythical goddess Gaia that would come to be associated with the stunning photographs of the whole Earth from space. What we see in these political cartoons is *Target Earth*, the Earth as the target of nuclear war. I would argue that this is the true origin of the icon we have come to know as the whole Earth, as the feared victim of nuclear weapons. The threat of nuclear war created a narrative of global death, of collective death, of a death that would encircle the globe, ignorant of the political borders we humans had imagined as so real, had in fact, fought and died for.

Considering the challenges of the new Atomic Age, Albert Einstein advised in 1945, "The situation calls for a courageous effort, for a radical change in our whole attitude, in the entire political concept. . . . Otherwise human civilization will be doomed."[35] In the arguments of such booklets as *One World or None*, there is the seed of the vision that blossomed into the beautiful icon we call the whole Earth. At first that vision seemed dark and apocalyptic, but once the idea was in our collective consciousness it started to grow: we began to see that this vision of the Earth as *one*, as *whole*, carried with it some very deep and ultimately empowering perspectives. The political cartoons studied above answered this call even as it was being made; they carried the first faint blue glow of the vision of the whole Earth forward into American society.

# Notes

1. Fred Hoyle, *The Nature of the Universe* (Oxford: Blackwell, 1950).

2. NASA website, www.nasa.gov/topics/earth/earthday/gall_whole_earth.html.

3. Harlow Shapley, "It Must Be Peace On Earth," *Parent's Magazine* (December 1945), 14.

4. P. C. J. van der Krogt, *Globi Neerlandici: The Production of Globes in the Low Countries* (Utrecht: HES Publishers, 1993), cartography.geog.uu.nl/research/phd/vandergrogt.html. This work is taken from van der Krogt's dissertation.

5. "Global Changes Benefit Globe Maker," *Business Week* (September 22, 1951), 98.

6. Gary H. Kitmacher, "Astronaut Still Photography During Apollo," www.hq.nasa.gov/office/pao/History/apollo_photo.html, August 2004. See also Neil Maher, "Shooting the Moon," *Environmental History* 9:3 (July 2004): 526-31.

7. NASA website, www.nasa.gov/vision/earth/features/bm_gallery_3.html.

8. Stewart Brand, "'Why Haven't We Seen the Whole Earth Yet?" in Lynda Obst, ed., *The Sixties: The Decade Remembered Now, By the People Who Lived It Then* (New York: Random House/Rolling Stone Press, 1977), 168.

9. Author interview, Stewart Brand, Sausalito, California, March 2006.

10. From webpage "Whole Earth Button," on Stewart Brand's website, web.me.com/stewartbrand/SB_homepage/WholeEarth_buton.html.

11. "Orbiting the Moon Christmas Eve," *Apollo Expeditions to the Moon.* www.hq.nasa.gov/office/pao/SP-350/ch-9-6.html.

12. Archibald MacLeish, "Bubble of Blue Air," *New York Times*, December 25, 1968, 1.

13. Author interview, Stewart Brand, Sausalito, California, March 2006.

14. Stanley Kubrick, director, *2001: A Space Odyssey*, 1968 (MGM). The film premiered in Washington, D.C., on April 2, 1968, two days before the assassination of Martin Luther King Jr.

15. Kubrick's photographs of the partial Earth were from the Air Force Cambridge Research Laboratories. See Jerome Agel, ed., *The Making of Kubrick's 2001* (New York: New American Library, 1970), 321.

16. In the novelized version of the film, Arthur Clarke includes a sequence at this point in which nuclear weapons are launched from the Earth, but the Star Child simply eliminates them, thus posing the new human as able to transcend the nuclear dilemma. See Arthur C. Clarke, *2001: A Space Odyssey* (New York: New American Library, 1968).

17. Stewart Brand, ed., *Whole Earth Catalog* (Menlo Park: The Portola Institute, 1968). See also Fred Turner, *From Counterculture to Cyberculture: Stewart Brand, the Whole Earth Network, and the Rise of Digital Utopia* (Chicago: University of Chicago Press, 2006).

18. Steve Jobs, "You've Got to Find What You Love," Stanford University commencement speech (June 15, 2005), news-service.stanford.edu/news/2005/june15/jobs-061505.html.

19. *Whole Earth Catalog*, 1.

20. Jack Lewis, "The Birth of the EPA," originally printed in the *EPA Journal* in November 1985, reprinted at epa.gov/35thanniversary/topics/epa/15c.htm.

21. Barbara Ward, *Spaceship Earth* (New York: Columbia University Press, 1966), 15. See also Barbara Ward and Rene Dubos, *Only One Earth: The Care and Maintenance of a Small Planet* (New York: W. W. Norton and Co., 1972).

22. Buckminster Fuller, *Operating Manual for Spaceship Earth* (Carbondale: Southern Illinois University Press, 1969), 50.

23. James Lovelock, *Gaia: A New Look at Life on Earth* (Oxford: Oxford University Press, 1979), 6

24. Ibid., 6.

25. Ibid., 9.

26. Ibid., 10. Golding would win the Nobel Prize in 1983.

27. *New York Times*, August 12, 1945, Sec. 4, 4E. They are reprinted there from three different newspapers, the first from *The Newark Evening News*, the second from the *New York Times* itself, and the third from the *St. Louis Post-Dispatch*.

28. *New York Times*, August 12, 1945, Sec. 4, 6E.

29. *New York Times*, August 12, 1945, Sec. 4, 6E.

30. *St. Louis Post-Dispatch*, Oct. 10, 1945, 2C.

31. *The Saturday Review of Literature*, March 30, 1946, 8.

32. Reprinted in, Herbert Block, *The Herblock Book* (Boston: Beacon Press, 1952), 33.

33. Reprinted in, Herbert Block, *Herblock's Here and Now* (New York: Simon and Schuster, 1955), 193.

34. Dexter Masters and Katharine Way, eds., *One World or None* (New York: Whittlesey House/McGraw Hill Book Co., 1946), 25.

35. Albert Einstein, "The War Is Won But Peace Is Not," *Essays in Humanism* (New York: Philosophical Library, 1950), 65–68. This is reprinted from an address originally presented at the Fifth Nobel Anniversary Dinner at the Astor Hotel, New York City, December 10, 1945.

# CHAPTER 10

# Nuclear Culture

*Judy Hiramoto*

## Nightmare in Paradise

I was born in Tokyo and raised in a bicultural Japanese American family in Hawaii when it was a paradise for children. We went swimming, relished juicy mangoes from our backyards, and had the run of a friendly neighborhood. However, I was terrified about the threat of nuclear war. The evening news showed Khrushchev with his shoe in hand telling Americans, "We will bury you!" I believed him. Why else would we practice duck-and-cover exercises at school diving under desks with our noses to the gritty floor, placing hands over our necks in total submission. Magazines and newspapers featured articles about fallout shelters. I tried to persuade my parents to build one in our backyard.

I had nightmares about nuclear war, often lying awake wondering when the attack would come. When I told Dad about my fear he replied that there was nothing to worry about because if the bomb hit us, we'd all die. Even as a child, I knew there was something very absurd and frightening about his response.

The possibility that Hawaii would be the target of a nuclear missile was not far-fetched to me as a child. After all, the Japanese bombed Pearl Harbor (only a short drive from my home), and Americans dropped atomic bombs on the Japanese. One night in December, the air-raid siren wailed. I sat terrified with my parents on the sofa, staring at the Christmas tree, fearing that at any minute we would be blown up into smithereens. That hour before the false alarm was announced was the longest one in my life.

I thought that since there may be no future there wasn't any point in planning a career or even having a fixed residence. I went to an alternative college and spent several semesters traveling. After graduation, extended residencies in South

America and Asia became a way of life. The nuclear threat was far from my mind in remote ruins of the Andes and temples in the Himalayas.

> There are no longer problems of the spirit. There is only the question: When will I be blown up?
>
> William Faulkner[1]

# Hiroshima

Japanese wondered why Hiroshima was a haven from bombing raids during much of World War II. They thought it was spared because it was a beautiful city, Truman's mother was living there, or because Americans had future plans for it. They wondered if Hiroshima was on American maps.[2]

In the installation $7 \times 7 = 49$ there are seven rows of ceramic wishbones with seven bones in each row. The numbers four and nine are considered bad luck since they contain Japanese homonyms for "death" and "suffering." Hence, too much luck turns into bad luck. The shape of wishbones resembles the Japanese character for "human." Each wishbone has a tag typed with synonyms for "hope," "search," "help," or "aid." Large pieces of broken wishbones are tagged with synonyms for "illness" and "mutilation" while smaller ones are marked with words relating to "death."

On the morning of August 6, 1945, a group of children took turns diving in the river for a bell. In the few seconds that a boy was submerged under water, the atomic bomb exploded. When he surfaced, his friends were dead, and life in Hiroshima had changed forever. In *Ground Zero* aerial views of Hiroshima similar to what the American pilots saw before and after the bombing are projected alternately on a circle of salt symbolizing purification. Survivors witnessed victims with skin hanging from their bodies walking in a circle like ghosts with outstretched arms similar to dancers in bon festivals that are held in August to commemorate deceased ancestors.[3] Silhouettes of ghostly folk dancers glazed with yellow paint float on the wall of the installation.

Americans changed the culture of war. Harry Truman stated, "[The atomic bomb] is used to wipe out women and children and unarmed people, and not for military uses,"[4] which is a violation of Article 22 of the Hague Convention.[5] General Dwight Eisenhower was opposed to using the atomic bomb because he felt that the Japanese were ready to surrender and did not want America to be the first to use such a devastating weapon.[6]

The vivid imagery in haiku written by witnesses of the atomic bombs inspired *Mu* (meaning "nothing") that expresses the last wishes of victims for water, a tomato, a slice of watermelon, and first aid. The wishes, often unfulfilled, are represented in this installation as objects placed high above the supplicants' hands. One of the haiku described ten fingers outstretched towards the sky holding nothing.[7]

Atomic bombs not only destroy cities but also breast tissue of young girls that is highly susceptible to radiation.[8] In the digital print, *Target*, the domed form on the left depicts the first atomic detonation at the Los Alamos test site. The middle image is a map of Hiroshima as the target city. The image on the right is an x-ray of cancerous breast tissue.

In *Mutant Spring* text on the sculpture expresses a mother's anguish for an innocent child who was exposed *in utero* to fatal doses of radiation.[9] Sickly green eggs represent radiated embryo. The empty basket suspended in the sky is lined with feathers alluding to deceased babies. A brown eye embedded in the ground represents victims gazing up at the sky while a blue eye has the American bird's eye view of the lurid mushroom cloud.

People in Hiroshima thought that plants would not grow here for seventy years. Miraculously some plants regenerated themselves a few weeks after the bombing, including morning glories, lilies, and feverfew, as John Hersey noted in *Hiroshima*. In *Garden for a Nuclear Age*, I cultivated these and other drought resistant plants in my San Francisco garden thinking that if a nuclear bomb exploded over this city, the garden would survive. A ton of pebbles represent the intersection of the Ota and Motoyasu Rivers that was the target for the bomb.

Glazed tiles with wishes of neighbors hang from a redwood fence. A six-year-old girl wished for apples. A high-school freshman hoped for lasting friendship. A neighbor wanted health, happiness, and harmony for the community. The garden provides a site where my neighbors and I remember Hiroshima through small personal rituals. On August 6 and 9, just as residents in Hiroshima and Nagasaki splash water on sidewalks, I water the garden and pebbles remembering victims who jumped into the river to escape heat and fire and those who wished for water to drink. Children visit the garden with their friends to tell them the story of Hiroshima and the garden.

*Memory Garden*, a mixed media work on paper, depicts a design plan for my garden layered with a map over it of the Hiroshima target area. The garden links my sense of place in San Francisco to Japanese history. Oppenheimer and many other scientists taught at California universities. The bomb was shipped from San Francisco to Tinian Island where it was loaded onto the plane, Enola Gay. Also, my family immigrated to Hawaii from a city near Hiroshima during the Meiji era. My sense of history is expanded when I think not only of Japanese American history, but also of a historic heritage that stretches back thousands of years.

# The Scientists

The digital image, *S-1* (which was a code name for America's atomic bomb project), is in the form of an exclamation mark. It contains acronyms, information and quotes regarding America's nuclear culture. Comments about the atomic bomb range from Rollo May's "You can't hate magic"[10] to Robert Oppenheimer's "The atomic bomb is shit."[11] A passage from George Orwell's novel *1984*, "Under the spreading chestnut tree / I sold you and you sold me," alludes to the recriminations of the scientists during the McCarthy era. Many scientists loved music, and several were talented musicians. During the countdown for the Trinity test, the music of Tchaikovsky's *Nutcracker Suite* could be heard on the airwaves. Excerpts from the score are placed on alternate lines with text. The triangle at the bottom is a detail from Vermeer's painting *Balance*, in which a woman holds empty scales representing a harmonious life as an antidote to the apocalypse depicted in a painting behind her.

I wondered about the nature of scientists who could make such a devastating and inhumane weapon. Debra Rosenthal and Hugh Gusterson describe their chilling mindset in a contemporary weapons laboratory. One scientist claimed, "Achieving an objective attitude is difficult. But once you get the knack, it becomes a hard habit to break."[12] Another claimed that he had only classified thoughts for the past four years.[13] The scientists devised complex devices to unleash atomic energy and yet the majority did not consider human or environmental consequences except in dry, abstract terms. When asked if there was any downside to the atomic bomb, Robert Oppenheimer sardonically responded, "The limitations lie in the fact that you don't want to be on the receiving end of one."[14]

I. I. Rabi, a physicist who worked on the atomic bomb project, said, "[The scientists] treated human beings as matter."[15] In *As Matter* the equation $E = mc^2$ is written repeatedly on the blackboard. Many of the scientists who worked on the atomic bomb project were also professors. "M" for matter is replaced with images of Japanese people, a corpse, and a shadow of a man imprinted on a wall. Victims are objectified in iconic photographs with close-up shots of their bodies rather than as individuals located in a particular time and place.

*x Killed y II* is composed of sentences in which the subject represented by "x" are men involved in the atomic bomb project from conception to detonation. They include Robert Oppenheimer, Franklin D. Roosevelt, Harry Truman, Secretary of State James F. Byrnes, General Leslie Groves, and the bomber pilot Paul Tibbetts. The object of the verb "killed" is "y," represented by Japanese women and children, guinea pigs, rabbits, chrysanthemums, and cities.

When scientists realized the magnitude of suffering caused by the atomic bomb, some of them became physically ill. Oppenheimer himself went to President Truman and claimed, "I have blood on my hands."[16] In *Oppenheimer's Sink*, the viewer is asked to imagine him washing his hands under the faucet gushing with water tinted red to represent blood and wiping them on the linen towel printed with names of Hiroshima victims, including Koreans and Americans. On each side of the sink are five rows of shelves that are part of the I-Ching hexagram, "Splitting Through." Bars of soap are imprinted with rationalizations for the use of the bomb ("defense," "democracy," "security," etc.) The sixth shelf at the top forms an unbroken line in this hexagram with bars of soap inscribed with effects of the atomic bomb including "mutilation," "incinerate," and "exterminate." A recording chants the names of victims.

I was surprised to find that Oppenheimer had many other interests in addition to physics. He read the *Bhagavad-Gita* in Sanskrit, enjoyed equestrian pursuits, and appreciated fine dining. His charisma motivated the best scientists to work at a grueling pace to complete the atomic bomb. However, his sharp and caustic wit gave him little patience with government officials who nursed grudges against him.

The Cold War and the McCarthy era brought with it a culture of secrecy and recriminations. Oppenheimer was accused of being disloyal to America when he was hesitant about supporting the hydrogen bomb project. In *x Sold y*, photographs depict friends, colleagues, and relatives who informed on each other during the Oppenheimer trial. Those who had negative testimony about Oppenheimer included nuclear physicist Edward Teller, General Leslie Groves, Atomic Energy Commissioners Lewis Strauss and Thomas E. Murray, FBI agent Boris Pash, J. Edgar Hoover, and Joseph McCarthy. Oppenheimer informed on his wife Kitty, his brother Frank, sister-in-law Jackie, friend Haakon Chevalier, and former students Rossi Lomanitz and David Bohm. In the painting *Sweet Land of Liberty*, photographs of the informers and the accused are paired as musical chords to the song that begins with "My country, 'tis of thee, sweet land of liberty, of thee I sing."

> When we beat the Nazis, we emulated them. I include myself. I became callous to death. I became willing to risk everything on war and peace. I followed my leaders enthusiastically and blindly. . . . We fought the war to stop fascism. But it transformed the societies that opposed fascism. They took on some of its attributes.
>
> Philip Morrison[17]

# America's Undeclared War

America conducted an undeclared war against its own citizens through the detonation of bombs at the Nevada test site. Fallout not only affected those living near the site but was carried by wind currents to places like Mandan, North Dakota, and upstate New York, where children's teeth showed a high concentration of radiation from drinking milk produced by cows who ingested grass dusted with fallout. Graphs documenting the amount of radio-nuclides in milk in Sacramento, St. Louis, and New York[18] inspired the sculpture *Milk Teeth*. The graphs are reproduced as white three-dimensional peaks placed in a pan of milk.

"I never saw a prettier sight; [the bomb blast] was like a letter from home or the firm handshake of someone you admire and trust," wrote Clint Mosher, a Utah columnist in 1951.[19] The naiveté of Americans in the 1950s regarding the dangers of fallout and radiation is expressed in *God Bless America*. Monochrome blue photographs double as music notes which are placed on a staff of red lines. Photographs document America's nuclear culture when news reporters passively sat as an audience to explosions near the test site, exposing themselves to radiation. A Miss Atomic contestant is depicted posing behind scanty cloud forms. Other photographs depict cheerful families in fallout shelters, children obediently practicing duck-and-cover exercises, and the deadly mushroom clouds. The irony is that "from the mountains, to the prairies, to the ocean white with foam" the government unleashed toxic fallout over the country as its citizens sang, "God bless America, my home, sweet home."

*Home on the Range II* illustrates the musical score of the lyrics, "And the skies are not cloudy all day." Color-enhanced photographs document the effects of atomic testing in Nevada of houses collapsing, mushroom clouds booming, and irradiated plants and cattle.

I felt like an archeologist as I created this series excavating quotes and images from the twentieth century to exemplify what a bizarre culture America has become. I would like these images and text to circulate in visual culture to memorialize this dark chapter in history. Walter Benjamin stated, "Every image of the past that is not recognized by the present as one of its own concerns threatens to disappear irretrievably." In *Nuclear Journal*, *Nuclear Culture I*, and *Nuclear Culture II*, duotone photographs of atomic detonations in Hiroshima, Bikini, and the Nevada test site provide the background for notes from research on the post-atomic age, which are placed on alternate lines with quotes from other eclectic reading including literature and history to create a surreal third effect of associations.

The arrogance and sense of entitlement of American officials as well as the western bourgeoisie contrast with testimonies of nuclear victims who express how they remain physically debilitated and emotionally scarred after they were used as guinea pigs. Dr. Robert Conrad conjectured, "Perhaps we could give each exposed (Utirik) person $100.00; I believe this would quiet their dissatisfaction."[20] Thomas Jefferson claimed, "Life is the art of avoiding pain,"[21] while a Hiroshima victim spoke of "keloid of the heart" and "leukemia of the spirit."[22]

Nuclear testing in the South Pacific disrupted several Pacific-islander cultures. The American military persuaded Bikini islanders to relocate to other islands temporarily for the cause of peace that they claimed necessitated testing hydrogen bombs. The islanders agreed in good faith. However, they were unable to return to Bikini due to high levels of radioactivity. The head of the Enewetak community said to Americans, "You live with gold and money and we have to depend on land and whatever life we can find on land and in the water. Without them we are nothing."[23] People fell into a dependent relationship for American subsidies similar to the cargo cult where Pacific Islanders prayed for American planes to deliver food and other necessities.

The acculturation of the Bikini islanders with their colonizers led to a hybrid mix of Japanese, American, and nuclear culture. Dances were a combination of bon dance and hula.[24] The installation *Cargo Cult* was inspired by elaborate festivities at Christmas in Bikini where a tree shaped like a bomb or missile was filled with dollar bills, boxes of matches, bars of soap, and detergent like a piñata.[25] The Christmas tree remains bare in this installation. Goods and money suspended from the sky never reach the people. Fish die marooned on sand, and nets are empty. The islanders' harmony with nature is disrupted, and American aid is never enough to truly compensate them. A silent video documents a series of nuclear explosions in the South Pacific. It concludes with footage played in reverse where the nuclear genie returns to his bottle as an expression of wishful thinking.

> The bomb first was our weapon. Then it became our diplomacy. Next it became our economy. Now it has become our culture. We've become people of the bomb.
>
> E. L. Doctorow[26]

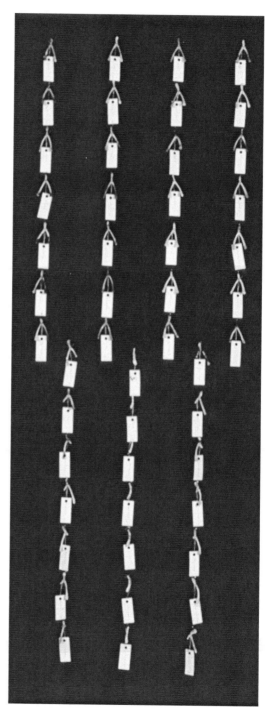

**Figure 10.1.** *7 × 7 = 49*, 1996, ceramics, paper and mixed media, 64"h × 21"w × 17"d (Image rights owned by Judy Hiramoto)

**Figure 10.2.** *Ground Zero*, 1998, projected slide images, wood, salt, 77"h × 70"w × 60"d (Image rights owned by Judy Hiramoto)

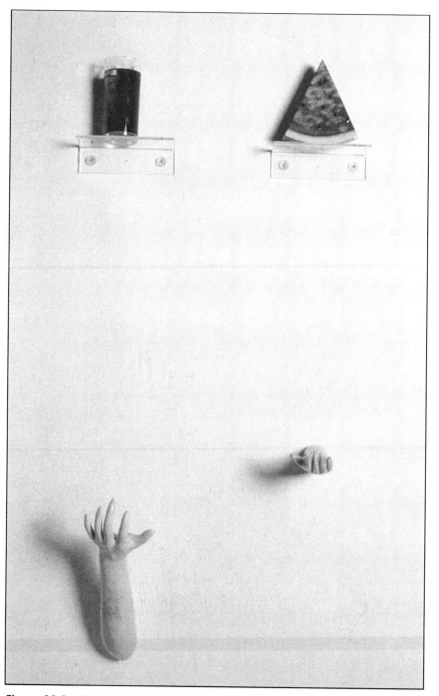

**Figure 10.3.** *Mu* (detail), 1995, ceramics and mixed media, 84"h × 72"w × 14"d (Image rights owned by Judy Hiramoto)

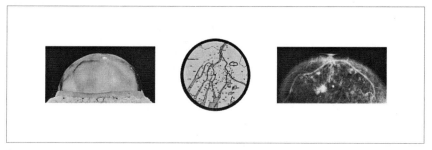

**Figure 10.4.** *Target*, 2000, digital print on watercolor paper, 6"h × 19"w (Image rights owned by Judy Hiramoto)

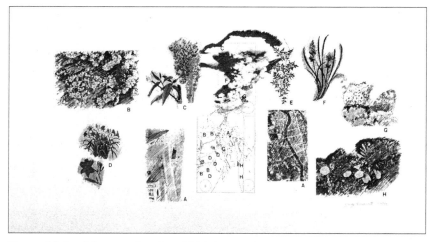

**Figure 10.5.** *Memory Garden*, 1997, ink on Coventry vellum, 15"h × 33.5"w (Image rights owned by Judy Hiramoto)

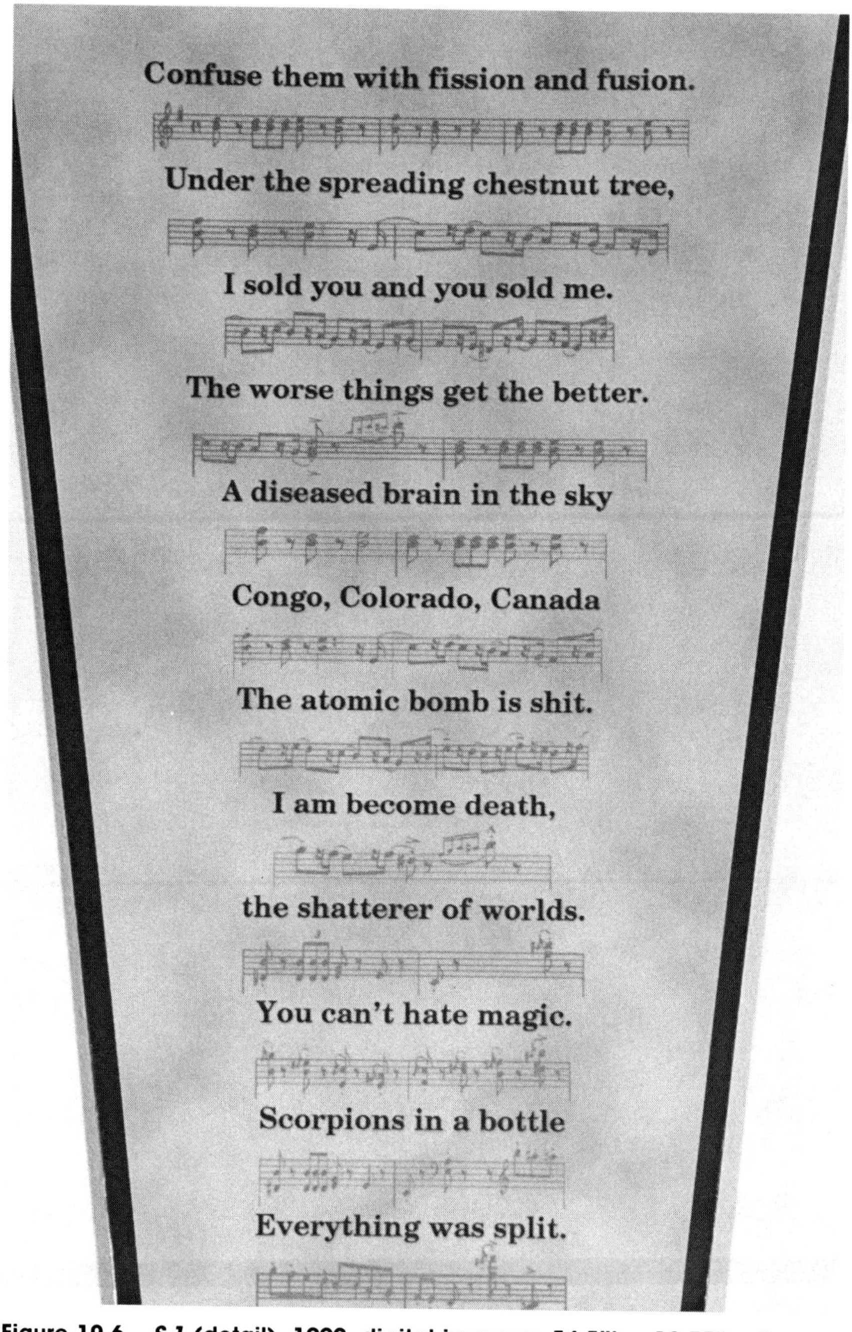

Figure 10.6. *S-1* (detail), 1999, digital imagery, 54.5"h × 10.75"w (Image rights owned by Judy Hiramoto)

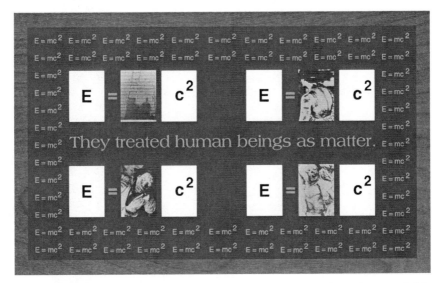

**Figure 10.7.** *As Matter*, 1999, digital print, 18"h × 29.5"w (Image rights owned by Judy Hiramoto)

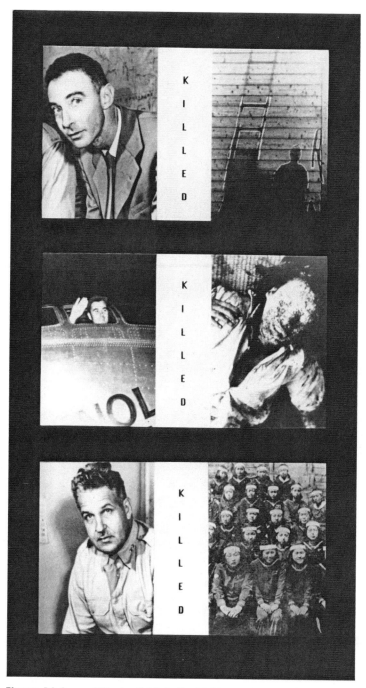

**Figure 10.8.** *x Killed y II* (detail), 1996, photographs and text, 29"h × 24"w (Image rights owned by Judy Hiramoto)

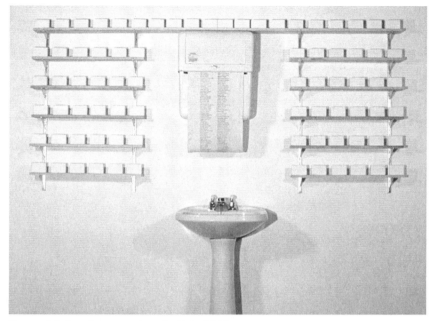

**Figure 10.9.** *Oppenheimer's Sink*, 1997, sound, sink, water dyed red, linen towel with text and dispenser, soap, wood and shelving units, 71"h × 79"w × 17"d (Image rights owned by Judy Hiramoto)

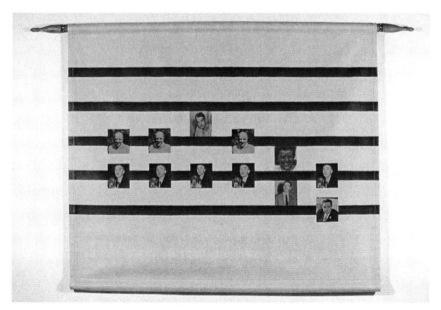

**Figure 10.10.** *Sweet Land of Liberty*, 1998, mixed media on canvas, 41.5"h × 61"w × 2"d (Image rights owned by Judy Hiramoto)

Figure 10.11. *Milk Teeth—Sacramento, St. Louis, and New York* (detail depicts Sacramento), 2001, ceramics, enamel paint, stainless steel, and milk, 43"h × 118"w × 12"d (total installation dimensions) (Image rights owned by Judy Hiramoto)

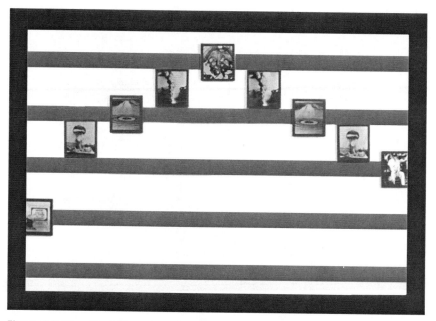

Figure 10.12. *God Bless America* (detail), 1999, photos, Plexiglas, plastic, 25"h × 127"w (Image rights owned by Judy Hiramoto)

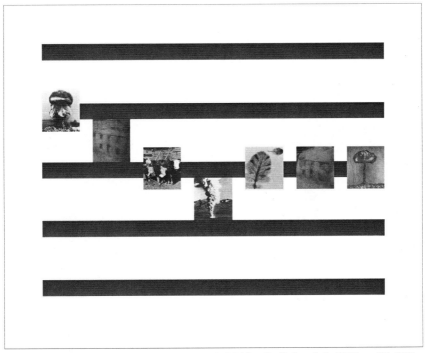

**Figure 10.13.** *Home on the Range II*, 2002, digital print, 33"h × 26.25"w (Image rights owned by Judy Hiramoto)

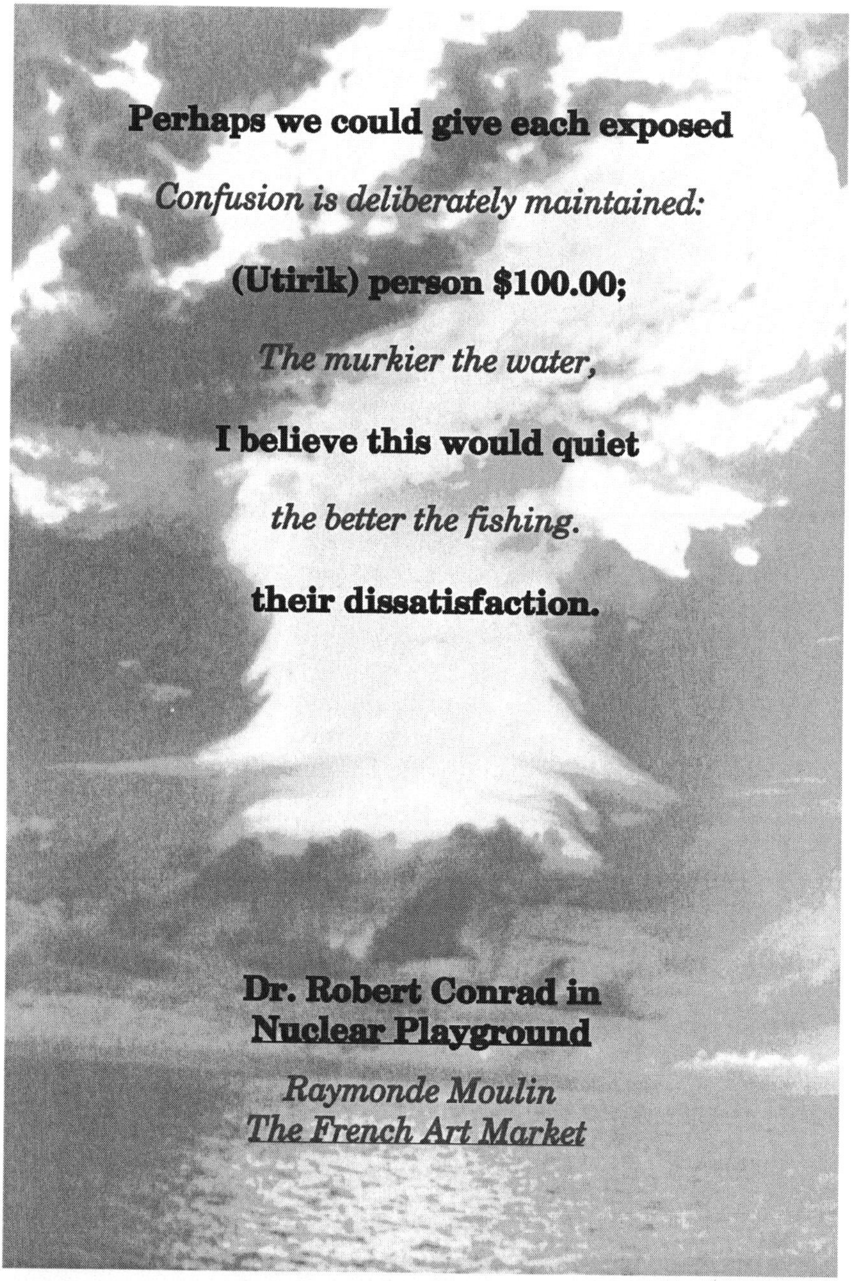

**Perhaps we could give each exposed**

*Confusion is deliberately maintained:*

**(Utirik) person $100.00;**

*The murkier the water,*

**I believe this would quiet**

*the better the fishing.*

**their dissatisfaction.**

**Dr. Robert Conrad in**
**Nuclear Playground**

*Raymonde Moulin*
*The French Art Market*

Figure 10.14. *Nuclear Culture II* (detail), 2000, digital print on watercolor paper, 25"h x 36"w (Image rights owned by Judy Hiramoto)

**Figure 10.15.** *Cargo Cult*, 2001, video and mixed media, 87"h × 84"w × 34"d (Image rights owned by Judy Hiramoto)

# Notes

1. Lifton, Robert Jay, and Greg Mitchell, *Hiroshima in America: Fifty Years of Denial* (New York: Grosset/Putnam, 1995), 345.

2. Gerson, Joseph, *With Hiroshima Eyes: Atomic War, Nuclear Extortion, and Moral Imagination* (Philadelphia: New Society Publishers, 1995), 46.

3. Selden, Kyoko, and Mark Selden (eds.), *The Atomic Bomb: Voices from Hiroshima and Nagasaki* (Armonk, N.Y.: M. E. Sharpe, 1989), 4, 6.

4. Rhodes, Richard, *Dark Sun: The Making of the Hydrogen Bomb* (New York: Simon & Schuster, 1995), 327.

5. Lifton, *Hiroshima in America*, 25.

6. Rhodes, Richard, *The Making of the Atomic Bomb* (New York: Simon & Schuster, 1986), 688.

7. Selden, *The Atomic Bomb*, 144.

8. Yamazaki, James N., *Children of the Atomic Bomb: An American Physician's Memoir of Nagasaki* (Durham, N.C.: Duke University Press, 1995), 116.

9. Linner, Rachelle, *City of Silence: Listening to Hiroshima* (New York: Orbis Books, 1993), 51.

10. Lifton, Robert Jay, *Death in Life: Survivors of Hiroshima* (Chapel Hill: University of North Carolina Press, 1991), 52.

11. Rhodes, *The Making of the Atomic Bomb*, 42.

12. Rosenthal, Debra, *At the Heart of the Bomb: The Dangerous Allure of Weapons Work* (Reading, Mass.: Addison-Wesley, 1990), 143.

13. Gusterson, Hugh, *Nuclear Rites: A Weapons Laboratory at the End of the Cold War* (Berkeley: University of California Press, 1996), 92.

14. Rhodes, *The Making of the Atomic Bomb*, 758.

15. Szosz, Ferenc Morton, *The Day the Sun Rose Twice* (Albuquerque: University of New Mexico Press, 1984), 77.

16. Stern, Philip M., *The Oppenheimer Case: Security on Trial* (New York: Harper & Row, 1969), 90.

17. Henrickson, Margot A., *Dr. Strangelove's America* (Berkeley: University of California Press, 1997), 40.

18. Fowler, Eric B. (ed.), *Radioactive Fallout, Soils, Plants, Foods, Man* (Amsterdam: Elsevier Publishing Co., 1965), 163.

19. Ball, Howard, *Justice Downwind: America's Atomic Testing Program in the 1950's* (New York: Oxford University Press, 1986), 49.

20. Firth, Steward, *Nuclear Playground* (Honolulu: University of Hawaii Press, 1987), 143.

21. Frost-Knappman, Elizabeth (ed.), *Bully Pulpit: Quotations from America's Presidents,* (New York: Facts on File, 1988) 132.

22. Linner, *City of Silence*, 22.

23. Firth, *Nuclear Playground*, 35.

24. Carucci, Laurence Marshall (*Nuclear Nativity: Rituals of Renewal and Empowerment in the Marshall Islands* (Dekalb: Northern Illinois University Press, 1997), 23.

25. Carucci, *Nuclear Nativity*, 182.
26. Gusterson, *Nuclear Rites*, 1.

# Bibliography

Ball, Howard. *Justice Downwind: America's Atomic Testing Program in the 1950's*. New York: Oxford University Press, 1986.

Carucci, Laurence Marshall. *Nuclear Nativity: Rituals of Renewal and Empowerment in the Marshall Islands*. Dekalb: Northern Illinois University Press, 1997.

Firth, Steward. *Nuclear Playground*. Honolulu: University of Hawaii Press, 1987.

Frost-Knappman, Elizabeth (ed.). *Bully Pulpit: Quotations from America's Presidents*. New York: Facts on File, 1988.

Fowler, Eric B. (ed.). *Radioactive Fallout, Soils, Plants, Foods, Man*. Amsterdam: Elsevier Publishing Co., 1965.

Gerson, Joseph. *With Hiroshima Eyes: Atomic War, Nuclear Extortion, and Moral Imagination*. Philadelphia: New Society Publishers, 1995.

Gusterson, Hugh. *Nuclear Rites: A Weapons Laboratory at the End of the Cold War*. Berkeley: University of California Press, 1996.

Henrickson, Margot A. *Dr. Strangelove's America*. Berkeley: University of California Press, 1997.

Lifton, Robert Jay. *Death in Life: Survivors of Hiroshima*. Chapel Hill: University of North Carolina Press, 1991.

Lifton, Robert Jay, and Greg Mitchell. *Hiroshima in America: Fifty Years of Denial*. New York: Grosset/Putnam, 1995.

Linner, Rachelle. *City of Silence: Listening to Hiroshima*. New York: Orbis Books, 1993.

Rhodes, Richard. *Dark Sun: The Making of the Hydrogen Bomb*. New York: Simon & Schuster, 1995.

———. *The Making of the Atomic Bomb*. New York: Simon & Schuster, 1986.

Rosenthal, Debra. *At the Heart of the Bomb: The Dangerous Allure of Weapons Work*. Reading, Mass.: Addison-Wesley, 1990.

Selden, Kyoko and Mark Selden (eds.). *The Atomic Bomb: Voices from Hiroshima and Nagasaki*. Armonk, N.Y.: M.E. Sharpe, 1989.

Stern, Philip M. *The Oppenheimer Case: Security on Trial*. New York: Harper & Row, 1969.

Szosz, Ferenc Morton. *The Day the Sun Rose Twice*. Albuquerque: University of New Mexico Press, 1984.

Yamazaki, James N. *Children of the Atomic Bomb: An American Physician's Memoir of Nagasaki*. Durham, N. C.: Duke University Press, 1995.

# CHAPTER 11

# Nuclear Fear 1987–2007

## HAS ANYTHING CHANGED?
## HAS EVERYTHING CHANGED?

*Spencer Weart*

Where does popular nuclear culture stand today? I'm trying to study this using the approach of the cultural historian: to construct a picture of current thinking by looking through the record of what people have been exposed to in the past. I am concerned here with the record of the past twenty years. This is our period, and it is a distinct period in the history of our subject.

Two events of 1986 mark the start of the current period, separating it from all that went before. The first was the disastrous release of radioactivity from the Chernobyl reactor in Ukraine, then part of the Soviet Union. Causing grave harm within its region and provoking fear or even panic all across Europe, the disaster transformed debates over nuclear energy.

The second event was détente between capitalist and Communist powers, first signaled in the 1986 summit meeting in Iceland, shadowed by the Chernobyl disaster, where the leaders of the United States and the Soviet Union made clear to the world that they were determined to severely reduce their nuclear arsenals. The fall of the Berlin Wall in 1989 and the other great events of those years confirmed that the world could breathe a huge sigh of relief: no longer was it plausible that a nuclear world war might break out at any hour.

Of course, the history of nuclear culture did not begin in 1986. It did not even begin in 1945 with the apparition of the first atomic bombs. I have written of all this before. By a helpful coincidence, it is not only twenty years since the transformation of debates over nuclear energy and the end of the Cold War, but also twenty years since I finished writing a book many readers of this chapter will have seen, *Nuclear Fear.*[1] So what I have to say here could be called a new chapter added onto the book. Of course, since the late 1980s when my book was published, others have found things to say about nuclear imagery in the Cold War era. I'll be drawing on some of these new thoughts about old history in this discussion of contemporary nuclear imagery.

# Theory: Emotion and Cognition

First, some theory. Our understanding of the psychological significance of imagination has developed significantly in the past twenty years. In *Nuclear Fear* I relied upon what we understood in the 1980s about how humans think with images. The model was associationist: if we see A in conjunction with B enough times, then the pair become associated in our thinking. Thus nuclear bombs become associated with military officers, scientists, mad scientists, monsters, and so forth. And each of these in turn brings in its own associations—for example, the scientist as all-knowing and all-powerful authority evokes associations reaching back to early childhood struggles against parental authority. Once you start looking for such things in productions like nuclear-bomb movies, they are uncomfortably obvious. This model, while drawing upon Freud and Jung and their followers, is fundamentally behaviorist, even Pavlovian. It appeals to biology without actually understanding the neurological mechanisms it assumes.

Since the mid-1980s it is precisely in the area of neurological mechanisms that psychology has made the most progress. This is partly thanks to advances in psychopharmacology and the study of brain lesions, but still more to the amazing new techniques of Functional Magnetic Resonance Imaging, which allow scientists to actually observe exactly which regions of the brain are active during specific cognitive and emotional processes.

The model that is emerging preserves everything from the associationist model but adds something to it, what should perhaps have been obvious—emotion. An image is associated not only with other images, but with emotions. The monster, for example, evokes fear, and, depending on circumstances, perhaps other feelings such as astonishment or disgust (the original Godzilla in the end became associated with a feeling of tragic sorrow at its death, and in later incarnations was viewed almost with affection).

When scientists today say an image is associated with an emotion, they mean it is connected to the body itself. Fear, for example, includes eyes widened, lips drawn back, a wrenching in the stomach, sweating, and even trembling. Indeed, as Henry James noted many years ago, you cannot really remember an abstract emotion: it is the body state that you vividly remember—or, in modern parlance, that deposits a trace as resonances in your neural circuitry.

An important thing we have come to understand is that the memory of emotions extends an influence all the way to the most refined logical thinking. Our evolution (to appeal to another area of study that has made important advances recently) shaped brains that would help us survive on the African plains, where decisions had to be made with limited information and less time. The result is a set of interconnected organs functioning through many shortcuts, means of thought that usually function with astonishing efficiency, although they can be tricked into error under special circumstances. The emotional punch associated with fire would be a help in running from a conflagration in the grasslands, but it can push people to their deaths as they crowd at one escape from a burning room, too preoccupied to look for other ways out. But emotion usually benefits thinking. There is good evidence that without an emotional component, our thinking cannot proceed efficiently at all. Unfortunate people whose damaged brains do not connect the emotional memory organs to the cognitive organs prove to be incapable of making commonsense decisions.

Bear with me, I will return soon to nuclear culture. But first I need to note that scientists now generally recognize (as first described by Charles Darwin) that our animal selves have a specific repertoire of basic emotions—things that are not only feelings in the brain but that have particular effects in our bodies down to the chemical level The classic Darwinian list is short: happiness, sadness, fear, anger, surprise, disgust. Each of these six produces a characteristic pattern in the faces of every brain-intact human on earth, and even apes. To be sure, there are other emotions that also produce effects on the body, if not always so visibly, including embarrassment and lust. But the classic six are all we need for this inquiry.

Indeed for our purposes we can concentrate on only two: fear and disgust. These emotions produce a powerful visceral reaction, right into our guts. More important, they leave an indelible trace in the brain (which has in fact been located, in an organ called the amygdala). A single powerful experience can be enough to make the association permanent—this is the physiology behind post-traumatic stress disorder. Allow me to give a minor example from my personal experience. Some years ago, in the Alaska wilderness, I had to cross an ice-cold river in flood. I lost my footing, was swept away, and nearly died. For years after that, the sight of water running in a river would instantly bring into my mind not only the event, but visceral fear. Note that this differs from Pavlovian association, which relies on repetition: one incident is enough.

These brain mechanisms evolved to make the most of actual life experience, but in the modern world it looks like the mechanisms are often activated by vicarious experiences. Especially in watching movies, we may be flooded with emotions. Recent experiments show that our brains use "mirror neurons" to represent actions that we observe: if you see a picture of someone's face being slapped, neurons are active in the same brain regions as if your own face were slapped. Although the science is not entirely clear, it's plausible that such vicarious experiences can act much like real experiences to cause permanent changes in the brain's emotional and thinking circuits. There's more: it was reported this January that the organ of the brain that organizes memories (the hippocampus) also organizes imagined experiences. I don't suppose an imaginary trauma will ever leave as powerful an impression as a real trauma. But it does now seem plausible that imaginary events can leave permanent physiological traces that will affect our thinking using the same pathways as memories of actual events. This suggests how the media, and most of all movies, can permanently influence our ways of thought. But we don't need brain science to understand that movies have power, something we have all felt ourselves. That's probably why critics of nuclear culture so often concentrate their studies on movies.[2]

Some features of this mechanism are particularly important for nuclear culture. The physiological embedding of emotion is strong and immediate with fear, but much weaker for shame, lust, or even happiness. The demands of survival in our evolutionary past have given special power to memories of terrifying events. The one other emotion that has such an effect is disgust. For example, a study of birds that tried just once to eat a Monarch butterfly, and were sickened by its poison, found that those birds would never again touch a Monarch. Disgust, like fear, is a bodily state that in a few seconds can imprint the brain for a lifetime. Think of the iconic 1954 movie *Them!* with its gigantic mutant ants. In the way they evoked both fear *and* disgust—in other words, horror—we can see why the movie had a lasting impact on all who saw it.

Closely related, especially in issues involving radiation or anything else perceived as polluting, is moral "disgust." It is probably no coincidence that we use the same word for that feeling as we use for physical revulsion. New evidence indicates that our emotional response to injustice and the like makes use of brain pathways that originally evolved to help us reject poisons. At some deep level, a cheater and a cockroach produce much the same reaction.[3] Moral and physical disgust reinforce one another in matters like the debate over nuclear wastes, a major political theme of our current period, which I discuss below.

We might also hope for some scientific illumination of the *opposite* of these processes, the cutting-off of cognition from emotions. As I said, this separation leads to impaired thinking, perhaps an absence of thinking and certainly a failure to make decisions. This is a problem that has been much discussed by students of nuclear culture, called *denial* or *numbing*. I'm not aware of work on classical denial by neurophysiologists, but I suspect it can be explained in terms of biological brain processes, probably the same ones that produce hysterical blindness in some traumatized people. I don't want to press this, though. It's been pointed out that we find it only too easy to accuse other people of being in denial or being numbed. Maybe they don't happen to agree with us about the politics of nuclear devices. Or maybe they have just reasonably decided not to spend time obsessively worrying about nuclear problems.[4] If the public has not been talking much in recent years about nuclear war, we should hesitate to invoke numbing or denial. While these may well apply to many individuals, for the public as a whole there are other explanations—historical explanations.

# A New Nuclear Period

The history of our current period, a new and distinct era of nuclear culture, begins with the 1986 Chernobyl disaster. Curiously, in the long run it made for *less* anxious debate over nuclear reactors. That is not because of numbing or denial. The disaster was well acknowledged as a public trauma, especially in Europe where some people as far away as Italy and England feared for their personal safety. It is still very well remembered—you can hardly read anything about nuclear power today without running across the word "Chernobyl." But a prompt practical effect was to close down the controversy over nuclear power in most countries. In the United States, the Three Mile Island accident in 1979 had already gone far to halt plans to build new reactors to generate electricity, and the mood was shifting that way in other countries too. After Chernobyl, nations from Sweden to Egypt cancelled their ambitious plans or even determined to gradually phase out existing reactors. That calmed down public controversy and its attendant propagation of frightening imagery. To be sure, there were nations like Japan and France where expansion continued. But these nations, fiercely determined to be independent of foreign fuels, and with political systems that largely prevented public outcry from reversing the decisions of technological elites, could not sustain an intense and prolonged anti-nuclear controversy.

Chernobyl also silenced the utopian proponents of nuclear power. Although radiant claims about nuclear prosperity were already in decline by the mid-1980s (especially as the oil supply crises of the 1970s faded from memory), some people had continued to push for a tremendous expansion. After 1986, whether nuclear reactor construction stopped altogether or proceeded with extreme caution in a "business as usual" manner, the reactor industry did little to fuel the fires of controversy. Moreover, the nuclear industry recognized that it could not survive if it had more such accidents. Going even beyond governments, the industry imposed on itself a strong tightening of safety standards, and this in turn has helped to prevent more disasters. The public memory is short, a new generation is growing up that never knew a world without nuclear electricity, and in the absence of new grave accidents the reactor industry is coming to seem like just one more normal industry—hazardous to be sure, but what industry is not? Emissions from the main alternative source of power—coal—were looking increasingly harmful to public health and the planet's climate.

I have found a good series of polls on nuclear acceptance only for the United States. In the 1980s, the number of citizens who accepted getting electricity from nuclear energy was roughly equal to the number who opposed it. After 1988 there was a slow and steady divergence, and by mid-2005 we find 70 percent of adults in favor and 24 percent opposed to "the use of nuclear energy as one of the ways to provide electricity in the United States." Perhaps more important, those strongly in agreement (32 percent) now greatly outnumber those strongly opposed (10 percent).[5] In sum: in a seeming paradox, the worst civilian nuclear disasters in history ultimately brought a decline in public concern about nuclear power.

The much greater historical turn of the late 1980s, of course, was the end of the Cold War, culminating in the astonishing disintegration of the Soviet Union. Less spectacular but not less important was the growing accord and interdependence between the Western capitalist and Chinese economies. Everyone agrees that all these developments damped the fears of nuclear war that had raged in the early 1980s. As a practical measure of the declining risk, the number of stockpiled nuclear warheads, which peaked in 1986 at the fantastic level of seventy thousand, fell rapidly. According to new treaties, by 2012 barely four thousand would be deployed on strategic delivery systems anywhere in the world.

It is possible that fearful nuclear talk was due for a decline in any case. We know that attention to nuclear war was in remission during the late 1960s and 1970s. After the 1963 peak of the Cuban Missile Crisis, followed by a ban on nuclear bomb tests that put fears of fallout to rest, the heights were not approached again until the nuclear freeze movement of the early 1980s. In the decades between, people might have told you they were afraid of war if you asked them about it, but the issue was not salient, not something most people would bring up spontaneously or would see often in the media. This sort of cyclical exhaustion has been noted in other issues too; one can imagine a magazine editor saying, "Not that again! Everybody's heard all that, bring me something new." In the 1970s political activists had turned public attention toward the war in Vietnam and environmental pollution. After the 1980s people found new things filling the limited amount of space available for worry and agitation, such as genetic engineering, climate change, and especially terrorism.[6]

We can trace statistically a decline of references in the American media. A search on the term "nuclear" of the full texts of the *New York Times*, *Washington Post* and *Time* magazine, using Google's news archive, finds the expected peak in usage in the early 1980s (to be precise, 1983). A low was reached in 1995–1997, with less than half the references seen at the peak. There followed a modest revival, probably mainly from reports on the Indian and Pakistani weapons programs and the radiation spill in Japan I mentioned below. The terrorist attack of 9/11 kept the numbers rising, and a new peak of "nuclear" references was reached in 2003, roughly two-thirds as high as the 1983 peak. The numbers have declined slightly since.[7]

The Gallup organization directly asked Americans to reveal their fears, or to be precise, how likely they thought a nuclear war would be in the next ten years. From 1981 to 2001 there was a real change: the fraction who thought a war was "very likely" to come soon declined from 19 percent to 8 percent, while the fraction who thought it "very unlikely" rose from 23 percent to 33 percent.

Thus there was not only a decline in media attention to nuclear war, but also a genuine decline in worry. Note however that the change was not great: there remain a lot of people who will be afraid about nuclear war if it's drawn to their attention, even if there has been much less in the news to do that. Both media attention to terrorism and worry about terrorism meanwhile rose, of course, even before 9/11 but especially afterwards.[8]

Outside the immediate news, we are used to looking to movies to see what people have worried about—or what movie producers think they are worried about, and I suspect the producers know that as well as anyone. Two people who have studied movies with nuclear themes exhaustively, Jerome Shapiro and Mick Broderick, agree that such movies have not gone into any great decline since the late 1980s.[9] Meanwhile the rise of a new medium—computer games—has given a whole new way for people to experience at least one important theme that has been common in movies relating to nuclear war: the post-nuclear-apocalypse world as a locus for battles with degenerated savages. From a cursory look at popular novels I again get an impression of no great decline in the number that have some kind of nuclear theme.

It is easy enough to find examples in our period of popular works carrying exactly the same mythical themes that were widespread before 1986. The three immensely popular and influential *Terminator* movies, for example, feature a genocidal computer whose ancestry can be traced back to a famous 1967 science fiction story and indeed much earlier; the most recent, *Terminator 3: Rise of the Machines* (2003), ends with barrages of rockets exploding in mushroom clouds—imagery that for all the benefits of modern computer graphics resembles the half-convincing special effects of the 1960s.[10]

A year ago, one of the most popular American television shows featured a dramatic emergency with a familiar plot: the threat of a deadly leak at a nuclear power station. As I write this, American television is playing three major and successful series on nuclear themes that would have seemed overdone already in the 1970s. In *Jericho*, townspeople in mid-America deal with criminal marauders and secret agents in the days following the nuclear destruction of many of the nation's cities. In *24*, a secret agent is pitted against terrorists who explode a nuclear bomb in Los Angeles and plot to explode more. The third show, *Heroes*, has as its dramatic center the efforts of its "heroes" to prevent the nuclear bombing of New York City.[11]

# Nothing Has Changed?

Has nothing changed? It's a familiar fact that mythical images are immortal, or at least have been since the spread of printed books. When witchcraft, astrology, and a thousand other scraps of nonsense remain alive in many minds, we can hardly expect rapid changes in nuclear imagery. It was already clear twenty years ago that this is an extraordinarily powerful complex of images, perhaps the most powerful ever described. In my *Nuclear Fear* book I explained how countless nuclear images are linked together through an ancient theme, what I called the theme of transmutation. This embodies universal myths of world apocalypse, played on an external and global stage, and correspondingly—on an internal and individual stage—the universal theme of personal renewal. The mushroom cloud, the mandala-like symbol of the atom, the pictures of a devastated and unpeopled city, the promises of marvelous atomic-powered airplanes—all these images and many more have strong historical and contemporary connections with themes of magical transformation. And versions of all of these things are still to be seen in contemporary culture.

To analyze nuclear imagery, it is particularly rewarding to focus on the figure that stands at the center of the complex in living form. In my book I concentrated on the monster and mad scientist, which are of course different aspects of the same thing—Frankenstein the creator and the monster, Dr. Strangelove, and Godzilla are all dedicated to the cause of universal destruction. And we know that their aim, conscious or not, is to go *through* the destruction of the world and the dark night of the soul, to emerge reborn—although we do well to fear them, for all too often the creature will remain stuck in the dead zone of utter negation.

Looking back on this description, I find that I left something out which will turn out to be especially important in talking about the current period of nuclear imagery. As usual the most important facts about symbols are right in front of our noses. The image of the nuclear monster, like all major mythic characters, has a double character (myths are often powerful because they express within themselves two opposites that otherwise cannot be reconciled). The traditional counterpart of a monster is a dragon-slayer: the hero found in myths of every culture. In nuclear imagery the matter can be more complex, with beasts matched not against heroes but victims—like that figure next to St. George in many paintings, the one helplessly chained as a sacrifice. The full meaning of such a symbol is not found in one or another of its elements, but in setting them all together. For example, as Yuki Tanaka and others have pointed out, the prototypical nuclear monster, the original Japanese Godzilla, had a dual character: as well as a raging monster, he was himself a tragic victim of the hydrogen bomb test that drove him from the ocean depths.[12]

I am indebted here to the work of Michael Ortiz Hill.[13] In studying many dreams with nuclear thematic content, reported by nearly a hundred people, Hill found frequent accounts of a mythic struggle with a personalized bomb, symbolized in countless ways. But surprisingly, the dreamer does not often fight by matching the bomb-monster's magical force with the corresponding power of a hero or heroine. Sometimes the dreams show only a victim. More often the dreamer wins a kind of victory simply by living on: the Hero as Survivor. This is the simplest form of passage through the dark valley, without being transformed or reborn but finding enough victory in just getting through. In other cases the dream-hero does better, managing for example to prevent nuclear war. Most commonly this is not through force, but through craft and subterfuge. The bestial monster's counterpart is its opposite even in its mode of fighting, suggesting the immemorial Trickster, found in many folk cultures. Perhaps our modern nuclear apparition is just too overwhelmingly strong, too invested with the satanic powers of apocalypse, to be speared like a dragon.

This is not to say that the monster must always charge into an ignorant and bestial rampage—Dr. Strangelove, like old Lucifer himself, can have a cold and terrible intelligence. Nuclear imagery takes many forms. The point is that the bomb, the monster, the mad scientist, the missile-launching military officer, and all their kin form only one aspect of a larger mythical complex, almost always matched by an opposing figure. This opponent can range from tragic victim to clever victor, although most often it is both, the victim who triumphs simply by surviving.

If I and most other cultural critics tended to fail to properly discuss this important figure, I suppose it is for the usual reason we miss such things: it has seemed too obvious and familiar to mention. Indeed, it is the most familiar figure of all, for the bomb's mythic opponent typically represents none other than ourselves.

To see how ubiquitous this is, just think of one modern archetype that has been extensively discussed: James Bond, who spans the nuclear age from the early 1960s down to the present. The majority of Bond films, from *Dr. No* (1962) onward, have had important nuclear content. Typically the villain aims to wield nuclear weapons for personal gain, perhaps even intending to set off a world conflagration. And typically the secret agent thwarts him partly through ingenuity and partly just by surviving attacks from the villain's minions.

We find a variant of the theme in some post-nuclear-apocalypse productions, like the archetypal 1981 movie, *The Road Warrior* (the second of three *Mad Max* movies). Here motorcycle gangsters serve as an incarnation of the infantile and bestial civilization-destroying monster. And after much heroics, in the end the victory is through cunning. The same theme repeats in our own period in the survivor-hero of the 1997 movie *The Postman*, who finds that simply delivering mail can create conditions to defend civilization against savage gangsters.

But as I said, there are many ways to portray the basic dichotomy of this multiform creature. If the villain is often himself clever, the opponent may be guileless. A few critics have drawn attention in particular to how often children show up in nuclear productions. "Without a question," says Hill, "children are the largest discernible group of people that inhabit the dreamscape of Apocalypse. Children appear in over a quarter of the dreams I've collected." The child often represents the war-monster's innocent victim, but it is often a survivor, or even a protagonist who helps prevent war.[14] This is exactly what we would expect in a transmutational complex of imagery that centers on rebirth, a word that necessarily calls up the image of a child.

Consider one of the early, and still among the most widely cited, nuclear fictions: *A Canticle for Leibowitz*, first published in 1959. Its ending features the miraculous awakening of Rachel, an innocent child who was in a sense, as the author puts it, immaculately conceived. Thus she is a Christ-figure, with a potential to redeem the world. Jump now to 2006 and another novel by a popular writer set in a post-apocalyptic world, Cormac McCarthy's *The Road*. His world is one of the bleakest ever described, a gray and shattered land that lacks even birds—the very seas are covered with ash. And the presentation of human nature, even for the cynical McCarthy, is dismal. To represent the failings that brought about the apocalypse, motorcycle gangs will not suffice: he shows hopelessly degenerate thieves, cultists, savages, slavers, and cannibals. Yet the final figure of the book is a young boy, subtly presented as messiah-like. He represents the fragile survival of an innate morality. With an unquenchable drive for goodness, at the end the boy not only survives but grows within a reviving family, community, and natural world. Again the old, old story—transmutation and rebirth in the passage through ultimate darkness.

# Everything Has Changed?

So has nothing really changed? My answer is that *everything* has changed. At least for a large part of the public, an ever-growing part of the public: the younger generation. Roughly speaking, that means everyone born after 1980, people who mainly encountered the ideas and images of nuclear energy only in the years after 1986. These children (many of them are full adults by now) did not grow up in a world where talk of nuclear war, radiation, nuclear reactors, and so forth showed up frequently in the news, and even sometimes in personal relations, in a context full of anxiety.

In terms of simple knowledge, I would suppose that younger people know much less about nuclear weaponry than people of the Cold War generations, although I'm not sure whether that matters much. Most people never had more than a limited and distorted factual knowledge. I only know of one study of what young people are now taught in their schoolbooks. Sam Walker looked into the way American textbooks describe the decision to bomb Hiroshima, and found much the same combination of brief facts, half-truths, and outright myths that had been the common understanding of Americans since the 1950s. The forces behind such ignorance were displayed in 1995 when the Smithsonian's Air and Space Museum in Washington, D.C., attempted to mount a detailed historical exhibit to describe and explain the Hiroshima bombing. Passionate objections by World War II veterans and politicians left nothing of the lengthy exhibit script beyond a few spare sentences.[15]

As for the actual effects of a nuclear bomb, the Cold War generations learned a lot from news accounts and from vigorous efforts by governments to inform their publics for purposes of civil defense. These reasons for explaining facts no longer exist. I suspect that most young people know little about nuclear war beyond a general feeling that it is extremely bad. For example, I believe that Hersey's 1946 book *Hiroshima* is still often used in schools (a 1985 *Library Journal* review called it "absolutely essential for collections from junior high on").[16] It is a fine work for conveying a general understanding of devastation at the 1950s fission-bomb level. But it has nothing to tell about the complex paradoxes of deterrence, or the facts of warfare by missiles with multiple fusion-bomb warheads. In short, overall I believe the knowledge base has changed little except to shrink. If I ask what the younger generation knows of the nuclear balancing act of the Cold War—which ended before many of them were born—I suspect their response would have less to do with textbook facts than with the lurid adventures of James Bond and the agonizing decisions of fictional nuclear submarine commanders. This gives us a hint about where the balance of imagery may be shifting.

But what about the emotional base? Modern technology has brought something new into play: the ubiquitous electronic media. Surveys tell us that television and other on-screen entertainment takes more of our children's time than schoolwork does. All the famous old nuclear movies are easily available, along with countless new but derivative productions. This has, by the way, made a profound difference even in my own scholarship. In the 1980s, when I did the research for my *Nuclear Fear* book, it was difficult to see an old mutant-monster movie. I had to scan the newspaper television guide every week and set my alarm to wake me well past midnight so I could blearily take notes. Now I can order up a movie on DVD by mail.[17]

If the new media influence modes of scholarship, all the more do they influence, notoriously, modes of apprehending entertainment. It has long been remarked that the small screen of television in a lighted living room gives a more detached experience than an enveloping movie. Still more distancing from immediate emotional experience are movies on DVD. You can pause the show, freezing a frame while you fetch a cola. You can view a sequence repeatedly to catch some nuance of acting or an amusing error in the continuity of how a shirt is buttoned. And you can look at the extra features—ludicrous outtakes, a documentary revealing the trickery behind the special effects, and so forth. All this makes for a less intimate and less impressive encounter with the story.

One new medium, however, is extremely immersive: computer games. The young person who plays them (and they are mostly young people, that is, younger than thirty-five or so) feels his heart pumping, sweat springs to his forehead—he knows terror and exhilaration. But the game repertoire is notoriously limited. There have been a few nuclear strategy games, but chess-like strategy as such is too cold-blooded to bring an emotional engagement with nuclear horrors. The most popular such series, called simply *Nuclear War*, is what reviewers called a "fun" game with a "light-hearted approach" full of "wacky humor."[18]

More important culturally, and more popular, is a well-known genre of "first-person shooter" games that feature gun battles in the post-apocalyptic ruins of cities or blasted deserts. Arguably, playing a game in which you are shooting at savage gangsters or mutant monsters will leave stronger emotional traces even than watching *The Road Warrior*. This is another hint about where the balance of imagery may be shifting. We can trace the theme back to nineteenth-century tales of action after the fall of civilization, where you identify with a protagonist who is not a victim nor even a bare survivor, but a warrior in a world rich with opportunities for sex and combat. The emotions such games evoke are far from those that millions of people felt, for example, at the conclusion of the 1959 movie *On the Beach* as the camera slowly scanned the unpeopled streets of a dead city.

As I have noted, polls do show a significant if partial decline in Americans' worries. Those in the polls I mentioned were adults, whose attitudes were mostly formed during the Cold War, and it would be interesting to know what younger people feel. Back in the early 1980s, when the nuclear freeze movement and the crotchety belligerence of Reagan and Brezhnev were much in the news, a number of researchers asked American adolescents what they thought about nuclear war. Many youths reported that they thought about it often and seriously, and a majority believed a nuclear war was likely in their lifetimes. Majorities also doubted they would survive such a war.[19] So far as I know, nobody has repeated such surveys in the post–Cold War period. I take that as significant; presumably those who watch adolescents don't see the kind of problems that were so noticeable in the 1980s. The current generation of students does not seem to me anywhere near as worried about nuclear war as the 1980s students. Still, we can't say whether the anxiety has really gone away, or whether it is quietly present but gets little attention, as tended to happen in the 1970s.

I have talked about some specific ways that modern media may affect nuclear culture, but we can also think in a more general mode. The post-Chernobyl and post–Cold War period is known to many cultural critics as the "postmodern" period. The term "postmodernism" has many meanings and implications, but a few of them are particularly important for our inquiry. Most of them can be summarized in one term: referencing. From children's cartoons to rap music, productions of the postmodern era are soaked in references to earlier works. Children today are likely to have their first encounter with, say, radioactive monsters not from seeing one directly portrayed in a horror movie, but from clever references in television shows. How many have first met a nuclear reactor in the introductory sequence of the perennially popular cartoon show *The Simpsons*, featuring a lovable but amusingly incompetent reactor operator?

Referencing is all the more distancing when, as now often happens, it is ironic. Of course the rise of the ironic mode is not a strictly postmodern phenomenon. The 1964 film *Dr. Strangelove* and other works of the Cold War period already displayed themes of black humor and disdain for mainstream society, themes we can trace as far back as the Dada movement during World War I. In our postmodern period, however, irony is no longer a shocking position taken by rebellious intellectuals: it has become a standard position. Producers of entertainment flatter the audience that they are "cool" (both up-to-date and cool-headed), sharing in a knowing and amused depreciation of the old themes. The monster is not seen as an actual monster but as a representation of a quaint concept, something that might have seemed scary to our parents but not, heaven knows, to us. *Dr. Strangelove* deployed its black comedy for deadly serious purposes (Kubrick originally meant to do a tragedy of war begun by mistake, and the underlying drama shows through). Postmodern products by contrast deploy satire for little purpose but fun.

An example is Bart Simpson's favorite comic book characters, Radioactive Man and his sidekick Fallout Boy. What exactly are we seeing here? Well, it is Bart Simpson, a fictional cartoon character, looking at another character that we are expected to understand is even *more* fictional. While Bart acts like a real boy, we are not supposed to suspend disbelief in taking his comic book as realistic; the comic is meant to stand for an entire genre. So the representation of a boy reads a representation of a genre: namely, the genre of fictional superheroes, who themselves represent—well, we don't quite remember what, something people used to take seriously.

The prototype for this approach appeared already in 1982: the documentary *The Atomic Café*. It remains well known, and has taught many in the younger generation to see "duck-and-cover" training as a ridiculous aberration. In fact the training was, at least initially, a rational deployment of World War II sheltering techniques to prepare for the World War II level of destruction that would have resulted from an attack with the few atomic bombs at hand in the early 1950s, before the advent of hydrogen bombs. But now that we have hydrogen bombs, who remembers that?

More recently the playful approach to old nuclear themes is perhaps best seen in sophisticated art products. Takashi Murakami's exhibit and book *Little Boy* gives some striking examples, like Kenji Yanobe's ludicrous warrior suit—a set of mechanical trousers referencing on the one hand futuristic plans for armored soldiers, and on the other hand Godzilla.[20]

I'll just mention one more feature of referencing. Theorists of postmodernism point to a growing confusion between the reference and the thing referenced. In pure postmodern culture, the reference can even take precedence over the original: the simulacrum can be more meaningful than the actual object. Nuclear imagery is uniquely well adapted to this culture, for as many have pointed out, it is precisely as representation that nuclear weapons exert their influence. After 1945, national establishments did not manufacture bombs to explode them over cities, but to awe or intimidate people (and not only enemies). Today, in the early years of the twenty-first century, geopolitical positions are profoundly shaken when one or another nation simply threatens to deploy nuclear weapons without having actually built any. Arguably, the Bomb (not bombs, but "the Bomb") was the first great postmodern object—or should I say image—but object and image are so entangled here that we can no longer make such a distinction.

The trend is clearest in the profusion of what are sometimes called "avatars" (from the computer simulation world). The avatar was created to represent a character or thing, but it can come to be the chief reality itself, more active and important than what it represents. This form of confusion infects historical knowledge itself. Who has a more "real" place in the history of the twentieth century—Charlie Chaplin or his character, the Little Tramp? Increasingly, people's historical memory even of actual events has its roots more in television docudramas or wholly fictional movies than in nonfiction texts. When we think of the Korean War, do we recall the Battle of Pork Chop Hill, or *M\*A\*S\*H*? This is not entirely new (how many have held images of the French Revolution derived from Dickens's *Tale of Two Cities*?). But cultural observers argue that referencing has become more pervasive and fundamental.

The changes wrought by postmodern modes should be understood in terms of what we understand about the workings of the human brain. In modern media, the cognitive associations between images that were created in the twentieth century remain, but not so the emotional associations. In the cartoons children watch, nuclear radiation can still be linked with a crazed scientist and a three-eyed mutant—but not often with gut-wrenching terror and nausea.

# Nuclear History, 1987–2007: Reactors

Now let us move from theory to the history of events in nuclear imagery, and actual nuclear practices, since 1986. I'll start with events and images relating to civilian nuclear power, and then turn to nuclear weapons. I'll finish with a few words on what the imagery may have meant in practical terms: in other words, first I'll talk about how history influenced imagery, and then I'll talk about how imagery influenced history.

The history of civilian nuclear power since 1986 is straightforward. After Chernobyl, when the public and governments determined to proceed with far more caution, the nuclear industry itself agreed. Reactor operators and investors realized they needed a much better safety regime, if only to protect their investments (at Three Mile Island, reactor operators with normal training had lost a billion dollars in half an hour). It was not enough just to obey government regulations—or as had sometimes happened, pretend to obey them. For the industry to survive, it would have to make sure there were no more Chernobyls. In the United States, already after the Three Mile Island accident in 1979, the industry had set up its own safety institute and rigorous procedures. After Chernobyl, Europe followed. The Japanese were not directly threatened by radioactivity from either accident, and procedures in Japan remained lax. The natural result was several accidents, culminating in a 1999 radiation spill at the Tokaimura fuel processing plant that killed two people and contaminated hundreds. This brought unprecedented public criticism of the authorities, which I think has led to tightening of safety procedures, but this is so recent that as a historian I can't comment on how far it's gotten.[21]

What is clear is that safety measures have improved enough to prevent, at least so far, any accidents on remotely the scale of Chernobyl. To bring the history up to the present, for several years now business journalists have been reporting a revival of optimism within the nuclear industry. Plans are underway in several nations for expansion, with some hoping for a large expansion. The reasons are practical. It is now generally agreed that the world's ever-climbing demand for power cannot be met indefinitely with oil; the only disagreement is when oil production will reach its peak—some say in thirty years, some say next year. That leaves only two realistic options for building new electrical generating stations: coal or nuclear. Coal is currently cheaper, but nuclear will become cheaper if governments require coal plants to meet strict pollution standards. It will be costly for coal plants to curb their deadly emissions of smoke and other wastes. Beyond that looms a rapidly growing demand for power plants that emit no greenhouse gases.

This does not turn back the clock to 1960, when negative images of reactors were balanced by utopian promises of an atomic-powered world. The proponents of nuclear reactors no longer try to deploy millennial promises. And the armory of images wielded by their opponents has grown. The most important new image is Chernobyl, that is, the abandoned city itself. In my 1988 book I discussed the history of one particularly important nuclear image, the empty city. For centuries, ruins in paintings and stories had stood for a downfall of civilization, usually connected with moral decay. In their emptiness the ruins also represented the individual as dead and forgotten, the familiar and emotionally potent concept of physical and even spiritual death. Now such an image appears before the world in the actual city of Chernobyl, the vacant apartments and silent streets. News accounts, television documentaries, and art productions by photographers and others have brought the sights repeatedly into view. It is another example of the remarkable ability of nuclear energy to give factual reasons for links to primitive myths. Mutants and death rays and arrogant scientists and all that are only a few of the associations that have both real and fantastic aspects; now here is one more, a strong association between civilian nuclear reactors and the vision of an empty city.

This is one example of how the balance in our current period is different from the balance through most of the post–World War II period. In a process that began in the early 1970s and was completed by the end of the 1980s, the double-sided public image of nuclear reactors shifted until the negative side became overwhelmingly predominant. Pictures of a gleaming white containment dome and the soaring geometry of cooling towers were something the industry had once presented as a promise of the clean and efficient scientific-technological paradise to come. But the immense scale and geometrical perfection and even the whiteness of the cooling towers could evoke (like Melville's white whale) an ambiguous meaning: an emblem of mysterious, overwhelming, and inhuman powers.[22] By the 1980s, particularly after photographic coverage of the Three Mile Island accident settled on the cooling towers as icons, these images had been welded to frightening emotional experiences. Today when an artist or journalist shows a white cooling tower, it is understood to be ominous.

The Chernobyl accident was manifestly not an atomic-bomb type of explosion. It did little to strengthen the old fears of such reactor catastrophes, but it did greatly strengthen the slightly newer association of reactors with large-scale radioactive contamination. (The history of this, covered in *Nuclear Fear*, involved a transfer of worries over bomb tests to concern over radioactivity releases projected in worst-case reactor accident scenarios.) The associated imagery can be seen in science fiction stories of a world after nuclear war, where the empty city often stands within a larger radioactive Dead Zone. This is a symbol of devastation well expressed in the term "Ground Zero" (created, of course, in a "Year Zero"), a vision of the utter negation of civilization, of people, of life itself. The Dead Zone was connected with reactor accidents only in an abstract fashion before Chernobyl, for example, in technical statements about how many square kilometers might be contaminated in the worst case. After Chernobyl it all came to seem horribly real. No matter that wildlife flourishes around Chernobyl, or that to picture a zone where life is actually nearly extinct you should visit a site of conventional pollution, like the barren regions downwind from metal smelters. People were more impressed by radioactive contamination, which resonated so strongly with thoughts of mutant monsters, forbidden secrets, and universal devastation.

Contamination of any kind has a particularly powerful impact. I noted the meaning of contamination already in *Nuclear Fear*, explaining the close connections to issues of pollution in the wider sense, including social stigmatization as well as psychological problems with deep roots in infantile fantasies and anxieties. Since then, the question of public reaction to threats of contamination has become prominent in the literature of nuclear and other industrial risks, and scholars have advanced our understanding of the matter.[23] In particular, the sociologist Kai Erikson and the political scientist Jessica Stern have emphasized how the invisibility and incomprehensibility of modern industrial pollution make it especially impressive. Chernobyl is only one of many cases where a large population was traumatized by something they could not see or feel. (The prototypical cases are the hibakusha of Hiroshima and Nagasaki.) Many have not even known for sure whether or not they have been harmed. And their uncertainty never ends: they feel they are somehow damaged for life. Moreover, unknowns have a natural psychological connection with secrecy, a theme that immediately evokes distrust of authorities. Distrust redoubles when the authorities are in fact secretive (perhaps silent only from ignorance, but that is rarely believed). Worse, authorities have often been evasive or actively deceptive. The victims of pollution, Erikson concludes, suffer "a lasting numbness, bleak outlook, estrangement (from those not co-victims at any rate), absence of trust in human institutions, even a feeling that nature itself is unreliable: a change in sense of self and worldview."[24]

Stern pointed out that the feelings of distrust and estrangement in cases of industrial contamination are redoubled because pollution is linked with poison. Poisons are "dreaded on inborn grounds, an actual visceral aversion to poisonous substances."[25] This is the basic emotion of disgust, one of only two things that can cause a single experience to leave a powerful and permanent imprint in the very structure of our brains. The other such thing is, of course, fear. An experience, *whether direct or vicarious*, of poisoning can evoke both physical fear and disgust—that is, horror—leaving an indelible imprint. Some circumstances can redouble the imprint if, as new studies suggest, transgressions of our moral code evoke much the same physical feeling of disgust as we feel toward sickening substances. Poisons are not only secret but treacherous: whether the transgressor slips a toxin into your wine or releases vile substances into your environment, it is a revolting violation of basic human trust.

The imagery has recently been enhanced by another real-world connection. There was widespread publicity in November 2006 when a former Russian intelligence officer, Alexander Litvinenko, suffered an agonizing death through poisoning by polonium. Traces of polonium found around London and in other countries, perhaps posing health risks to dozens of other people, added to the horror. This foul deed surely intensified the public's association between radioactive substances and gruesome death by secret poisons. *Time* magazine attributed "Litvinenko's excruciating and sinister death" to the effects of "a Chernobyl" inside him, and Litvinenko's father said his son "was killed by a little nuclear bomb."[26]

Along with the old associations between radiation and reactors and bombs, there was something new here: a close connection between radioactive poison and spies. This reinforces an important feature of the post–Cold War period that I have already hinted at, a strengthened association between fears of radioactive contamination and the imagined world of secret agents and terrorist criminals. In particular, experts have frequently warned that a well-organized gang might find a way to release the radioactive wastes stored near reactors. Still more likely, terrorists might steal radioactive material at some point in the nuclear fuel cycle and use it to contaminate a large area with a so-called dirty bomb (we cannot escape overt references to the most primitive notion of pollution, dirt itself).[27] This topic is so important that I will defer discussion to a separate section.

With the shift of attention to other problems, overt concern about reactor accidents has declined. A few serious incidents have come to public notice, like the Tokaimura accident in Japan, and a revelation in 2002 that corrosion in an American reactor (Davis-Besse), detected only by chance, had gone nearly far enough to threaten a meltdown. But these incidents were small enough to have only a modest public impact, and they are now seldom recalled, except within the industry and by anti-nuclear activists.

Anti-nuclear activism has been limited. Opposition to nuclear energy began as a local issue, and it was again local opposition that raised the greatest obstacles to civilian nuclear energy from the 1990s onward. Public concern came to focus on noxious radioactive substances—not at individual reactor sites as in the 1970s, but at places where officials hoped to bury the entire industry's wastes. In the United States, the main political attention has gone to a stumbling government effort to certify Yucca Mountain, Nevada, as a repository for nuclear wastes. The high-handed attempts to impose a national problem on one locality drove many people in Nevada into vehement opposition, but elsewhere most citizens paid little heed. Similarly, in France the 1990s saw protests verging on violence in places under consideration as waste repositories, and in 2004 substantial protests were mounted in both France and Germany against the transport of nuclear wastes—an entire transport route could be seen as a "locality" at risk. Here and everywhere else, regional opposition to permanent waste repositories has prevented any solution to the problem. But it has done little to slow the continued operation of reactors, with the wastes stored in temporary repositories.[28] New reactors could be built if they were placed where they would not arouse intense local opposition—in some countries because the reactors were put next to ones already operating (where the neighbors had grown accustomed to the plant, or even held jobs in it), in other countries (like China) because opposition could be repressed.

A 2006 poll of thirty nations found that on average the world public is almost evenly divided on their willingness to see nuclear reactors built to replace fossil fuel plants. (The support is weakest in European nations like Germany and France.)[29] I haven't yet found a series of polls that would show how this has changed over time outside the United States, comparable to the polls mentioned above that found Americans shifting toward acceptance after the 1980s. But I suspect that as awareness of fossil fuel problems has grown, in many countries nuclear reactors are now somewhat more acceptable than they were immediately after Chernobyl, or even in the early 1980s before Chernobyl.

As noted above, probably some of the fear has drained from the reactor image because of the industry's record of success in avoiding scary large-scale disasters for the past two decades—a long time for public attention and memory. The younger generation, at any rate, was not directly traumatized by Chernobyl. Moreover, I believe (and with many others have presented evidence) that much of the anxiety about nuclear reactors has been a displacement of anxiety about that other potentially devastating technology, nuclear weapons. Observers could predict that as fears of a nuclear world war faded, putting explosions and fallout farther from conscious reflection, anxiety about reactors would likewise decrease.

There may also be a more subtle force at work. Most great images gain their potency from a creative tension within them, the endless and impossible effort of combining and reconciling opposites. When the promises of a radiant atomic-powered future faded away, some of the energy went out of the opposing image too—in the practical politics of campaigns against expansion of the industry, and perhaps at a deeper level of consciousness. I suspect that nuclear power has become *prosaic*, a technology that more and more people, and especially younger generations, will evaluate mainly on the technical and economic merits.

We see this working out in *The Simpsons*. Both in the opening sequence and in a number of episodes that have appeared over the years, the nuclear reactor is central to the fictional city of Springfield. It provides the city with electricity but is hardly seen as benign; at any moment the careless operators may set off a devastating explosion. Meanwhile radioactive emissions engender a three-eyed fish and other monstrosities. But in the children who watch these episodes, does anything strike them with a visceral shock of fear or disgust? Far from it: the greedy industrialist who owns the reactor, the hapless operators, and the goofy-looking fish are all elements of the show's highly satisfactory program of satirizing almost everything in sight with a wink and a chuckle.[30] Next week Springfield is still there, reactor and all. In this postmodernist city, everything is bad and nothing is serious.

So much of the emotional power has leached out of nuclear accidents that expert media producers have rethought some of their mythical figures. It is like what happened in 1945, when it was revealed that Superman's superpowers (and weaknesses) were all connected with atomic rays—only now it went in reverse. Comic book fans place great store in the "origin story" of their heroes, so it is significant that the owners of Spiderman—who in his 1962 debut got his amazing powers from the accident of a bite by a radioactive spider—realigned him in his 2002 movie, conferring his powers from a genetically modified spider. Other comic book characters, notably the Hulk, were similarly reassigned. In the 2001 remake of the *Planet of the Apes* movie, humanity was felled by genetic engineering instead of the nuclear war implied in the 1968 original; the 1995 movie *Twelve Monkeys* featured a society devastated and driven underground by a virus instead of the nuclear war of its 1962 inspiration, *La Jetée*. In short, for an image of uncanny magic, whether to bestow amazing powers or to destroy civilization, biology has tended to displace nuclear physics. I have not taken time to seek statistics of news articles, but one can scarcely doubt that reactor accidents and similar problems of civilian nuclear power have had far less media play, in our current period, than genetically modified crops, artificial cloning, engineered viruses, mad cow disease (BSE), and other novel epidemics . . . and the list goes on. To take one direct measure of what is currently on the World Wide Web, a search on Google (1/24/07) for pages containing the three words "nuclear," "science," and "pollution" found 4.2 million pages, whereas the combination "biological," "science," and "pollution" turned up 7.6 million.

This change points to another reason for the decline of intensity in anti-nuclear politics. In any period there is only so much outrage and activist effort that can be mobilized. Other issues have become more salient, and for good reason, as new moral issues and technological perils came into view, not only matters like genetic engineering but a variety of visible threats to entire ecosystems, culminating in global warming.

But there is one complex of issues, loosely linked to nuclear reactors, that did become much stronger in our period: weapons proliferation and terrorism.

# Nuclear History, 1987–2007: Weapons Proliferation and Terrorism

I call weapons proliferation and terrorism a complex of issues rather than two separate issues, for in the post–Cold War period they became inseparably entangled. Through the 1980s, the threat of proliferation of nuclear weapons to new states was seen mainly in the context of a possible use in war. If Egypt or South Africa or Argentina should get nuclear bombs, people feared that their government might use them if they got into a war with a neighbor. Beyond this, many worried that such local use could trigger a wider war that might destroy civilization. That concept was probably more prominent in thriller novels and secret-agent movies than in rational political science discussions. Still, everyone understood that objections to the use of nuclear weapons had become almost a sacred taboo. Once the line was crossed—perhaps, for example, in the Mideast where the United States and the Soviet Union had important interests—might the conflict escalate into a general exchange of missiles? With the demise of the Cold War this fear dwindled. But a new fear rose in its place. The dictators of nations like Libya and Iran were known to favor and support certain terrorist organizations. If these nations learned how to make nuclear bombs, might they not teach their protégés, or even give them a bomb?

The fastest way to get nuclear material suitable for a bomb is to extract plutonium from fuel irradiated in a reactor. Proliferation, many experts believe, is the most serious of all genuine risks associated with nuclear reactors. There has been enough news in the past few decades, connecting reactors with proliferation of nuclear weapons to third-world dictatorships, to keep this concern before the public. Prominent stories have ranged from Israel's 1981 bombing of the Osirak reactor in Iraq, forestalling the production of plutonium, to the 2006 North Korean explosion of an actual device using plutonium from a reactor. The Pew Research Center for the People and the Press has regularly conducted surveys of "Public Attentiveness to News Stories." A score over 20 percent is relatively high—Americans notoriously do not pay much attention to foreign news—and since the late 1980s scores well above that level have been recorded for news stories about nuclear weapon proliferation in Pakistan, North Korea, Iran, and Iraq. Significantly, the *only* nuclear-related news attended to by the pollsters and their respondents since the U.S.-Soviet arms reductions of 1991 were stories about weapons in third-world dictatorships.[31]

The public is responding to an important trend in our period, a genuine rise in the risk posed by nuclear technology held by third-world regimes. This becomes particularly worrisome when the regime is infected with some combination of tyranny, irrationality, and fanaticism. All these elements appeared in news accounts (whether accurate or not) of the so-called rogue states—an adjective evoking the image of a vicious and uncontrolled beast—Libya, Iran, Iraq, and North Korea. And it is precisely tyranny, irrationality, and fanaticism that are also fundamental to images of terrorism. I've already mentioned some ways that civilian nuclear technology has become linked to secret agents and terrorists, to the mythical world of James Bond and the real world of Al Qaeda: the polonium poisoning of Litvinenko, the fear that terrorists would attack a reactor, or that they would steal radioactive materials for a "dirty bomb." Experts described all these as genuine threats.

The largest threat, experts explained, came from the former Soviet Union, where tons—not kilograms, tons—of bomb-grade material were unaccounted for. (It was not even known how much plutonium and highly enriched uranium existed anywhere, for Soviet officials had probably lied about meeting their production targets.) Many of the fragmentary post-Soviet nations, including sections of Russia itself, displayed third-world levels of corruption, disorganization, tyranny, and fanaticism. An example of the news this has generated, not unique, was the announcement just last month that a Russian had gone to the gang-infested republic of Georgia to sell weapons-grade uranium to an agent he thought represented a secret Muslim organization.[32]

Even more worrisome were revelations from Pakistan, where reactors have been producing significant amounts of plutonium. In 2004 the founder of that program, Abdul Q. Khan, confessed that he had engaged in transferring nuclear weapons technology to Libya, Iran, and North Korea. It was almost exactly like the plots of thriller novels where a scientist, motivated by greed or religious fervor, steals secrets and gives them to a terrorist gang. Many observers questioned whether Khan could have done his nefarious work without the knowledge of Pakistan's government. Here was a new idea: a regime might, so to speak, steal weapons technology from itself, to place in the hands of evildoers out of ideological affinity or sheer financial greed.

Of course a regime might not rely on terrorists but deliver its weapons directly. Considering how they treated their own citizens, and the delusional nature of their thinking, what would hold back Saddam Hussein from bombing Tel Aviv if he had the means, or Kim Jung Il from destroying Washington? Among these proliferation concerns, the most historically important were fears that Iraq would get nuclear weapons. A great shock came in 1991 when United Nations inspectors dramatically discovered that Saddam Hussein had come all too close to producing bombs. The Iraqi weapons program had been successfully hidden from the world, and only the dictator's mistake in invading Kuwait too soon had brought the collapse of his effort. Even the world's most pessimistic analysts had been fooled. Might they not be fooled again? The idea was a weight on the minds of all observers, and especially intelligence analysts. It was one of several factors that led to the tragic intelligence failure of 2002, when many American analysts thought it likely that Iraq was getting back on the road to a nuclear armory.[33]

At this point we are no longer talking about reactors. In the usual fashion of such discussions we have slid, almost without noticing the transition, to the history of nuclear weapons themselves. But there is little more to say about the history of nuclear weapons as such since the end of the Cold War. The arsenals of the two major powers were cut roughly in half and then frozen. There have been a few controversies in the United States over plans to design a new generation of weapons, and over deployment of antiballistic missiles (of which more later). But the history of public attention to nuclear weapons has its center elsewhere in the post–Cold War period. People have not worried much about weapons held by the familiar sort of political and military authorities. They have worried chiefly about weapons in the hands of terrorists. If they also worry about proliferation to rogue nations, it is largely for fear that those weapons might get into the hands of terrorists.[34]

Anxieties about terrorism are not new, but they have grown. In 1996, shortly after a shocking blast killed 168 people in a government building in Oklahoma City, a poll of Americans found that 72 percent of them believed there was a chance that terrorists could attack a U.S. city with a weapon of mass destruction. A different poll two years later found that half of all Americans believed that terrorists would explode a nuclear bomb in the United States within the next ten years. But the majority at that time did not feel a personal concern: in the 1996 poll, the 40 percent who said they felt some worry (including 13 percent who worried "a great deal") were outnumbered by the 59 percent who said they did not worry at all. We may conclude that lots of Americans, not unreasonably, thought a bombing was likely *somewhere* but probably not where they themselves lived. Similarly, in the 1998 poll about two-thirds thought a nuclear war was likely somewhere in the world by 2008, but only one-third thought the United States would be involved in such a war.[35] Overall, what we see in the 1990s is a modest level of concern about nuclear war and a somewhat higher level about nuclear terrorism.

A more detailed view comes from a consistent series of polls run by the Gallup organization over the years. They found that the fraction of Americans who worried about terrorism declined from the 40 percent in 1996, right after the Oklahoma City bombing, to 25 percent in 2000. After the 9/11 attacks the number leaped to 60 percent, but after a few years this fell back, and worry is now again at the 40 percent level. Overall we see significant but not overwhelming fears, perhaps comparable to what people felt during the Cold War outside of a few periods of urgent crisis. For balance, note that Americans, and also people in other developed countries, currently rate war, economic troubles, and several other issues above terrorism as a concern, placing terrorism alongside second-rank problems like the environment and education. (People in most of the less-developed countries are even less likely to mention terrorism as a concern.)[36]

There is a special emotional power, however, in the image of the bomb-wielding villain or villainous group. Unlike nuclear war and reactor wastes, this factor in nuclear imagery not only retains its traditional power, but has grown stronger than ever during our period. To understand this we need to look at a consequence of the ending of the Cold War that is subtle, yet of the greatest importance.

The end of the Cold War meant the waning of enemies. For the West, there was no longer a fearfully powerful and aggressive Soviet Union. Nor, as China turned to reform, was there a world communist movement for people to worry about. This had echoes all across the political spectrum, for the collapse of one side of a dichotomy drains energy from the other side. Russians and Chinese were no longer warned against capitalists who schemed to enslave them. In the West itself, for half a century the socialist left's enmity of capitalists had been sustained by visions of Soviet greatness and by the worldwide Soviet propaganda machine. It became harder to maintain the fervor against corporate villainy. In particular, during the 1990s as the opposition to the nuclear reactor industry weakened, the image of industrial corporations as despicable enemies also dimmed.

Why do I call this waning of enemies an event of the greatest importance? Because there is good evidence that people *must have* enemies. Social cohesion is strongly advanced by having an "outgroup" (in sociologists' language) that we, the ingroup, must oppose—an enemy that threatens us and draws us together. Personal selfhood similarly has a need for an "other," a type of person who stands for everything that we are determined not to be: we partly define ourselves by what we hate. (Perhaps the others in fact embody mainly projections of what we really are but try not to see, but that is by the way.)

I'm not sure about other countries, but at least in the United States in the 1990s I feel there was a need for an enemy that settled on criminals. Violent and sometimes clearly irrational campaigns targeted drug dealers, child molesters or simply criminals in general. Another campaign opposed immigrants; after all, foreigners have always been chosen for the role of enemy other. Moreover, immigrants in countries like France and Russia were said to be especially responsible for crime, while Americans debated specifically "illegal immigrants"—again, lawbreakers. And then of course there were the supreme criminals: terrorists.

I have already taken note of the many tales about nuclear terrorists. Mick Broderick, among others, has pointed to a good description of the theme in a pure state (a neat case of postmodernist referencing) in the 1996 movie *Austin Powers: International Man of Mystery*. When Dr. Evil's ingenuity for concocting evil schemes fails him, he tells his cohorts: "Oh, hell, let's just do what we always do. Let's hijack some nuclear weapons and hold the world hostage."[37] Other motives of fictional terrorists have included revenge, political ideology, religious fanaticism and plain insanity. I have mentioned the current television show *24* and could cite many others. Let me note only the most popular recent nuclear-terrorist production, the 2002 movie *The Sum of All Fears*. It was based on a

1991 novel by the bestselling author Tom Clancy, in which Islamic terrorists blast Baltimore with a stolen nuclear bomb. Working in the wake of the 9/11 attack, the movie's producers did not want to add to anti-Muslim hysteria. So they fell back on the old standby of a neo-Nazi terrorist group that devastates Denver. (This is one of the stories in which the terrorists' aim is to set off a larger war, in this case by casting the blame on Russia.)

The threat of terrorist attacks has scarcely engaged high culture, or even pop culture, in ways similar to earlier reactions to the threat of nuclear war. I find little use of imagery with the power and complexity of the ancient theme of apocalyptic transmutation, so psychologically rich and culturally deep. The narratives we have now are simple secret-agent fantasies. Their history is easily traced back, through the Cold War fables of James Bond and his colleagues to the adventure stories that proliferated after World War I and even earlier. These are simple tales of a hero (or less commonly, a band of heroes) against a villain (or more commonly, a gang of villains). To be sure, some of our best writers have given us novels that attempted to get into the mind of the terrorist—a project already undertaken by Joseph Conrad and Emile Zola, among others, back in the days of the anarchists.[38] But on the whole, nuclear terrorism has not inspired great novels, movies, and other art in the way that nuclear war did.

The victor over the terrorist has a counterpart, certainly, in nuclear war literature, namely in the survivalist fantasies that also pit hero against villain. The secret agent is in fact often a survivor, triumphing over all sorts of threats. There may even be some personal growth through these travails, as in the transformation of an ordinary fearful woman into a tough fighter, which is the dramatic core of the first *Terminator* movie. But these dramas scarcely approach the transmutational theme that was central to most nuclear stories of earlier decades, the many forms of an ancient passage through death and the underworld with hopes for rebirth into full humanity. The secret agent in fact prevents the apocalypse. He (or, rarely, she) remains stuck in a childish world of secrets, violence, and enemies. In this regard the secret agent is cousin to the manly gun-wielding survivors of post-apocalyptic fantasies—a genre popular in cheap thriller paperbacks and computer games that flourished in the 1980s and 1990s, well remembered if less often seen today. These right-wing militant survivors were not transformed by the nuclear disaster, unless to become coarser and more violent.[39]

In sum, when we look for images that connect with deep emotional memories, in the Cold War period we find them in the contexts of war and technology: the military officer and his missiles, paralleled by the mad scientist and his monster. In the post–Cold War period, postmodernism has cut these off from their emotional roots. It is, I believe, a related but different image that evokes visceral terror: the terrorist. With his unpredictable explosives and secret poisons, he can evoke as much anxiety and irrational aggression as the warriors of the Cold War, although he does not, for better or worse, carry all the other rich associations of apocalypse and rebirth.

The image of the nuclear terrorist has gained emotional power in recent years, but has also undergone some changes. In the usual manner of images, it has shed none of its old associations—going back to nineteenth-century mad scientists and anarchists—while it has acquired some important new associations.

The most important psychological connection is with suicide. To be sure, the nineteenth-century terrorist and mad scientist might both die in their attempts to wield blasphemous powers. But they seldom embraced suicide. That idea entered modern history definitively in 1983 when Shi'ite militants killed themselves deliberately while bombing a U.S. Marine barracks in Lebanon. Since then the tactic has become notoriously common, primarily in the Muslim cultural sphere but also, for example, by Tamils in Sri Lanka. A chief implication of suicide bombing, as one observer pointed out recently, is that "by design, it unsettles the question of deterrence. . . . To make the challenge to deterrence even more stark, a suicide bomber . . . is willing to kill innocent bystanders." That can include even one's own people, as when, for example, a fanatic Sunni bomber welcomes the death of even the most orthodox Sunnis as fellow "martyrs."[40]

The idea of suicide has been part of nuclear weapons imagery since the 1960s, if not earlier. As I discussed in *Nuclear Fear*, all-out nuclear war was frequently described as "suicidal," a thought evoking strong associations that range from infantile fantasies to the spiritual theme of passage through death. The image of the nuclear warrior embracing death was perfected in the cowboy-pilot riding a bomb to catastrophe in *Dr. Strangelove* (caricatured in an animation that was the opening sequence of the first *Nuclear War* computer game). Most people eventually understood that precisely because the strategy of "mutually assured destruction" (often abbreviated MAD) was suicidal, it had to be shunned in the real world. Modern terrorism has turned that on its head. Suicidal bombing has become a strategy that fully rational people not only accept, but actually perform, again and again.

The idea is profoundly disturbing even as an abstract proposal, and for many adults a mention of suicide will also connect with potent personal memories. Add to this the horrific pictures of carnage everyone has seen in the news, and it is clear we have an image at least as frightening as the most monstrous creatures of past fictions. And if that holds for the terrorist in general, so much the more so if we add nuclear weapons. Besides bringing its own heavy burdens, the nuclear image complex facilitates associations with the older themes of evil gangs with their masterminds—from Dr. No back through the comic-strip villain Ming the Merciless (1934– ) to the pulp-novel master criminal Dr. Fu Manchu (1912– ). These figures, if not exactly scientists themselves, wielded advanced scientific powers, and connect us onward to the Frankensteinian mad scientist. This immediately connects us to the crazed destructive monster from which it is only a short step full circle back to the modern terrorist.

In this quick tour of villains I have not yet talked about the most common of all, the foreigner. Immigrants and terrorists who have slipped in and live among us are bad enough, but we are still more prone to fear entirely foreign evildoers. In the minds of many Americans and some other Westerners, this role has been taken in recent years by Saddam Hussein, Kim Jung-Il of North Korea, and the rulers of Iran. These rulers nicely fit the old archetype of Ming the Merciless—himself the emperor of a rogue state—not to mention the countless actual despots in world history. Saddam was seen, rightly enough, as a torturer and warmonger, while Kim Jung-Il and the Iranian theocrats have been pictured as preposterously irrational violators of human rights. (In other nations, similar stereotypes have attached to U.S. President Bush.) These leaders may be despised for violating peoples' rights, but it is when they threaten to build nuclear weapons that they are feared.

Once again nuclear imagery shows an uncanny tendency to reflect imagery in actual facts. The old psychological association of criminal terrorist with evil mastermind with wicked despot starts to look like simple reality in concerns that a despot might hand a nuclear weapon to a terrorist. To be sure, few political scientists believe that any rational government would actually give bombs to terrorists. But the fear is precisely of what an irrational despot might do. And it must be said that the actual leaders of states can hardly boast that all their actions are perfectly rational. Still less can we feel safe about what elements within a corrupt regime might secretly do, driven by fanaticism or greed. It has become difficult to separate the sober warnings of government counterterrorism experts from thriller novels and television dramas.

But is it truly realistic to imagine suicidal terrorists actually using a nuclear weapon to destroy thousands, or hundreds of thousands of lives? Even in fiction, during the Cold War period the criminal who got a bomb was more likely to act as the fictional Dr. Evil planned, aiming only to extort money or otherwise wield personal power. This relatively kindly view of human nature has been overthrown. The first blow came when members of the large Japanese cult Aum Shinrikiyo released poisonous gas in a coordinated attack on five subway trains in Tokyo. A dozen people were killed and hundreds more harmed, but the cult had intended to kill far more. Ultimately they aimed for nothing less than global apocalypse. If anyone still doubted that there existed groups who not only desired to kill on a very large scale, but could mobilize the will and persistence and technical means to do so, they were answered by Al Qaeda in the 9/11 attacks.

I think the destruction of the World Trade Center had its deepest impact on public thinking by showing that horrors of human will that had been scarcely credible must be taken as fact. What was truly terrifying was not that terrorists might pull off another coup that would kill thousands: it was the discovery that a far worse attack was truly possible. As the director-general of the International Atomic Energy Agency put it shortly after: "The willingness of terrorists to commit suicide to achieve their evil aims makes the nuclear terrorist threat [appear] far more likely than it was before September 11." A writer reflecting back on events went further: "The reason 9/11 was so traumatizing for all us, I believe, is that the vision we all had of the World Trade Center collapsing in a horrible cloud is that for us it was effectively the mushroom cloud that we have been dreading for a generation."[41]

Many noted that the pictures of airplanes, billowing clouds and smoking wreckage resonated with familiar imagery of bombardment. Reporters immediately used the language long associated with nuclear Apocalypse—"gates of hell," "like a nuclear winter."[42] The site of the attack was quickly named "Ground Zero," a term long associated with Hiroshima. Within a few years the phrase "nuclear 9/11" emerged as a common shorthand term for what many fear. A search of the *New York Times* and *Washington Post* news archives for the combination "nuclear" and "terrorist" finds a steady level of references from the mid-1980s up to September 2001, and then an immediate six-fold increase with little decline since.[43]

Of course, terrorists can deploy biological or chemical means to kill many people, and more easily. When governments talk about such things, whether for terrorists or foreign governments like Iraq, they tend to use the phrase "weapons of mass destruction." The phrase conventionally includes chemical and biological weaponry, but note that in fact those are weapons of mass mortality. The word "destruction" clearly points straight at nuclear weapons. The phrase is not entirely a euphemism for nuclear bombs, but it leans deeply in that direction.

In the public mind, nuclear terrorism does trump all. As Tom Engelhardt has pointed out, the mailing of letters with deadly anthrax spores, which horrified Americans soon after the 9/11 attacks, and which demonstrated the potential for a biological assault of vastly greater magnitude, has been largely forgotten.[44] A search using Google of pages on the World Wide Web that contain variations of the word "terrorist" and the phrase "nuclear weapon" turned up about six million pages, whereas searches for variants of "terrorist" and "biological weapon" got only two million, and "chemical weapon" or "poison gas" fewer still.[45] In short, not only the greatest nuclear worry of our time, but one of the greatest of all worries, is that terrorists might somehow get their hands on nuclear weapons.

Some experts in geopolitics would disagree, arguing that it is in fact very unlikely that a terrorist group would be able to get a workable bomb. A simpler and perhaps more likely threat is that some nuclear-armed regime will decide to lob a few bombs.

This too has found a response that is hard to distinguish from fantasy. We might call it "war from the skies." The missiles boasted by North Korea are to be countered by antimissiles. If diplomatic and economic pressure fail, we are told that Iran's bid to assemble materials for constructing bombs may be countered by air strikes, not excluding the possibility of nuclear bombardment to shatter underground facilities. An Israeli air strike in actual fact destroyed Saddam Hussein's first attempt to get plutonium (the Osirak reactor), and the bombardment of Iraq by airplanes and missiles was a prominent feature of both Gulf Wars and on many occasions in between.

I bring this up because it points to an interesting feature of nuclear imagery that I only became aware of recently, although on looking back it can be seen to have a long history. The nuclear warhead streaking down from the heavens is symbolically more than a missile. The thunderbolt—like the three zigzags clutched in a mailed fist that formed the Strategic Air Command symbol often seen in the 1950s—is an ancient symbol of divine retribution. All the Indo-European peoples had a thunder god, and his cousins are found wielding lightning in other cultures as far afield as Japan. Even farther back, folklorists have identified a widespread theme of battle in the heavens, where a shaman mystically ascends to fight or plead on behalf of his tribe. This is linked to the very ancient human theme of magical flight. In such fashion, as various observers remarked, the SAC bomber pilot took on the god-like role of fighting on behalf of his people.

We would expect the sky-warrior, like all important symbols, to be complex and multivalent. And so he is. The aggressive urges of the bomber pilot, and later the missile launch officer, are also embodied in the anthropomorphized bomb or missile itself (contributing to the unforgettable power of the image of the pilot straddling his bomb). All this brings up associations with the mingled image of mad scientist and robotic monster. The robot or other strange creature doing battle in the skies was a popular figure in the Cold War period, especially in Japan. Astroboy, the popular 1951 Osamu Tezuka manga robot (in the original Japanese, Atom Boy), was joined by mechanical Transformers and many others. An especially acute use of the themes is found in an underappreciated American animated movie, *The Iron Giant* (1999), which climaxes with the flying robot acting as an anti-nuclear-bomb missile.

These machines are on our side, protecting us. But didn't I say the robot-monster represents the worst enemy? In *Nuclear Fear* I explained how robots typically embody a blank absence of human feeling, the frozen world-destroying soul-death that lurks at the nadir of the transmutational passage. There is a paradox here, well illustrated by the dramatic turn in the second *Terminator* movie (*Terminator 2: Judgment Day*, 1991), where the homicidal robot played by Arnold Schwarzenegger in the first movie returns as a protector, although still a robot. Once again to see what is happening we should trace back the history.

The 1991 Terminator robot, the Iron Giant, and Astroboy all share something with their forebears back to the Tin Woodsman of Oz and Pinocchio: they are struggling to become human. Seeking a heart, a conscience, and true life, they are coming through to the other side of the darkness. I suspect this psychologically powerful context has become associated in many minds with nuclear missiles, although the resonances are not easy to see. What is clear is the appeal of the image of machines warring in the skies to protect us from nuclear-armed foreign enemies.

# Consequences

Much of this may sound like an ethereal academic exercise in folklore analysis. Yet it has important consequences in the real world of blood and money. Consider the war in the heavens—or "Star Wars," as the 1983 antimissile Strategic Defense Initiative of the Reagan administration was nicknamed immediately, spontaneously, and durably. Most experts understood and explained that the original scheme of space lasers (ray weapons, in fact) could never work. Indeed they never did, and the research was abandoned after vast expenditures. Other schemes rose in its place, and although the technical skepticism remained, so did the budgetary largesse. In the last few years the United States actually constructed missile defense facilities even after attempts to test them in practice failed, as experts predicted. The facilities are not even built to defend against any actual threat. For they are acknowledged to be impotent against a Chinese or Russian salvo, and the North Korean missiles for which the defenses are nominally designed do not presently exist.

There are various opinions about why the United States government has spent many tens of billions of dollars on technologies that don't work. One explanation is that certain leaders, blinded by faith in technology and anticommunism, believed that scientists could do what they were told to do. Another view is that since a large majority of Americans believed that scientists could indeed built a working defense, the program was an easy way to get tax dollars to maintain a flourishing military technology industry. In other words, it was "welfare for the rich," as one physics laboratory leader told me (after conceding that missile defense lasers were unfeasible and saying "I'll take the money" anyway). A third view maintains that it was all a bluff to force the Soviet Union to concede that it could not match the United States in military technology. Whether deliberately or not, the missile defense program probably did have some effect in that direction (I have seen an intelligence report, predating the initiative, that emphasized Russians' admiration of American technology and their fear of being taken by surprise by a new Manhattan Project). Note that in each of these explanations, what matters is the symbolic impact of the simple assertion that a missile defense would be created. Thus the "Antimissile" is a pure postmodern object, operating as a representation, like the "Bomb" itself—only more so, since nuclear bombs actually work. If strategic missile defense continues to absorb billions of dollars, it is less because of technological reality than because it stands for a heroic defense with miraculous science-fictional powers.

An entirely different area in which symbolism is at least as important as technological facts is the reaction to radioactive materials from civilian technology. Here nuclear anxieties have been found to contribute directly to morbidity. The best-studied case is the Chernobyl disaster. Direct and immediate deaths numbered about thirty; estimates of the total deaths eventually expected range from hundreds to several thousands over the lifetimes of the survivors. But they do not call themselves by the positive term "survivors." They identify themselves, and are officially identified, as "victims," subject to all the problems identified for the hibakusha and similar traumatized groups. According to the most definitive study, "the mental health impact of Chernobyl is the largest public health problem unleashed by the accident to date." A large population became, and to this day remains, highly anxious, with serious consequences for their health going well beyond the observed thyroid disorders and other direct damage. Many of the "victims," convinced they are damaged, have become fatalistic and are careless about alcohol and other risks. Many have psychosomatic disorders.[46]

Another clear case of damage caused by nuclear fear happened in Goiania, Brazil, in 1987. Two men who were salvaging scrap metal released radioactive material from a discarded cancer therapy device. Children played with the glowing material and spread it around. Several hundred people were contaminated and four died. But the matter went far beyond what would have been a rather routine accident if nonnuclear chemicals had been to blame. The entire Goiania region and its people were stigmatized: "Hotels in other parts of the country refused to allow Goiania residents to register, airline pilots refused to fly with Goiania residents on board, automobiles driven by Goianians were stoned. . . . The sale of products manufactured in Goiana dropped by 40%." The economic and social damage persisted for a month or more.[47] For a neater demonstration that nuclear fear can have proven economic effects all by itself, we can point to a lawsuit by landowners in New Mexico, who won compensation when interviews showed that the value of their property was lowered by proximity to a route proposed for the transport of nuclear wastes.[48]

The stigma of radioactivity has had much broader consequences in the reaction to civilian nuclear reactors. Since the late 1980s, the chief impediment to building more reactors has been public pressure. This has been exerted less through direct political action, than by raising doubts in industrialists and bankers who might plan to build a reactor, but worry that regulation and lawsuits would delay or halt it after great expense. As I pointed out in my 1988 book, already by that time the public was especially anxious about nuclear waste, associating it with evil and uncanny pollution—poison, in short. Radioactive waste of course really can cause cancer and genetic mutations even in small amounts. So can many other common industrial products. Since the 1980s while no new nuclear reactors were built, there has been a steep rise in generation of electricity through the burning of coal. Fossil fuel wastes have long been known to be deadly, and in the past two decades scientists have found that they are even worse than we thought. For example, a recent report showed that microscopic soot particles, in the concentrations often found in cities, radically increases the rate that mature women die from heart attacks. It seems likely that tens of thousands of premature deaths would have been avoided if nuclear power plants had been built instead of coal burners—an outcome partly due to the irrational fears evoked by the symbolic associations of nuclear products. And this is to say nothing of the carbon dioxide that will linger in the atmosphere for hundreds of years, contributing to global warming, as eminent scientists were already warning twenty years ago.[49]

There are other possible consequences of nuclear imagery that are more speculative, but, if they are true, even more important. I have said enough about how terrorism has gotten tangled up with the nuclear complex of emotions and myths. For Americans in particular this became a deeply emotional connection as a result of the national trauma of 9/11, when nearly everyone spent many hours obsessively watching images of catastrophe. Tom Engelhardt and others have pointed out that the video clips, endlessly replayed on television, struck people as resembling special effects in disaster movies. No doubt the live images gave a stronger emotional kick than movies ever did.[50] Within hours the entire nation became—to use a cliché that here applies exactly—paralyzed by fear. I think it is undeniable that reasonable concerns, serious as they were, were overshadowed by violent emotions, although diminished somewhat in proportion to people's distance from the American East Coast. Everywhere the impact of the events was redoubled because they aroused all the powerful old associations of nuclear imagery. Some of the indelible effects on thinking had little to do with factual reasoning.[51]

Nobody can tell how much of the subsequent "war on terrorism" has been driven or facilitated by nuclear fear. But none can doubt that nuclear fear has been a major factor. To some extent the fear of the nuclear terrorist is reasonable, but I hope that I have shown that it is also associated with images and evokes emotions leading far from rationality.

It is even clearer that nuclear fears played a significant if not dominant role in facilitating the Bush administration's mobilization of public opinion to support the invasion of Iraq in 2003. The president and others in his administration spoke of all types of "weapons of mass destruction," but they could expect the greatest impact when they warned specifically of a "mushroom cloud." These repeated warnings were based on flimsier reasons than the assertions that Iraq might wield chemical weapons (which it had already done) or biological ones (which are easy to conceal). The most notorious example was the State of the Union address preceding the attack, when the president asserted that Iraq had tried to procure African uranium. It later emerged that American intelligence services had previously told the White House explicitly that this claim was baseless. Evidently the administration was prepared to risk its reputation (and in the end did do grave harm to its reputation) by distorting facts in order to arouse nuclear fear.[52] It is an open question whether the administration could have won enough public support to invade Iraq if everyone had understood that there was no prospect of an Iraqi nuclear bomb.

The complex of post–Cold War associations that I have sketched in this paper, with its deep resonances of fear and disgust—nuclear poisons, monstrous cultists, renegade scientists, magical weapons, evil tyrants, suicidal terrorists, and all the rest—this is not found only in computer games and television thrillers. The complex of imagery walks in the real world, to no good result.

# Notes

1. Spencer Weart, *Nuclear Fear: A History of Images* (Cambridge, Mass.: Harvard University Press, 1988). I am preparing a new work drawing on the 1988 book, the present essay, and other material, for publication by Harvard University Press in 2011.

2. Antonio R. Damasio, *Descartes' Error: Emotion, Reason, and the Human Brain* (New York: Avon, 1994). K. Szpunar et al. *Proc. Not. Acad. Sci.* 104 (2007), 642–47.

3. The evidence is summarized by Paul Rozin et al., "From Oral to Moral," *Science* 323 (2009), 1179–80.

4. Jerome Shapiro, *Atomic Bomb Cinema* (New York: Routledge, 2002), 307–8, 312–15.

5. Ann Bisconti, "Record High 70 Percent Favor Nuclear Energy," Nuclear Energy Institute, 2005, www.nei.org/documents/PublicOpinion_05-07.pdf (12/13/06). Note that the poll only asked people about accepting nuclear power at all, not whether they would prefer it to wind or solar power (very few would) nor even whether they would prefer it to fossil fuels.

6. The idea that there is only a limited "news hole" in the media is well accepted. There is some evidence that individual mental "space" for worries is also limited—for example, Joseph I. Constans et al, "Stability of Worry Content in GAD Patients: A Descriptive Study," *Journal of Anxiety Disorders* 16 (2002), 311–19.

7. news.google.com/archivesearch, accessed September 2006. Details on request.

8. Compiled from brain.gallup.com. Details on request.

9. Mick Broderick, "Is this the Sum of Our Fears? Nuclear Imagery in Post-Cold War Cinema," in S. C. Zeman and M. A. Amundson, eds., *Atomic Culture: How We Learned to Stop Worrying and Love the Bomb* (Boulder: University Press of Colorado, 2004), 144; *Atomic Bomb Cinema*, 14–15.

10. Harlan Ellison, "I have no mouth and I must scream," frequently anthologized. The first *Terminator* appeared in 1984, the second in 1991. See Paul Brians, "Terminator vs. Terminator," published online only, 1991, www.wsu.edu/~brians/science_fiction/terminator.html (accessed 1/12/06).

11. *The West Wing*, Warner Brothers–NBC and many other networks worldwide, "Duck and Cover," first aired January 22, 2006. *Jericho*, CBS-Paramount (2006–2008). *24*, Fox (sixth season, winter-spring 2007). *Heroes*, NBC (2006– ).

12. Yuki Tanaka, "Godzilla and the Bravo Shot: Who Created and Killed the Monster?" *Japan Focus* (2005), www.japanfocus.org/products/topdf/1652.

13. Michael Ortiz Hill, *Dreaming the End of the World: Apocalypse as a Rite of Passage* (Dallas: Spring Publications, 1994).

14. Mick Broderick, "Rebels with a Cause: Children versus the Military Industrial Complex," in Tim Sherry and A. Seibel, eds., Youth Culture in Global Cinema (Austin: University of Texas Press, 2006); *Dreaming the End of the World*, 59; *Atomic Bomb Cinema*.

15. Samuel J. Walker, "History, Collective Memory, and the Decision to Use the Bomb," in M. J. Hogan, ed., *Hiroshima in History and Memory* (New York: Cambridge University Press, 1996).

16. Review quoted on Amazon.com (viewed 2/8/07), at which time the 1989 reprint held the respectable sales rank of 4,343.

17. That is, from Netflix. A detailed synopsis can usually be found online in Wikipedia or another web source. I have actually viewed only a few important movies, to catch subtleties that would escape a simple synopsis. Note that for the purposes of this essay it is usually more significant how a work is perceived, summarized, and critiqued (whether on the Internet or elsewhere) than what its actual contents may be.

18. *Nuclear War* series, New World Computing, released 1989, concluding with *Ground Zero*, a fan-made remake, 1997. Reviews from www.thehouseofgames.net/index.php?t=10&id=49 and www.the-underdogs.org/hame.php?id=3857 (accessed 1/07). NOTE: I give this as an example of my online research; I am not documenting all my research here. Given the mutability of the Internet, readers may do better to search the Internet or Wikipedia and find their own references for these topics.

19. Robert Coles, *The Moral Life of Children* (Boston: Atlantic Monthly Press, 1986).

20. Takashi Murakami, *Little Boy: The Arts of Japan's Exploding Subculture* (New York: Japan Society Press; New Haven, Conn.: Yale University Press, 2005), 65.

21. Mindy L. Kotler and Ian T. Hillman, "Japanese Nuclear Energy Policy and Public Option," Houston: James A. Baker III Institute for Public Policy of Rice University, 2000.

22. The chapter on "The Whiteness of the Whale" in *Moby Dick* is a remarkable early example of image analysis.

23. E.g., Paul Slovik, *The Perception of Risk* (London: Earthscan, 2000), 342.

24. Kai T. Erikson, *A New Species of Trouble: Explorations in Disaster, Trauma, and Community* (New York: Norton, 1994), 226–42 and passim; Jessica Stern, *The Ultimate Terrorists* (Cambridge, Mass.: Harvard University Press, 1999).

25. *The Ultimate Terrorists*, 35–37.

26. J. F. O. McAlister, "The Spy Who Knew Too Much," *Time* (December 18, 2006), 32; Walter Litvinenko, quoted in *New Scientist* v. 192 no. 2581 (December 9, 2006), 9.

27. The large literature on these issues is itself a sign of their prominence. One good summary is *The Ultimate Terrorist*. Another example is Graham T. Allison, *Nuclear Terrorism: the Ultimate Preventable Catastrophe* (New York: Times Books, 2004).

28. Allison M. Macfarlane and Rodney C. Ewing, *Uncertainty Underground: Yucca Mountain and Nation's High-Level Nuclear Waste* (Cambridge, Mass.: MIT Press, 2006); for France, Jon Palfreman, "A Tale of Two Fears: Exploring Media Depictions of Nuclear Power and Global Warming," *Review of Policy Research* 23 (1997): 23–43; Palfreman, "Why the French Like Nuclear Energy," *Frontline* (PBS-WGBH) website, www.pbs.org/wgbh/pages/frontline/shows/reaction/readings/french.html (accessed 12/13/06).

29. With an average 20 percent "strongly favor" plus 29 percent "favor," the United States public was relatively favorable. University of Maryland Program on International Policy Attitudes, "Current Energy Use Seen to Threaten Environment, Economy, Peace," July 2, 2006, www.worldpublicopinion.org/pipa/articles/btenvironmentra/227.php?nid=&id=&pnt=227.

30. Almost but not quite everything: government nuclear regulators seem exempt from criticism. Mick Broderick, "Releasing the Hounds: the Simpsons as Anti-Nuclear Satire," in J. Alberti, ed., *Leaving Springfield: The Simpsons and the Possibility of Oppositional Culture* (Detroit: Wayne State University Press, 2004).

31. Search of data on the terms "nuclear," "atomic," "weapon," "reactor." The highest peak was 40 percent attentiveness to UN inspections in Iraq in 2003. Libya's abandonment of its weapons program in 2004 was noted by a lower but not negligible 14 percent. The only other nation mentioned was China, whose quest for U.S. nuclear technology got 21 percent attention in 1999; people-press.org/nii/bydate.php.

32. *The Ultimate Terrorism*, 1999. *New York Times*, Jan. 25, 2007.

33. "Shaken by the magnitude of their errors, intelligence analysts were determined not to fall victim again to the same mistake." Commission on Intelligence Capabilities of the United States Regarding Weapons of Mass Destruction, "Report to the President of the United States" (Washington D.C.: GPO, 2005), www.wmd.gov/reports/index.html.

34. Besides the polls noted below, this is based on my personal reading of news articles in recent years.

35. 1996 poll: Pew Research Center for the People and the Press, "Public Apathetic about Nuclear Terrorism," April 11, 1996, people-press.org/reports/display.php3?ReportID=128 (accessed 1/8/07). 1998 poll: Keating Holland/CNN "Poll: Many Americans Worry About Nuclear Terrorism," www.cnn.com/ALLPOLI-TICS/1998/06/16/poll/ (accessed 1/3/07).

36. Gallup: from brain.gallup.com. A more specific 2003 poll found four Americans in ten said they often worried about the chances that terrorists may attack the United

States with nuclear weapons. Pew Research Center for the People and the Press, "Two Years Later, the Fear Lingers," September 4, 2003, people-press.org/reports/print .php3?PageID=735. World survey: www.globescan.com/rf_gi_first_01.htm. A more recent U.S. survey (January 2007) is at www.galluppoll.com/content/?ci=26470 and further polls can be readily turned up with Web searches.

37. "Is this the Sum of Our Fears?"

38. Joseph Conrad, *The Secret Agent* (1907), a masterpiece; Emile Zola, *Paris* (1898), a failure; recently, e.g., John Updike, *Terrorist* (2006).

39. Thomas M. Disch, *The Dreams Our Stuff is Made of: How Science Fiction Conquered the World* (New York: Free Press, 2000). Notable series were Jerry Ahern, *The Survivalist* (1981–1993), many reissued as audio cassettes in 2003–2005, and William Johnstone, *Ashes* (1983–2002).

40. Noah Feldman, "Islam, Terror and the Second Nuclear Age," *New York Times Magazine* (October 29, 2006), 53.

41. Muhammad el-Baradei, quoted in John Tagliabue, "A Nation Challenged: Atomic Anxiety. Threat of Nuclear Terror Has Increased, Official Says," *New York Times* (November 2, 2001). Or as a government commission coldly put it, "the dangers of underestimating our enemies were deeply underscored by the attacks of September 11, 2001." "Report to the President of the United States." "Traumatizing": James Carroll on "Morning Edition," National Public Radio, May 30, 2006.

42. Tom Engelhardt, "9/11 in a Movie Made World," *The Nation* online (September 25, 2006), www.thenation.com/doc/20060925/engelhardt/2, gives these quotes from the *New York Times*.

43. news.google.com/archivesearch (accessed September 2006). I included terrorist(s) and (-ism).

44. "9/11 in a Movie Made World."

45. Accessed September 11, 2006. The methodology here is complex because I had to remove overlaps by searching on different combinations of the terms. The first group included "nuclear weapon" (2.8 million all by itself), "nuclear bomb," "atomic bomb," and "dirty bomb." The second group included "anthrax" (1.0 million), "smallpox," "biological weapon," "germ," and the term "virus," which got nine million combinations but most of these seemed to be computer viruses or descriptions of terrorism itself as a virus (Google conveniently included "terrorism" and "terrorists" in "terrorist" searches). "Chemical weapon" and "poison gas" minus overlaps got only about 730,000 hits. Also, the search found about 29.5 million pages with "terrorist AND bomb," including 12.2 million for "terrorist AND bomb AND (nuclear OR atomic)," along with about 13.8 million for "terrorist AND bomb NOT nuclear NOT atomic."

46. Chernobyl Forum, 2003–2005, 36, quoting Chernobyl Forum report on Health. See 14, 20–21, 41. These problems are partly caused by the permanent displacement of people from their homes and the economic depression brought on the disaster. But the displacement and depression were themselves caused partly by fear of radioactive contamination, a fear more widespread than in many chemically contaminated regions.

47. See J. S. Petterson, "Perception vs. Reality of Radiological Impact: The Goiania Model," *Nuclear News* 31 (1988), 84–90; *The Perception of Risk*, 270.

48. J. Flynn, "Nuclear Stigma," in N. Pidgeon, R. E. Kasperson and P. Slovik, eds., *The Social Amplification of Risk* (Cambridge: Cambridge University Press, 2003), 341–42; see also "A Tale of Two Fears," 37.

49. Notably J. Hansen in 1988. See Spencer Weart, *The Discovery of Global Warming* (Cambridge, Mass.: Harvard University Press, 2003). A 2009 National Academy of Sciences study estimated ten thousand deaths per year in the United States from coal pollution.

50. One witness: "the first, irrational thought that came into my staggered mind was that someone was making a blockbuster disaster movie." Daniel Mendelsohn, "September 11 at the movies," *New York Review of Books* (September 21, 2006), 21. www .nybooks.com/articles/19292. See discussion in "9/11 in a Movie Made World"; Anthony Lane, "This is Not a Movie," *New Yorker* (Sept. 24, 2001), 79–80.

51. I claim an unusual outside viewpoint: on September 11, I was backpacking in the Colorado wilderness and I first heard of the fall of the World Trade Center on September 15. I saw the video clips another week later.

52. Frank Rich, *The Greatest Story Ever Sold: The Decline and Fall of Truth from 9/11 to Katrina* (New York: Penguin Press, 2006), as summarized in frankrich.com/timeline .htm. Rich points out, for instance, in his *New York Times* op-ed column of February 4, 2007, that revelations in the perjury trial of I. Lewis "Scooter" Libby show the importance the White House placed on this ploy.

# Index

# About the Contributors

**Mick Broderick** is associate professor and research coordinator in the School of Media, Communications & Culture at Murdoch University. His major publications include editions of the reference work *Nuclear Movies* (1988, 1991) and, as editor, *Hibakusha Cinema: Hiroshima, Nagasaki and the Nuclear Image in Japanese Film* (1996, 1999). Broderick's curated programs and digital media productions include the fifty-minute drama *Fugue* (2008: executive producer/actor); a digital diptych on the Rwandan genocide, *Exhale* (2007); and a touring exhibit of cold war material culture objects, *Atomicalia* (Japan 2009–2010). Two coedited anthologies, *Interrogating Trauma* and *Trauma, Media, Art: New Perspectives*, are forthcoming in 2010.

**John Canaday** is the author of *The Nuclear Muse: Literature, Physics, and the First Atomic Bombs* and *The Invisible World*, a book of poems set in Jordan and New England, which won a Walt Whitman Award from the Academy of American Poets.

**Tom Engelhardt** is an author, editor, and blogger. A long-time editor for such writers as Studs Terkel, John Dower, and Paul Boyer among others, his own books include *The End of Victory Culture: Cold War America and the Disillusioning of a Generation* and the novel *The Last Days of Publishing*. He is the editor of *Tomdispatch*, an online project of *The Nation* magazine, publishing some of the most influential writings on current American politics. His most recent book, *Mission Unaccomplished*, is based on his interviews first published on *Tomdispatch*.

**Carole Gallagher** is a widely honored and exhibited American photographer. Her book of portraiture of Americans involved with the nuclear weapon testing program in Nevada, *American Ground Zero*, was published in 1993 and reprinted in 1994. A traveling exhibition based on this work was exhibited internationally including exhibits at nine national museums. She is a cofounder of the Atomic Photographers Guild.

**Judy Hiramoto** is a visual artist based in San Francisco. Ms. Hiramoto teaches art both at Goddard College in Vermont and at San Mateo College in California. She has exhibited her work widely in the United States and her work is also held in a number of collections.

**Kenji Ito** is an associate professor at the Graduate University for Advanced Studies (Sokendai) in Japan. He is a historian of science and technology who has published on both the history of quantum mechanics and also on science in Japanese history.

**Robert Jacobs** is an associate professor at the Hiroshima Peace Institute in Hiroshima, Japan working on the history of nuclear narratives in American culture. He is the author of the book *The Dragon's Tail: Americans Face the Atomic Age*, published in 2009 by the University of Massachusetts Press, and numerous articles on American nuclear culture.

**Minoru Maeda** is an artist and animator living in Hiroshima. He teaches art at Anabuki Design College, Hiroshima.

**Naoko Maeda** is a painter and manga artist living in Hiroshima.

**Yuki Tanaka** is a professor at the Hiroshima Peace Institute in Hiroshima, Japan. His books include *Japan's Comfort Women* and *Hidden Horrors*. He has published extensively on Japan's war crimes during World War II, and is coeditor with Marilyn Young of *Bombing Civilians*, a history of air war published in 2009 by the New Press.

**Spencer Weart** is the director of the Center for the History of Physics at the American Institute of Physics in College Park, Maryland. A prominent historian of physics, his books include *Nuclear Fear*, *Never at War*, and *The Discovery of Global Warming*. He has published widely on both the practice of physics and cultural impact of science.